A Techno-Economic Analysis of the Port Transport System

JUNICHI IMAKITA

Visiting fellow St Antony's College, Oxford.

SAXON HOUSE

© Junichi Imakita 1978

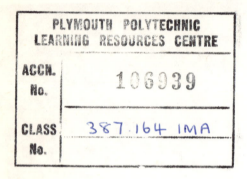
Published by

Saxon House, Teakfield Limited,
Westmead, Farnborough, Hants., England

 British Library Cataloguing in Publication Data

Imakita, Junichi
    A techno-economic analysis of the port
    transport system.
    1. Freight and freightage
    I. Title
    387.1'64   HE551

ISBN 0-566-00188-8

Printed in Great Britain by David Green (Printers) Ltd, Kettering, Northamptonshire.

A TECHNO-ECONOMIC ANALYSIS OF
THE PORT TRANSPORT SYSTEM

Contents

vi

List of Figures

List of Tables

1 Introduction

Scope of the subject

Transportation provides an infrastructure vital to economic growth. The demand for transport increases the faster the economy grows, requiring in turn all the more capability for moving goods and resources from places where their marginal utility is relatively low to where it is relatively high, in order to fulfil all sorts of physical as well as spacial economic activities. It is hardly surprising to note that transport accounts for between 10 and 20 per cent of the gross domestic products of most industrial nations. However, such figures doubtless are a great underestimation of the importance of transport, since the costs attributable to transport include notoriously hard-to-estimate, yet highly important costs such as those of time (e.g. travel time), pollution and environmental problems, and those involving other controversial external effects, to mention the more pertinent ones.

Transport is an integral part of production. It is not an end within itself, except perhaps where passengers alone are concerned, but rather an intermediary service activity. Reduction in transportation cost and time will result in greater production and even encourage new industrial ventures and a higher level of consumption. Investment in transport has such direct effects as the growth of employment, which leads to income growth as well as the redistribution of national income. But what is more apparent are such indirect effects as the removal of cost and capacity restraints to the development of the economy. For example, the transport system is the artery linking less developed areas, which happen to have ample resources (labour as well as raw materials), with other areas where the resources are needed for manufacturing industrial goods. And, of course, the latter goods then have to be moved to wherever they are demanded and consumed. If it were otherwise, resources would simply be left unutilised, and of no benefit to anyone.

The economic structure of a transport system also reflects many aspects of the country concerned, the degree of economic development, geographic and demographic features, the disposition of scarce as well as abundant resources, and so on. Transportation requirements can be met by various modes — roads, rail, inland waterways, sea, air — some of which may find themselves in direct competition with, or perhaps complementary to, the others, thus often creating problems of substitutability.

Each mode offers its own advantages — different infrastructures with different facilities, different speeds, different costs — but there are areas where these relative advantages diminish and overlap with one another. Railroads seem to offer cheap and efficient transport for large quantities of goods over long distances, whereas air transport provides the fastest, though most expensive, services more suited to small quantities of high value goods. Air transport is primarily concerned, nonetheless, with carrying people, partly because the capacity for handling cargo at air terminals has hitherto restricted the extensive use of this mode. The recent introduction of container technology, however, seems to have been a spur to encouraging wider use of air transport in this respect.

The general worldwide trend towards motorisation is reflected in the current dependence upon, and development of, the road networks in most countries. 'The relative importance of rail, sea and air transport varies from one country to another depending largely on geographical features, but almost everywhere the dominant form of transport is by road.' [1]

The breakdown of the *World Bank Operations* statistics on lending for transportation endorses this observation, pointing out that its cumulative lending through the financial year 1971 allocated nearly half (49 per cent) to highways, with railways standing at 38 per cent and ports at 10 per cent. This World Bank report concludes then that: 'Concurrently with the changes in geographic distribution, there has been a steady trend away from railways and in favour of highways in the modal distribution of transport lending.' [2]

Granted that motor transport is generally the most efficient mode for 'short' and 'intermediate' distances, what actually seems to have been behind this trend of road transport dominance is the fast growth of the world economy in the 1960s. To take the extreme, if a country is underdeveloped, with no industry and no factories, there is hardly any sense in building an expensive road or railway, while traffic volume remains too small to justify the investment. And it is no surprise that, in such cases, air transport is cheaper to adopt.

Needless to say, maritime transport has been an industry furnishing the lifeblood for sea-surrounded industrialised countries such as the United Kingdom and Japan. For the latter in particular, most of the raw materials essential for such a resource-poor country have, by necessity, had to be carried in, and industrial goods carried out, by sea transport alone. But surprisingly, this transport sector seems to have received a relatively small amount of attention among transport researchers, at least until recently. Following upon the surge of imports in gargantuan proportions into Middle Eastern countries — raw materials, industrial goods, entire plants, and so on — attention has inevitably been drawn more and more to this field, and especially to port development as the most important aspect of this phenomenon.

A port is the interface between the maritime transport and domestic transport sectors. And it plays a key role in the development of any economy, by no means excepting the land-locked nations (whose bulkier imports usually arrive by way of ports in neighbouring countries). Any inadequacy of a nation's port(s) will doubtless depress the level of throughput, to a level where it fails to meet the target set by national economic planning schemes. Such a situation, with ports unable to meet the demands imposed upon them, often manifests itself in the long ship queues currently prevalent in harbours everywhere, with much of the cargo having to be 'laid up' unwittingly in expensive vessels instead of in cheap warehouses.

At a conference for experts organised by UNCTAD in Geneva in April 1976, it was established that the average number of days a ship must wait for a berth in thirty ports which are regularly subject to port congestion has grown as follows:

Year	Days
1971	2.2
1972	2.3
1973	4.0
1974	4.8
1975	14.3
1976	40.5

These figures refer exclusively to general cargo vessels. The waiting period for bulk carriers in the same ports was often much longer. [3]

It is essential that any country determines as early as possible the right level of capacity it requires, and how much to invest in the sector, not only to help avoid such congestion but also simply because port investment involves lengthy planning delays, a large initial capital outlay, and a relatively long lag time before completion. What makes the problem of port planning all the more difficult is that not only does the traffic flow vary in volume over time, but also the pattern of flow may show a marked change as the degree of development of the domestic economy shifts from one stage to a more mature stage. The process is further complicated by changes in port technology such as specialised berths, roll-on roll-off type handling, and unitisation or assembly of packages.

Moreover, the 'capacity question' of a port cannot be answered solely within itself. A port is only a sort of 'gate' for imports and exports, and not the final site of either production or consumption, being merely a connection to the sea on one side and to inland transport facilities on the other. Therefore, the improvement of this intermediary system, without a commensurate consideration of these joint systems, will result in nothing more than a superficial improvement of the total transport system, without making adequate safeguard against the rise of bottlenecks at some points in the other connected systems. After all, the transport system is only part of an integral system for production and consumption; and the optimal co-ordination of all the interrelated transport systems is a task which must have first priority. It is no exaggeration to state that substantial economies in the maritime transport cost can be achieved through the improvement of the port transport system — provided also that the improvement is fully cognisant of its potential effects throughout the extended transport and industrial sectors which it serves.

The object of this study is to make an extensive analysis of the port transport system, and its economic implications, from the viewpoint of its fundamental functions described above, laying suitable stress upon co-ordination relative to other transport systems connected to it. It has long been a source of anxiety that

> ... there is no commonly accepted method of appraising proposals for investment in port facilities .... In some instances this lack of systematic appraisal techniques appears to have led to under-investment, over-investment or misplaced and mistimed investment. [4]

A brief glance at the literature on port operations and development brings this complaint into clear perspective.

One cannot point to a single up-to-date general text on the subject. Titles of books and essays dealing with particular aspects of the port subsystems and investment schemes do appear in the footnotes and bibliography whenever deemed essential. (Other references which have not been considered directly relevant to the present work may be found in the bibliographies of these books, as well as in the essays contained in such serials as the London School of Economics trimestrial *Journal of Transport Economics and Policy*). The few pertinent works in the Japanese language are descriptive, limited largely to statistical presentations and the identification of bottlenecks to smooth development, and have not yet reached the stage of comprehensive analysis.

When published works on a particular subject are sparse, one usually has recourse to unpublished university theses. But here also ports are scantily represented. In addition to those theses noted, a very few others may be found in the annual *Index to Theses Accepted for Higher Degrees in the Universities of Great Britain and Ireland*, and in the monthly *Dissertation Abstracts* (listing doctoral theses of major United States universities, plus a few in Australia, Canada and Europe). Ideas pertinent to the present study have been adopted in a few instances from other works, with appropriate credit given in each case. But except as otherwise noted, the concepts, and their development, presented here are my own.

The case of Japan presents a remarkable instance of the indifference with which the port industry can be regarded by both industry and government even for a nation totally dependent upon sea transport for its livelihood. The port as an entity has always been regarded as something set apart from the rest of the transport sector, not least because other forms of transport (road, rail and air) have come to form part of everyday life while most people never have any contact at all with a seaport. The port tended to be regarded as something that can 'take care of itself', a notion reflected even in the most recent transport texts (such as A. Prest's *Transport Economics in Developing Countries*) which treat the question of ports thinly if at all. Moreover, it was long thought that the era of 'high growth rate' would last forever. And since raw materials in Japan were very cheap in relation to the value of finished goods, the remarkable profits reaped during the boom period far over-shadowed whatever losses there were due to inefficiency in port operations. This complacency was rudely shattered in Japan following the 1973 energy crisis. As money became dearer, it was realised that the carefree days of cheap capital and high profits were a thing of the past, and that investment in future would have to be more carefully designed and appraised than ever. With the growth rate falling to nil, the cost of raw materials (all imported) on the rise, wage pressure remaining fairly high, and so on, the industrial as well as public sectors rapidly came to realise that, since other factors were often beyond their reach, the transportation system was one of the few significant components of production which was both entirely within the control of Japan itself and also capable of being profitably improved. The passing of the old 'never mind the price' attitude brought the efficiency of port operations under close scrutiny. And it is now generally accepted that in order to help restore at least a moderate growth rate, both public and private sectors will have to work towards a total co-ordination of all transport modes in order to draw the utmost advantage from available facilities.

Some reference will be made to policy strategies, investment planning, and other amorphous problems which can never be dealt with in as tidy and comprehensive a fashion as might be desired. But general investment planning, or even the means of formulating investment policy piecemeal, are questions which do not fall entirely within the scope of this work. We are more concerned here with the essential design of the port, in trying to understand its discrete parts and discrete operations, and the interrelations among them, in as orderly and as mathematically sound a manner as possible: And it is to be hoped that this presentation will furnish a few useful tools for making a systematic analysis in order to help, at least in some ways, to provide a clearer basis for the appraisal of port operations and future investment.

Recent developments in the analysis of port systems

The studies and plans for port development which have appeared in recent decades have frequently been received with acrimonious criticism. A 1960 report by T. Thorburn of the Business Research Institute in Stockholm declared that: 'Large investments in harbours throughout the world appear to be made to a large extent *intuitively* and not on the basis of rational economic calculations.' [5]

His opinion was echoed by a United Nations Conference on Trade and Development (UNCTAD) paper pointing out the lack of systematic evaluation techniques in this area, and in particular the failure in general to provide cost-benefit analyses. [6] In spite of the paucity of studies dealing with any or all of the subsystems involved in port management, the problem has nonetheless gradually come to be widely recognised, doubtless influenced by the ever increasing capital outlay involved. It was not until a few years ago that the importance of port pricing policy entered the limelight, as suggested by a World Bank report's advice to countries on the point of investing in new equipment and port capacity expansion.

> In the future the characteristics of shipping and port pricing in each case should be analyzed in more depth, to see what can be done with port pricing to regain benefits or to encourage behaviour on the part of shippers and shipping companies which will yield maximum benefits to the country. [7]

Partly because of the complexity of the port system as a whole, and because of the shallow nature of research which has often been undertaken, most of the studies in the literature at present do not attempt to tackle more than a single aspect of port activity, merely satisfying themselves by relating each aspect in a general way to the numerous other subsystems with which their own particular problem is integrated. Most of these studies fall into two categories; the 'case studies' which are derived from data collected in particular ports, and the 'theoretical studies' whose conclusions are usually derived from consideration of analytical models.

One of the early works which presents a comprehensive appraisal based on data from a real port project is a paper published in 1964 by the University of Malaysia on Port Swettenham. [8] The chapter dealing with an analytical treatment of the port project, as opposed to sheer statistical extrapolation of existing data trends, is based upon an application of queuing theory to be solved by the Monte Carlo method. A paper published several years later by the Economist Intelligence Unit Limited of London (EIU) provides a thorough exposé of the cost-benefit analysis of the same project, including a simulation model constructed in such a way as to take into account both the physical and the technological changes likely to happen in subsequent years. [9] In this paper, the authors made a comparison between Mettam's method, [10] which is an application of queuing theory, as opposed to the workable cost-benefit method using discounted cash flow (dcf) techniques. The EIU paper concluded that the complex characteristics of Port Swettenham and its traffic could more sufficiently be taken account of by applying a simulation model as opposed to the method proposed by Mettam. A similar type of treatment can be found in a study of port development in Korea by Lyon Associates, acting as consulting engineers in association with the EIU, in which the various arguments justifying a set of priorities for the project ports of Pusan and Mukho are evaluated. [11]

Most of the theoretical analyses of port systems are constructed by and large on the basis of queuing theory, a trend which is tersely examined by E. Edmond in his 'Uses and Abuses of Queue Theory in Port Investment Appraisal'. He points out that generally there tend to be only two considerations involved, because: 'the essential feature of these appraisals is the trade-off between estimated port costs supplied by the civil engineers and the costs of ship waiting times, including cargo inventory costs.' [12] A paper by P.Taborga published by the School of Engineering at the Massachusetts Institute of Technology, for example, develops and tests a model for a dynamic growth policy for a seaport in an undeveloped geographical region, using a simple type of dynamic programming to treat a case of a single homogeneous commodity flow. [13] The basic assumptions on which his model is built are as follows: (1) constant elasticities of demand with respect to all demand variables, (2) a constant marginal utility of income throughput, with the condition that revenues equal costs. The model actually constructed, because of its scope, does not attempt to analyse the complexities of the port system but is in fact an application of queuing theory. It represents the port as a set of multi-channels in parallel (in this case, a set of identical but independently operated berths), with an identical set of Poisson inputs and outputs, and for simplicity does not treat all the constituent subsystems and the linkages among them.

A similar approach dealing with port capacity requirements was taken by Jan de Weille and A. Ray in their 1974 article 'The Optimum Port Capacity', [14] which places emphasis upon the general problems involved in reconciling capacity with fluctuating demand. The authors carry out extensive calculations, achieving various numerical transformations as a result of manipulating their initial, basic insights. The validity of their assumptions is defended by the authors on the ground that quite a few reports have already attested to the Poisson distribution hypothesis upon which they depend. Examples, which might be noted here, of the construction of such models on the basis of the Poisson distribution hypothesis, with subsequent application to particular ports, include the work carried out by the Israel Ports Authority. [15] Another report by P. Omtvedt *On the Profitability of Port Investments* [16] published in Oslo, has been described as

> an elaborate exercise in queuing theory and is concerned with minimizing costs rather than maximizing either the profits of the port authority or the net social benefits of the project. Queueing theory has indeed a significant part to play in this field, but not a leading role. [17]

A similar approach has been followed by a Portuguese economist dealing with the port of Lisbon. [18]

An alternative to the application of queuing theory was introduced by J. Buckley and S. Gooneratne in their 1974 article 'Optimal Scheduling of Transport Improvements to Cater for Growing Traffic Congestion'. They argue in favour of using their 'average congestion cost' function as a function of the traffic flow, the shape of which depends on the particular traffic congestion process in operation as well as on unit vehicular costs. They also investigate some aspects of the determination of timing for investment in the face of changing traffic flow over a period of years. [19] Their idea of introducing a

8

congestion cost function was quickly taken up, and modified for somewhat more generalised applications, by W. Chang and others, who have built a model for the comprehensive planning of future harbour capacities. [20] In essence, the latter's work is devoted to the minimisation of the total cost for cargo transport (i.e. ship cost plus inland transport cost) by using non-linear programming. They assume the non-linear function for ship waiting cost to be dependent only on the flow of cargo. Their costs for ship waiting time, however, are derived on the basis of queuing theory. One of the reasons why ship waiting time costs are included in this comprehensive analysis is that such costs are passed on to the grain importers (to whom they make specific reference in the model) through surcharges and higher ocean transport rates. This problem, as they formulate it, is handled accordingly by linear programming.

One especially problematic area which the existing literature has hardly dared to tackle is the analysis of investment planning for a port facing a continuously shifting, price-dependent demand. Nonetheless, proposals for the use of dynamic programming towards this end have recently been put forward by J. Devanney and L. Tan in an article examining the coupling of expansion policies for a port with short-run pricing. [21]

The handiness as well as the usefulness of the various theoretical modelling techniques mentioned here have thus become keenly recognised in recent years; and a lot of work has been undertaken in this connection. This type of approach cannot be pursued to advantage, however, nor continue to be viable, without questioning the validity of the basic assumptions. One example is the widely accepted assumption of Erlang distribution for ship arrivals and service times, which is necessary in order to make the various models generally applicable. A reluctance on the part of some researchers to accept the validity of such assumptions has naturally given rise to a different type of approach, the simulation model.

It is the purpose of the simulation model technique to obtain the operational consequences of changes in port configuration, and to estimate as accurately as possible the systems implications of port investment projects. A fundamental difference exists between the simulated and the theoretical techniques. The basic idea of the simulation technique is to simulate the system in a computer using data actually collected from operational statistics of a particular port, whereas its theoretical counterpart, on the other hand, is concerned with building a model of the system which seems to answer certain questions as regards system operations in a general sense. The latter may be accomplished by substituting several simplifications in place of

9

complicated reality, trying at the same time not to destroy the fundamental feature while still extracting the essence of the system.

The simulation method has been extensively examined by the Transportøkonomisk Institutt of Oslo. The first version of its model was worked out under contract for UNCTAD in 1968, and tested on the Port of Casablanca. The extensively modified second phase of the model — carried out during 1971-73 under a joint project among UNCTAD, the Port of Bergen Authority, and the Institutt, and published in 1973 as *Port Development Planning* — is reported to have been tested successfully on the Port of Bergen in Norway. [22] The third version was further developed to allow simulations of several ports simultaneously, a project carried out by the Institutt alone, and published in 1974 as *A Simulation Model for a Multi-Port System.* [23]

In contrast to the Transportøkonomisk Institutt model, where the operational relationships are mostly based upon regression analyses from the actual data, various other researchers have attempted to imbed the Erlang distribution into their models. [24] They defend their positions on the ground that observed port operations throughout the world have shown the range of patterns found, in practice, to coincide with that of the Erlang family of distribution; and that since only two parameters — that is, parameter k and the mean value λ — fully determine an Erlang distribution, this method has the distinct advantage of placing few data demands on the user. For application to a particular port, nonetheless, such a statement seems to be a matter of putting the cart before the horse. One might also bear in mind Edmond's claims in his work on queuing theory in the same respect, where he notes that

> the number of berths where ship arrivals are random is rather small. The only deep sea trade where this may be true is the grain trade and possibly the ore trade. For tramp shipping on short sea routes it is probably true. Other trades are either organized on a liner basis with scheduled service . . . . This means the assumption of random arrivals at a berth is a poor one. [25]

Such views, if found to be correct in actual port operations, would tend to invalidate much of the academic groundwork already broken in this area. They nonetheless suggest that a further consideration of such distributions, examining the validity of opinions on both sides, might well be undertaken now to considerable advantage.

One gets the impression from much of the research so far published that theorists have tended to find such assumptions as the Erlang distribution quite handy and appealing, and so are tempted to 'reshape' the data (or at least assume that it will fit closely enough these distribution sets), so that the queuing theory will be readily applicable. This is not to say, however, that the queuing theory has little role to play in the course of analysis of the port transport system. In fact quite a few analyses in this work have made use of the basic concept of queuing theory. What should be stressed is simply that it is of vital importance to recognise the scope of the applicability of any theory; and the conclusions derived from the theory should be reappraised within this scope without any bias.

The questions raised here thus provide a challenging incentive as well as a starting point for my own research into yet another area, systems analysis for analysing the inextricably interrelated parts of the whole port system. This may not be regarded generally as so tidy and appealing as other methods of analysis. But it is nonetheless operational-oriented and, of perhaps greater importance, is designed and presented here in such a way that it will, it is to be hoped, find not only a wide application but also easy use by all those involved in port systems operations and planning.

Subsystemisation for an extensive analytical approach

Existing studies of port operations have tended to follow a piece-meal approach to systems analysis. This has not led to a generally satisfactory treatment of the problems of port development, in spite of the large quantities of data available. Two of the key difficulties seem to be the hesitancy of most investigators to make full use of mathematical modelling, and the tendency to regard port operations in terms of a few independent activities rather than in terms of a highly complex entity of subsystems. Examples of both weaknesses are provided in the United Nations *Berth Throughput*. The analysis of only a portion of the entity cannot lead to the creation of a full model, although each and every part must be regarded as a separate problem before one can proceed to study the interaction of all as a whole. In order to establish any formulae for optimisation one must have at one's disposal the means of seeking out the weakest links in a whole system, and the means of dealing with such bottlenecks in the context of restraints imposed by existing facilities, capital and labour. This requires the treatment of the port in a comprehensive fashion, both in each of its parts and as an integrated system.

An analytical approach is adopted here for several reasons. It can take advantage of the rough and unused data currently accessible,

11

while circumventing that which is regarded as unreliable. In particular, the data are published by the United Nations, the World Bank, and various national and international transport institutes. But much of what is available is either inaccurate or poorly organised. So the collection of data adequate for testing the model would require considerable time and effort. This does not, however, impede the construction of the model itself. The Transportøkonomisk Institutt of Norway, working in connection with UNCTAD, were previously following the analytical approach. But because of difficulties in mathematical treatment and formulation in their study of the Port of Bergen, they have switched to the computer simulation approach. Although I myself have conducted other research using computer simulation techniques, I have chosen not to use the latter approach because it would be too time consuming (requiring at least a year for a test run) and prohibitively expensive. The analytical approach, in contrast, is an open challenge which can be taken up with reasonable expectations for success by anyone prepared to carry the mathematical modelling involved beyond the limits formerly reached. From a practical point of view, therefore, the analytical approach seems to offer every advantage in terms of personal resources and time for a limited theoretical treatment which can be related to wide practical applications.

Not a great number of basic operations are involved in the flow of cargo through a seaport. Each will in due course be examined separately. But it might be useful at this juncture to give a very rough description of the divisions. Imported cargo is carried into the port area and up to the berth by ship, usually with a tugboat guiding it. Depending on the state of congestion the ship may or may not have to wait in the offing. After berthing, the cargo is unloaded onto the quay. It can then be taken directly to the inland transport terminals (e.g. rail or road); or it can be removed onto barges for further transport by waterways. There is also the choice of the 'indirect' route, moving the cargo into the storage system (sheds or warehouses) before transfer at a later time to inland destinations. Exported cargo, of course, follows the exact reverse process. For purposes of analysis, it has been thought best to break port operations down into no more than four basic operations, or groups of operations, which seems to be the most convenient division of units which can be treated effectively as entities.

1   *Navigation aids system.* The number of navigation aids is quite large — lighthouses, buoys, radio aids, harbour radar, leaders and leading lines, and so on. The only aid which is thought to require careful scrutiny here is the tug-berth system, particularly

12

because of its important role in the port time of the ship and also because tugs are indispensable to large ports for achieving overall optimality of port operations.

2   *Quay handling and transfer system.* The handling system is the true interface between marine transport and inland transport. It is the gateway and the sole corridor of the port system. Efficiency in the handling system depends not only on the handling rate at quay-side, but also on the extent to which the link-ups between this system and all subsequent ones are properly matched. Contrary to what might be supposed at first glance, an increase in handling rates would result in little improvement in overall productivity of the port, unless it were well matched by commensurate improvements of the incorporated system.

3   *Storage system.* The storage system provides a variety of services — transit sheds, warehouses, open shed, grain silos, container parks, and so on. Its very existence gives rise to a number of questions. What, for example, determines the cargo 'split' between direct and 'indirect' (i.e. by way of storage) routing? How does the storage pricing policy affect the behaviour of the port users, and thus affect port throughput capacity? The choices available allow this system to serve as a kind of 'buffer' between marine transport and inland transport. And its analysis in this light alone is often posed in parallel with the other alternative, the 'direct' route, for cargo requiring no storage at all.

4   *Co-ordination with inland transport.* Inland transport is the pipeline connecting the port with domestic markets (for imports) as well as production sites (for exports). The inland transport system *per se* lies entirely outside the scope and purpose of this work. The pertinent questions here about inland transport are those involving the ways in which it connects to the port, and its capacity in relation to the throughput capacity of the port. Without effective inland connections, the port cannot function. Thus the particular concern of this work must be to examine how efficient the inland transport system may be in carrying inbound cargo away from the port without delay, and in bringing outbound cargo into the port area.

Notes

[1]   J. Thomson, *Modern Transport Economics*, Penguin, 1974, p.51
[2]   *World Bank Operations: Sectoral Programs and Policies*,

Baltimore, 1972, p.154

[3]   Hinterland, Tweenmaandelijks Tijd Schrift, *Bimonthly Review*, XXVI, Antwerp 1977, p.13

[4]   R. Goss, *Studies in Maritime Economics*, Cambridge, 1970, p.158

[5]   T. Thorburn, *Supply and Demand for Water Transport*, Stockholm Business Research Institute, 1960, p.140 (italics added)

[6]   UNCTAD, *Development of Ports*, Geneva 1967, pp 28-32

[7]   *World Bank Operations*, p.174

[8]   U.A. Aziz, S.J. Gilani, Jock Hoe and Lim Ching Yah, *Traffic Flow through Port Swettenham, Projected to 1975*, University of Malaya, Department of Economics, Kuala Lumpur 1964. See especially part 6 for their analytical treatment.

[9]   I.G. Heggie and C.B. Edwards, 'Port Investment Problems: How to Decide Investment Priorities', in Institution of Civil Engineers (eds), *Conference on Civil Engineering Problems Overseas*, London 1968, pp 31-49

[10]   J.D. Mettam, 'Forecasting Delays to Ships in Port', *The Dock Harbour Authority*, no.558, April 1967, pp 380-382

[11]   Lyon Associates, Inc., *Korea Port Development Study, Draft Final Report: Determination of Port Development Priorities*, privately reproduced for the Republic of Korea and the International Bank for Reconstruction and Development, *ca.*1971

[12]   E.D. Edmond, 'Uses and Abuses of Queue Theory in Port Investment Appraisal', privately reproduced and distributed at the University of Liverpool Marine Transport Centre, 1975, p.1

[13]   Pedro N. Taborga, *Determination of an Optimal Policy for Seaport Growth and Development*, mimeographed, Massachusetts Institute of Technology School of Engineering, 1969

[14]   Jan de Weille and Anandarup Ray, 'The Optimum Port Capacity', *Journal of Transport Economics and Policy*, VIII/3, September 1974, pp 244-59

[15]   Israel Ports Authority, Reports and Statistics Center, *Yearbook of Israel Ports Statistics, 1963/64*, Haifa 1965

[16]   Petter C. Omtvedt, *On the Profitability of Port Investment*, Oslo 1963

[17]   R.O. Goss, 'Port Investment' in D. Munby (ed.), *Transport*, Penguin 1968, fn.8, pp 280-81. Goss mentions several additional works to which his criticisms are equally applicable.

[18]   F. Marques Da Silva, *Boletin do Porto de Lisboa*, no.150, 1963, which is mentioned in de Weille and Ray, op.cit., p.247

[19]   D.J. Buckley and S.G. Gooneratne, 'Optimal Scheduling of Transport Improvements to Cater for Growing Traffic Congestion',

Journal of Transport Economics and Policy, VIII/2, May 1974, pp 122-35

[20] W.H. Chang, L.S. Lee, S.J. Yang and C.G. Vandervoort, 'Harbour Expansion and Harbour Congestion Charges', *Journal of Transport Economics and Policy*, IX/3, September 1975, pp 209-29

[21] J.W. Devanney and L.H. Tan, 'The Relationship between Short-Run Pricing and Investment Timing: The Port Pricing and Expansion Example', *Transportation Research*, IX/6, December 1975, pp 329-37

[22] Frode Eidem, *Port Development Planning*, Oslo, Transportøkonomisk Institutt, 1973

[23] Frode Eidem, *A Simulation Model for a Multi-Port System*, Oslo, Transportøkonomisk Institutt, 1974

[24] See for examples Pedro N. Taborga, *Port Simulation Model (GSM) Release (I) User's Guide*, reproduced by the International Bank for Reconstruction and Development, 1974, and R.W. Gaisford, *A Simulation Model of a Large Multi-Purpose Sea Port and Its Application in Two Large International Sea Ports*, Rendel, Palmer and Tritton, Consulting Engineers, London, *ca.* 1970

[25] Edmond, 'Uses and Abuses of Queue Theory', p.18

2 Economic implications of port congestion

Part A. Causes and effects of congestion

In order to simplify the economic implications of congestion for both suppliers and users of services in ports, one might make a comparison with a seller of sweets at a kiosk in a country fair. The inconvenience of having to queue to buy at the kiosk does not seem terribly vexing, because the people who go to the fair generally expect 'congestion', indeed, some of them even go to enjoy it. The kiosk owner, however, to meet his required selling target, actually prefers a constant 'congestion' of customers, because an absence of it may mean in effect that he cannot meet his operating costs, including his opportunity cost of labour. It is of no importance that some customers, from time to time, may decide to go elsewhere to avoid the 'congestion', because the kiosk owner is fully occupied and could not have sold to them anyway (at least, not without increasing his own costs, such as by paying wages to an assistant).

Port authorities are not unlike the kiosk owner, in the sense that congestion caused by ships will mean that port operations are in constant motion, without any lapses which would automatically entail a stoppage of cargo inflow while incurring costs even for the time in which operations had to shut down in the absence of customers. Congestion of a minor degree, from the port authority's point of view, is therefore not an undesirable situation, as long as it does not slow down or hinder port operations but rather tends to keep them topped up. If congestion becomes heavy and chronic, then the port may profit by investing to provide more services which, in turn, will attract more traffic and thus greater revenues, provided that the new tariff scheme is sensibly worked out.

From the point of view of shippers, however, if the tariff (that is, the total of charges paid by shippers to the port for services) were fixed, they would obviously prefer to encounter no congestion whatsoever. Their ships could then always be guaranteed immediate servicing upon arrival in port. Yet, faced with no alternative transport

16

of much better efficiency, they will be ready to accept some congestion, at least to such an extent that under the existing tariff scheme it does not greatly disrupt the viability of their business.

If congestion becomes really heavy, however, the positions of both sides will be considerably modified. The shippers will lose money in various ways because of delays. And port authorities will be forced to seek remedies, either temporary ones (such as traffic regulation and control) or longer-term ones (such as the supply of new capacity). One of the effective temporary measures would be to introduce some form of rationing of services in order to eliminate marginal users, a tactic which often, but not necessarily, includes increases in the tariff. It is the problem of how to determine the tariff in the first place which is of great importance to the port authority, as well as the even more difficult mechanism of determining the exact increases in the tariff which will produce the desired effect of returning to the optimal utilisation of existing facilities. One has, moreover, few examples to use as guidelines, as there seems to be no agreement among either port authorities or users as to how to determine a proper tariff structure. In most cases port dues paid on ships and on goods bear no relationship to the actual cost incurred by the services rendered to them, and consequently do not reflect the true picture of the optimal allocation of scarce resources (that is, port facilities, including space and manpower).

The question of the tariff structure itself will be taken up in a later chapter. But here it would seem useful to confine ourselves to the individual problems involved, from both the shippers' and the port authorities' points of view, which will always have to be taken into consideration. One must thus examine the circumstances in which congestion tends to arise, and the steps which may be taken generally by port authorities to reduce it.

The mechanism by which the congestion phenomenon emerges can be put simply. It is the situation in which utilisation by the users leads to the relative saturation of the system. What is distinct about the congestion of ports, in contrast to that of inland transport, is that there can be as many distinct causes as there are distinct types of operation and equipment. Furthermore, not many of these components seem to be independent of the rest. (The outstanding ones would include channel depth, ship size, ship arrival pattern, cargo type, berthing speed, and storage capacity, to name the more important ones.) The seaport suffers, moreover, because of its own peculiar position in relation to bureaucracy and often to the people of many nationalities which it serves. 'Transport difficulties stem not just from overcrowded ports . . . but also from complex documentation procedures, inadequate communications facilities and even, at times, from a clash of cultures.' [1]

Marked externalities of congestion would include, for instance, increasing risk of collision, slower turnround time for ships, and thus incurred costs of tied-up ships and cargoes, delay of delivery of goods, and possible loss of market advantages. Each of these aspects must be examined from the viewpoint not only of the shippers and consignors, but also of the port authorities.

What makes it more difficult to tackle the problem is the port's supply characteristics, because the supply of services, unlike ordinary consumer goods, cannot be 'stored'. Besides, its capacity is relatively invariant in the short-run; and therefore a sudden jump in demand often cannot be coped with accordingly. If the phenomenon of fluctuation is of infrequent nature, some device (such as priority rules) could be introduced by consensus. But if it becomes a chronic profile, a proper rationing scheme of pricing seems necessary as a sensible means of identifying and eliminating the truly marginal users.

Some key points to be examined for attempts at resolving port congestion are listed below.

A. Operational improvement

    1   traffic regulation and control, including priority rules
    2   better organisation of the work force
    3   more efficient co-ordination of subsystems
    4   consolidated management information system
    5   simplification of paperwork (customs inspection, quicker notification of cargo arrivals, etc.)

B. Capital investment

    1   dredging and widening of channels
    2   construction of new berths and warehouses
    3   reclamation of land
    4   introduction and reinforcement of new handling facilities, plus labour consolidation

The limited scope of the present work does not permit a treatment of problems concerning management and traffic regulation *per se*. Traffic control could well receive analytical treatment, if the priority rules were given; but this seems impractical here because of the vast number of combinations of priority rules which might be formulated. Organisation of the work force is treated in the section below on allocation of labour. Co-ordination of the subsystems forms the basis of chapter 7. And various aspects of capital investment are discussed in the concluding chapter.

Some consequences of port congestion

There is no doubt that the problem of congestion produces serious repercussions of all sorts, not only within the countries concerned but also for the users of the ports. The most significant of all is probably that ships and cargo are liable to be tied up for fairly long periods, thus freezing capital as well as goods for nothing. During such periods, to make matters worse, time losses and damage or thefts and pilferage of cargo tend to occur more frequently than would otherwise be the case. And the entry of too many ships for anchorage within the mooring area of the port makes each one increasingly subject to collision. Such problems are encountered just in the short run. On the other hand, heavy congestion may result in a substantial diversion of traffic in the long run, or even stimulate the development of an alternative transport route, in both of which cases the host country may receive no share of the growing transport industry.

A variety of circumstances can lead to the crippling of port operations. For example, the food supply to India was put in question by strikers who forced India's ports out of work in 1975.

> Ships bringing food and fertilizers were among hundreds stranded in Indian ports today as more than 150,000 dock workers went on strike. . . . Unless the strike lasts for more than a week, the hold-up of grain ships is not likely to create a famine. . . . But the interruption of fertilizer imports could have a serious effect on plantings for the wheat crop due to be harvested next spring. [2]

Another cause is exemplified in the trouble facing the East African area. With the completion of the railway linking Zambia and Tanzania, the huge traffic expected from Zambia enormously heightened the pressures on the port of Dar-es-Salaam, which was already increasingly used by Zambia for its outflow of copper. Drastic political changes exerted a precipitate effect on routing, as explained by a Zambian copper concern.

> The port of Lobito and the Benguela railway were closed in August, 1975 following the outbreak of civil war in Angola. This route was handling about 50 per cent of the Zambian mining industry's import and export traffic. Its closure inevitably placed heavy pressure on Dar es Salaam which then became our main outlet to the sea. In September, 1975 limited use of the Tanzania-Zambia railway (Tazara) commenced,

19

supplementing the existing road transport capacity to the port.

After initial constraints, the transportation capability on the Dar es Salaam route improved but it soon became clear that the port could not cope with the sharply-increased throughput and port congestion reached disturbing levels. NCCM (Nchanga Consolidated Copper Mines Limited) exports were badly affected and the inflow of essential materials to the mines was severely disrupted. In the last few months (mid-1976), however, there has been a marked improvement in port handling performance at Dar es Salaam. This, together with growing Tanzara capacity, has produced encouraging results both in copper shipments and handling of imports. [3]

One could cite numerous cases in which similar sudden jumps in traffic, rather than gradual increases, have become imminent. The problem for such ports becomes especially acute when the expected increase brought about by the development of other transport facilities comes at a time when a huge backlog of goods has already been piling up at a port for some time.

Yet another reason for congestion is the big import surge which has become a commonplace in most of the Middle Eastern countries. The seven berths of Dammam, before the big import boom beginning in 1973, handled 1,308,878 tons. By 1975 it had added another six berths and pushed its tonnage up by 401,576 tons. An increase in the number of berths to forty-two by 1980 is planned, in anticipation of an annual tonnage of around seven millions. [4] If that target is met, it will mean an increase in tonnage capacity by more than 300 per cent in five years. In the meantime, priority has been given to ships carrying cement, a commodity desperately needed for the Saudi development boom. Even so, cement-bearing ships were reportedly having to queue for about sixty days for a berth, while general cargo ships were having to wait around seventy days.

One striking phenomenon which has in recent years appeared especially in developing countries where port facilities cannot keep up with demand is the loss of precious investment capital, partly through being needlessly tied up in commodities which cannot be unloaded and sometimes through payments of compensation. 'Congestion at the ports of the Gulf, the Red Sea and North Africa is added billions of dollars to the importing countries' payments, and tying up a considerable amount of freight capacity.' [5]

Regardless of whether delays are caused by lack of planning, coordination, or strikes, it is often the government that is called upon to pay a surcharge, or other form of compensation to help offset the losses incurred by shippers under conditions of extraordinarily

20

long delays. Perhaps the most remarkable case of heavy congestion ever faced by any country was that which began to build up in Nigeria in 1974. *The Observer* reported that

> More than 400 ships, 240 of them carrying cement, are stuck outside Lagos harbour. Most have little hope of unloading their cargo for up to two years. . . . But with shipowners going through a particularly lean time . . . the oil-rich Nigerian Government is forced to pay an average of £1,225 a day in waiting time. [6]

Among the several reasons for this situation, the outstanding one is the apparently irrational orders made by the Nigerian government for 16 million tons of cement, when the actual handling rate of the only available port was estimated at about 1.3 million tons a year. Extra wharf allocation was hurriedly scheduled to increase unloading by a factor of six, from 4,000 to 24,000 tons a day, although this was still only about half what was required for the momentary surge.

It is reported that surcharges resulting from port congestion cost Iran some one billion dollars during the financial year April 1975 to March 1976. In some countries, such enormous surcharges may easily offset the benefits being sought through the betterment of the transport system. For example, the reopening of the Suez Canal has certainly benefitted the countries of the Arabian Gulf region; but the gains deriving from speedier and cheaper deliveries are more or less offset by the surcharges incurred, as well as delays encountered because of acute congestion at nearly every port. To some extent, the same holds true for North African ports.

Port congestion must thus be seen as one of the foremost constraints to rapid development of any region. Its repercussions are far wider than first meets the eye.

> Acute port congestion has been the biggest infrastructure bottleneck, aggravating the life of the constructors, raising the cost of locally purchased building materials and leading to delays in implementation. . . . The lack of locally produced or available materials undoubtedly imposes a constraint upon the total construction output in the Middle East and poses many problems in the execution of individual projects. . . . The basic materials which greatly affect the pace of construction are cement, structural steel, rod reinforcement, and timber. [7]

The general shortage of skilled manpower for port operations is certainly not among the least of the causes of port congestion in some countries.

To implement the targets of their visionary plan the Saudis fore-

21

see the need to import no less than 500,000 expatriates by 1980. . . . as the momentum of development continues, the manpower shortage seems likely to become an even bigger constraint than it has been so far. [8]

Among the other crucial factors comprising the causes of congestion are poor handling facilities and equipment, and a lack of storage space. But in some cases, at least, provisional efforts have been made to provide some relief. 'The expansion of grain silos . . . plus the supply of new warehouse and lighting equipment to other (Algerian) ports . . . illustrate the priority the Government is giving to temporary measures to ease congestion until the bigger infrastructure projects can be completed. [9]

One cannot overestimate the direct repercussions to a country's economy arising from port congestion. The problem is partly a matter of causal effects — including a deterrent to the rapid development of the domestic economy through delays of vital cargo, and the diversion of traffic — and partly a matter of such after-effects as the surcharges incurred at great expense to the country.

Viewed from another angle, port congestion has its external effects upon the users of the port as well. For example,

Shin Nihon Shosen, a cargo shipping operator with 22 vessels of 10,000-15,000 tons, none of which was owned by the company but chartered from foreign ship owners, went bankrupt because of their tied up cargo off the Persian Gulf, solely due to the long chronic congestion there. [10]

This clearly illustrates how badly port congestion can hit the smaller shipping agents, who have tended to protest bitterly because of the needless costs they have incurred (including insurance and interest payments) as well as the tying up of their working capital.

But port congestion has a few positive aspects as well. It has occasionally led to a shift in demand, though temporary it may be, on technological equipment such as vessels, cranes, and so forth. A good example is the steady increase in the demand for 'ro-ro' (roll-on, roll-off) type vessels.

Middle East economies have greatly stimulated the growth of other transport systems as well as roll-on roll-off. Freight forwarders have invested large amounts of money and efforts into developing overland systems which in some cases use roll-on roll-off for one leg of the journey and in others are entirely by road. Freights forwarders are in business to try to guarantee door-to-door delivery for goods and have made considerable progress in minimising the risks and problems which have

22

become apparent in the past two years. [11]

At a time when the tanker business is in a deep slump, it is reported that Japanese ship building companies have nonetheless been receiving steadily increasing orders for these ro-ro type vessels from such countries as Liberia, Kuwait, West Germany, France and Sweden. One of the major reasons behind this tendency is explained as its advantage that ro-ro type vessels, in contrast to the traditional cargo vessels, can be handled with satisfactory efficiency even where ports are already rather congested and where port facilities are in relatively poor condition. [12]   But ro-ro vessels have their drawbacks, too.

> It is argued that the roll-on roll-off vessel is a short-term solution to a short-term problem, namely lack of quayside space for cargo shipping. Once the vast number of new berths are completed, many of them with container handling facilities, it is said that the roll-on roll-off ship will be defeated by the superior economics of its rivals, in particular a specialised container ship. [13]

Comparisons of this type of vessel to a specialised container ship reveal that the disadvantage of ro-ro lies in the fact that it is 'space inefficient', that is, containers despatched by ro-ro may have to be on wheels, which occupy space that could otherwise be used for more cargo. Nonetheless, 'several roll-on roll-off operators claim that they are there to stay'. [14]   And they apparently place their hope on the flexibility of roll-on roll-off ships as an advantage that will persist.

Port efficiency/inefficiency with respect to
ship turnround time

Port time, that is, time required for any ship to make all essential motions at port, plus any waiting time at anchor, may be divided for purposes of analysis into three parts.

1   Time spent at anchor: perhaps the greatest variable, due in great part solely to congestion

2   Time spent in internal manoeuvring: the sum of times spent in motion in the channel, waiting for tugs and pilots, shifting towards berths, and loss time before and after cargo handling

3   Cargo handling time: the truly productive time spent at a berth, from the commencement of cargo handling until its completion

The third of these encompasses the large number of subsystems treated elsewhere. The second is subject to improvement only within strict limits, as one cannot, for example, move ships too quickly within the port without danger of accidents.

It is thus the first point which is of particular concern to us here, as it is this time-consuming portion which is subject to the greatest variation, hence the greatest leeway for reduction of time. With port time occupying more than half of the time a ship spends on any voyage, it should be obvious that this facet is a matter of vital significance to any consideration of ship cost. And as congestion is the foremost culprit contributing to the high ratio of port time to total voyage time, it is to the question of the reduction of congestion itself that we should address ourselves here.

Arguments for the reduction of congestion in a port, hence some relief from ship delay, may be couched in terms of such 'benefits' as the avoidance of potential collision. This cannot readily be translated into money terms; and it is not likely to have strong appeal as a justification for the investment involved. A much more straight-forward benefit, and one of greater importance, is the improvement of ship turnround time.

> The current proportion of time spent in port by cargo liners appears to be about 60 per cent, and . . . if this could be re-duced to 20 per cent the cost of sea transport in a cargo liner could be reduced by between 18 per cent and 35 per cent depending on the route length. [15]

Port time may vary greatly depending on the efficiency of port operations, as pointed out in a comparison of two groups of ports to which Britain trades.

> The conventional cargo liners operating on the U.K. —India trade route spends on average some 67 per cent of their voyage time in port . . . (whereas) the time spent in port on those routes (from the U.K. to Australasia and the Far East) is scheduled at about 52 per cent. [16]

One should not, however, immediately jump to the conclusion implicit in the above quotations that the percentage of total ship time spent in port is a clear indicator of port efficiency. These percentages will vary widely depending on ship size, type, and numerous other factors, as indicated in table 2.1.

It is probably advisable to avoid the two extremes of (a) high efficiency *with* congestion, as opposed to (b) low efficiency *without* congestion. One may ask, then, by how much the time spent in port could be reduced, if the port can ensure both reasonably efficient handling and the absence of congestion at the same time. The

Table 2.1

Percentages of ship time spent at sea and in port [17]

	Passenger liners	Cargo liners	Deep-sea tramps	General purpose tankers
Per cent of time at sea	63	40	57	81
Per cent of time in port	37	60	43	19

percentages of times given in the table do not indicate the extent of deviation from any optimally efficient system. Theoretically speaking (although not realistically so), port time could be reduced almost indefinitely by installing some super-efficient handling system. One can also imagine a situation in which there are two types of handling equipment in the port. One may be 'slow' in its handling services, but at the same time offer the advantage of no queuing for the berths it serves. The other may offer a 'fast' and highly specialised type of service, but suffer from congestion at its berths. One may find, then, that for a ship which can use either of the two types of equipment, the latter alternative, in spite of its congestion, actually reduces ship time in port more than would the former, uncongested alternative.

One should, furthermore, not assume that the absence of congestion is any sort of indicator that the port is a particularly efficient one. The price of increased efficiency for a particular port may have been extensive capital investment, which in turn may have been followed by increases in the tariff, followed by a decrease in the use of that port by shippers, and so on. This circular sort of argument suggests that the port, in its efforts to achieve higher efficiency and reduce congestion, may have in fact realised only the latter half of its two goals, since the resulting idle-capacity under the absence of congestion would itself imply 'inefficiency' in operations. Alternatively, improved efficiency might induce a higher level of traffic flow than ever (in spite of tariff changes), thus opening the way to a return to the former congested state.

Carefully planned investment in mechanisation, palletisation (unitisation), intensified use of labour, and other improvements will certainly help ships to reduce the time spent in port, thus saving ship cost as well as enabling shippers to increase their earning power through increases in voyage frequency. If on the other hand the

25

mechanical equipment is a 'given' factor, not to be altered much in the short-run, then any reduction of congestion will be a straight-forward matter of reducing, by some other means, the average ship time in port. In either case, the percentages of time spent in port should not be a target in itself, but rather a by-product of investment decisions based on aggregate costs and benefits all around. Ultimately, capital costs for improving cargo flow must be appraised in the light of the potential benefits accruing to everyone: shippers, consignors, consumers, and the port itself.

Part B. Congestion and the consequent opportunity cost

The cost of delay due to congestion is usually regarded as the cost of capital tied up in terms of freight and vessels. However, operating cost is by no means of little significance. Labour costs, maintenance, depreciation, and overheads may all be increased. 'With fully utilized vehicles like most ships, aircraft and lorries, delay reduces the output of the vehicle over a given period and therefore raises the age-depreciation per vehicle-kilometre.' [18]

Delays to goods, whether on board ship or in storage, imply in general a longer stay within the port. This means the tying up of valuable commodities for 'unwanted' periods of time and, moreover, the necessity of higher insurance premiums. In addition to the direct costs incurred, of course, goods become more liable to loss, damage, theft, and pilferage.

Since the smooth operation of the working capital is disrupted, an opportunity cost is implied. One consideration of great significance must then be that of opportunity cost, where port authorities (or governments) are asked to pay compensation to shippers in cases of unreasonable delay to help offset their losses (in respect to what the shippers might otherwise have been earning had the ship been free to proceed elsewhere).

The mere existence of a vessel, regardless of what it is, or is not, doing, costs money. Just to be moored at anchor costs money. Capital thus tied up necessitates interest and depreciation; or there may be rental charges if the vessel is a chartered one. Not unexpectedly, most shippers are putting pressure on consignors as well as on port authorities to pay surcharges (or other compensation pay-ments) when congestion becomes unreasonably heavy, thus leaving vessels no choice but to wait for services.

For example, the Japanese shippers' conference reportedly agreed to place a 'congestion surcharge' on consignors in the Port of

26

Korramsharr in Iran, in addition to the normal freight rate, which meant in effect an 80 per cent increase in cost, in order to gain compensation for the formidable congestion there. Even so, this was said not to be enough to offset the costs incurred by the shippers due to delays estimated to be about four months in that port. However, as the congestion surcharge becomes larger, the price of imported goods rises accordingly, thus aggravating domestic inflation problems. And therefore it is not surprising to see port authorities bringing this matter into discussion within the shippers' conference, threatening to restrict port usage or to discriminate against the shippers in question unless the latter agree to reduce the rate of surcharge. [19]

Longer ship turnround time means less utilisation of vessels, and may lead to substantial loss of demand for freight in the market. This argument is often used as an adjunct in support of surcharge schemes, as an estimate of the opportunity cost of ship loss time. However, it is no easy task to estimate opportunity cost accurately.

Opportunity cost *could* be considered almost nil, or even 'beneficial' to the shippers, when the market is in a real slump. The supply of vessels would then far exceed demand, resulting in a massive surplus of ships which can find no cargo to carry. This situation became common in the tanker business subsequent to the 1973 energy crisis, and has often necessitated mooring or even scrapping.

In such event, shippers are understandably not unhappy if they are simply able to moor their vessels at anchor free of charge, with the opportunity cost of ship loss time being then reckoned almost nil. (The situation is similar to the opportunity cost of involuntarily unemployed labour in developing countries. In the latter case, opportunity cost is also nil, since there are no jobs anyway.) And in view of the slump period ahead, it is no wonder that an extraordinary number of ships were rushing recently to the Nigerian port of Lagos, where congestion was already entirely out of control. For those ships with no orders for cargo carriage, the prospect of a compensation-fund payment reported to be on the order of £40,000 per month per ship was a real attraction indeed, not to mention the free moorage.

At the other extreme, opportunity cost *could* be considered as high as that potential revenue which could otherwise have accrued from the potential freight transport. According to this line of reasoning, the vessel might have been put into operation if the market entered a boom period, thus topping up the demand for goods to be shipped. This type of reasoning can best be illustrated by the following model.

Ship journey cost model

A simple model will be considered here as a means of coming to grips with the essentials of the problem. An hypothetical ship is carrying cargo from the port of origin to the port of destination, then making the return trip in balast. For the sake of analysis, the following denotations are made.

W	ship size (dwt, fully laden)
K_{sp}	capital cost of ship (£)
n	trading life length of ship (from the day of purchase to the day of replacement) (years)
v_{sp}	ship speed (nautical miles/day)
D_{AB}	return journey distance between Port A and Port B (nautical miles)
a_w	crew wage per head on average (£/year)
N_{cw}	number of crew members employed
a_f	price of bunker oil (£/ton)
q_{cp}	consumption rate (tons/day) at normal cruising speed v_{sp_0}
ϕ	percentage of ship time spent at port in proportion to total journey time
T_{pt_1}	time spent at Port A
T_{pt_2}	time spent at Port B
b_f	freight rate (£/ton)
r_o	interest rate (%/year)
r_{is}	insurance (%/year)
r_{mt}	maintenance and miscellaneous (%/year)

The number of days spent per return trip at sea T_{sa} is

$$T_{sa} = \frac{D_{AB}}{v_{sp}}$$

(2.1)

Since the total ship time spent at port T_{pt} is

$$T_{pt} = T_{pt_1} + T_{pt_2}$$

(2.2)

the ratio ϕ is

$$\phi = \frac{T_{pt}}{T_{sa} + T_{pt}}$$

(2.3)

The annualised ship cost is calculated as

$$K_{sp} \cdot \left[r_o + \frac{r_o}{(1+r_o)^n - 1} + r_{is} + r_{mt} \right] \quad (\text{£/year})$$

The crew wages are $a_w \cdot N_{cw}$ (£/year). The fuel cost per return trip

is $a_f \left[\dfrac{v_{sp}}{v_{spo}} \right]^3 q_{cp} \cdot \dfrac{D_{AB}}{v_{sp}} = \dfrac{a_f \, q_{cp} v^2_{sp} D_{AB}}{v^3_{spo}}$ since fuel consump-

tion is a cubic function of ship speed. [20] Suppose that the demand for shipping is high and always on tap. This means the ship can set forth on another journey immediately it returns from the previous one. Therefore, theoretically speaking, the ship can perform as many as

$$\frac{L_a}{T_{sa} + T_{pt}}$$

journeys per year, where L_a is effective working days per year. The total cost for operating this ship is therefore

$$C_{sp} = K_{sp} \cdot \left[\frac{r_o (1+r_o)^n}{(1+r_o)^n - 1} + r_{is} + r_{mt} \right] + a_w N_{cw}$$

$$+ \frac{L_a}{T_{sa} + T_{pt}} \cdot \frac{a_f \, q_{cp} v^2_{sp} D_{AB}}{v^3_{spo}} \quad (\text{£/year})$$

(2.4)

whereas the freight revenue is

$$R_{sp} = b_f \cdot W \cdot \frac{L_a}{T_{sa} + T_{pt}} \quad (\text{£/year})$$

(2.5)

yielding profit

$$P_{sp} = R_{sp} - C_{sp} \ (\text{£/year}) = b_f \cdot W \cdot \frac{L_a}{\dfrac{D_{AB}}{v_{sp}} + T_{pt}}$$

$$- \left[\hat{r}_o K_{sp} + a_w N_{cw} + \frac{L_a}{\dfrac{D_{AB}}{v_{sp}} + T_{pt}} \cdot \frac{a_f \, q_{cp} v^2_{sp} D_{AB}}{v^3_{spo}} \right]$$

(2.6)

where $\hat{r}_o = \dfrac{r_o(1+r_o)^n}{(1+r_o)^n - 1} + r_{is} + r_{mt}$ (2.7)

In terms of the ship's profit per ton basis (p_{sp}), we get

$$p_{sp} = b_f - \frac{a_f q_{cp} v_{sp}^2 D_{AB}}{W v_{sp_0}^3} - \frac{\dfrac{D_{AB}}{v_{sp}} + T_{pt}}{W L_a}\left[\hat{r}_o K_{sp} + a_w N_{cw}\right]$$ (2.8)

It should be noted that p_{sp} (£/ton) is operating profit per ton basis, whereas P_{sp} (£/year) is operating profit on a per annum basis. Equation 2.8 shows that, if the cruising speed is not greatly changed to compensate for the delay at port, the rate of decrease in the profit per freight ton for operating the ship, in terms of the length of port time, is given by the coefficient $\dfrac{\hat{r}_o \cdot K_{sp} + a_w N_{cw}}{W \cdot L_a}$.

Practical example

Taking a practical example, suppose that a ship with capacity 200,000 dwt is operated at about 15 knots (1 knot = 1,852 metres/hour, and v_{sp_0} would thus be roughly 360 nautical miles per day), consuming 130 tons of bunker oil per day at £40 per ton, for a return voyage distance of 20,000 nautical miles. From our enumeration above:

W	= 200,000 dwt	a_f	= £40/ton
K_{sp}	= £20 millions	q_{cp}	= £130 tons/day
n	= 15 years	r_o	= 8%
v_{sp}	= v_{sp_0} = 360 nautical miles/day	r_{is}	= 3%
		r_{mt}	= 3%
D_{AB}	= 20,000 nautical miles	b_f	= £8 per freight ton
a_w	= £4,000 per crew member	L_a	= 365 days
N_{cw}	= 50 crew members		

30

From equation 2.7,

$$\hat{r}_o = 0.1168 + 0.03 + 0.03 = 0.177 \qquad (2.9)$$

$$P_{sp} = 6.56 - 0.051\,(T_{pt} + 55.56) \qquad (2.10)$$

If, for instance, the total port time (handling time plus delay) is estimated at about 60 days, the percentage of port time ϕ is 52 per cent, and the operating profit P_{sp} will be 67 pence/freight ton. The point of break-even time for operating this ship, in this case, is bound by the port time (from equation 2.10) at $\tilde{T}_{pt} = 73.07$ days. This means that if either or both of the operations of the two ports are disrupted for any reason, and the aggregate port time exceeds about 73 days, then an operating loss will be incurred. Moreover, the amount of loss with reference to total port time T_{pt} will increase as shown in equation 2.10.

Returning to the ship operating profit on a per year basis (P_{sp}), let us see what would happen if one of the ports experiences terrible congestion, with total port time expected to increase from 60 up to 80 days. For simplicity, the crew wage bill is assumed unaffected by the change of ship journey frequency; and the ship speed is not to be greatly changed to make up for the excess delays. (For the latter possibility, see below). From equation 2.6:

1 For $T_{pt} = 60$ days ($\phi = 52\%$)

$P_{sp} = £0.40$m/year

2 For $T_{pt} = 80$ days ($\phi = 59\%$)

$P_{sp} = -£0.21$m/year

If the ship does not get any benefit at all by this excess delay of twenty days, the ship operator may claim that this additional port delay is solely to blame for the disruption of the profitability of his ship's service. Namely, in this case he may claim that he could have *earned* £0.40 millions if only there had been no delay greater than 60 days at port, while at the level of 80 days the full utilisation of the ship has actually resulted in an operating *loss* of £0.21 millions. Therefore, he may claim a payment of the total difference between the two, or a compensation of £0.61 millions.

Operating profit sensitivity to variation in ship speed

This model can easily be elaborated to account for the effects of varying ship speeds as well. As expected from equation 2.6, there is a trade-off between the freight revenue and the fuel cost. The former increases as the ship speed increases, through quicker ship journey turnover, while the latter also increases to reduce the profit margin. The sensitivity of operating profit depends on ship speed as well as on port time, which is subject to change due to the degree of congestion at the two ports concerned in this model.

Using all the constants given in the practical example above, but leaving only v_{sp} and T_{pt} as variables, then one gets (from equation 2.6):

$$P_{sp} = \frac{584}{\dfrac{20000}{v_{sp}} + T_{pt}} - \left(3.74 + \frac{813.6\, v^2_{sp}}{\dfrac{20000}{v_{sp}} + T_{pt}} \times 10^{-6}\right) \quad (\text{£1m/year})$$

$$(2.11)$$

From this equation, one can construct figure 2.1. The figure shows the ship operating profit in relation to the ship speed, with port time as a parameter. Ship speed zero means the lay-up of the ship, thus incurring only the fixed cost (capital plus labour) with no freight revenues. (Mooring cost is not considered here.) For the three cases given in the figure, where port time is 40, 60 or 80 days, it can be readily seen that the ship operating profit (SOP) increases as ship speed becomes larger, but only up until a certain point, where SOP reaches its maximum, and beyond which it gradually decreases.

No profit can be realised from a port time of 80 days in this case, as shown by curve 3, no matter what speed is selected, as the curve never reaches the break-even point. In such event, the ship operator could try only to minimise the loss, by setting the ship speed, which is precisely determined from equation 2.6, so that it corresponds to the apex of the curve. Coming back to the original example, where ship speed was initially assumed to be fixed (point A of curve 2), we can see from the figure that the ship happens to be operated near the apex of the profit curve.

It is important to note that equation 2.6 gives a theoretically exact value of ship speed for the maximum SOP. But since the various constants are assumed to be only rough estimates anyway, one need not insist upon finding the *exact* apex of the curve, the calculation of which might even entail the use of a computer. It should suffice merely to understand the qualitative reasoning behind the model, and the desirability of choosing some point or other suitably near to the apex of the curve.

This general argument will hold, nonetheless, only where demand for ships is topped up. If, after its return, a ship has to wait before

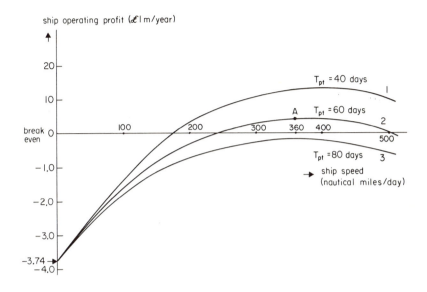

Figure 2.1   Ship operating profit in relation to ship speed with
port time as a parameter

getting another engagement, and incurred costs (e.g. a mooring
charge) then have to be paid in the interim, it may be to its advantage
to slow the rate of travel en route, regardless of the implications of
the theoretical model presented here.

Difficulties in evaluating ship time cost

In theory one could reach an evaluation of the cost of ship time by
any of several means.

1   Find the change of traffic demand in response to the
variation of delays inflicted upon it. If the delay becomes
large, then some traffic would diverge from this port to
other ports to avoid the incurred costs.

33

2   Present a variety of tariff schemes (price discrimination) for different types of services (e.g. priority system) from which the shippers may choose.

3   Estimate the opportunity cost (short-term and long-term of ship loss time) as accurately as possible from market conditions.

The first obviously cannot be examined for any practical purposes of analysis, owing to the inadvisability of imposing the conditions necessary to collect such data. A graphical representation showing the relationship between traffic volume and delay could be procured only by the artificial imposition by port authorities of varying amounts of 'delay', and then observing the effects on traffic volume. Such a technique would naturally result in financial losses all around, not to mention the likelihood of bitter criticism from users.

In reference to the second, it is very difficult to construct a basic tariff structure which truly reflects the actual cost configuration. For example, it seems difficult to establish a relationship between the size of ships and the actual cost incurred by them. The costs of a 10,000 ton ship are not necessarily exactly double those of a 5,000 tonner. In some cases, the length of a ship may be a better measure for reflecting cost, while in others the type of cargo, load factors, or type of handling facilities might be considered as well. In any case, even at the steady-state, the construction of such a scheme would take time; and in the presence of an ever-changing traffic profile, there would inevitably be endless confusion.

As for the third alternative, one can only half-heartedly suggest that port authorities make a stab at it, though they will doubtless encounter a tendency towards bias on the part of shippers to attempt to estimate the opportunity cost higher than it actually is.

None of these measures seems easy. Nonetheless, one cannot avoid tackling this evaluation task, so that the true picture of port congestion may be more fully understood, not only by port management but also by users of the port. A grasp of at least its economic implications may help to provide a basis for designing an adequate tariff scheme, and help break ground for the justification of new investment projects.

Notes

[1]   *The Financial Times*, 28 July 1976.
[2]   *The Guardian*, 17 January 1975.

[3]   Statement of the Nchanga Consolidated Copper Mines Limited, quoted in *The Financial Times*, 4 August 1976.

[4]   *The Sunday Times*, 30 November 1975.

[5]   *The Financial Times*, 16 February 1976.

[6]   *The Observer*, 26 October 1975.

[7]   *The Financial Times*, 28 July 1976.

[8]   Ibid.

[9]   *The Financial Times*, 16 February 1976.

[10]   *Nihon Keizai Shimbun*, 24 March 1976.

[11]   *The Financial Times*, 28 July 1976.

[12]   *Nihon Keizai Shimbun*, 24 March 1976.

[13]   *The Financial Times*, 28 July 1976.

[14]   Ibid.

[15]   Goss, *Studies in Maritime Economics*, p.153.

[16]   R.K. Saggar, 'Turnround and Costs of Conventional Cargo Liners: UK-India Route', *Journal of Transport Economics and Policy*, IV/1, January 1970, p.53. In all fairness to India, one should note, however, that this gap of 15 per cent is not so great as the raw statistic suggests, since the greater distances to the other ports (hence greater time spent at sea) tends to diminish the percentage of time spent in port when the latter is calculated in proportion to total voyage time.

[17]   Table adapted from Ministry of Transport, *Report of the Committee of Inquiry into the Major Ports of Great Britain*, HMSO, 1962, p.112.

[18]   Thomson, *Modern Transport Economics*, p.78.

[19]   *Nihon Keizai Shimbun*, 6 November 1975.

[20]   S. Gilman and G. Williams, 'The Economics of Multi-Port Itineraries for Large Container Ships', *Journal of Transport Economics and Policy*, X/2, May 1976, p.141.

3 Analytical approaches to the navigation system

Introduction

The inadequacy of tug services is often the subject of complaint by port users, who are always quick to suggest the use of more tugs, or else of more powerful ones, as a remedy. Such a solution would appear to be simple and straightforward enough, if the only consideration were that of avoiding delay. 'The effective use of a navigational aid can achieve an improvement in the operating conditions by increasing the level of safety in the area and by decreasing the delay experienced by a vessel in making its passage to or from its berth.' [1]

But from the port authority's viewpoint, the number of tugs which can reasonably be provided is, of course, affected by both port revenues and fluctuations in trade. [2] If a sufficient number of tugs were always available to handle all ships requiring their services at peak traffic periods, there would certainly be a surplus of tugs for the greater part of the year. This is clearly one of the many cases in which the aim must be to strike a happy medium. It has been argued that the large ports seem to have an advantage in this respect. [3] But one can indeed determine 'adequate' levels of tugs for a simple port system. It would therefore seem worthwhile to investigate the towage system in terms of the relationship between the level of vehicle (tug) employment and the efficiency of the service (ship time being taken as a basic measure of the latter).

Brief survey of ship activities in port

Before attempting to analyse the navigation system and the tug related ship activities, it would be useful to enumerate these tug-related activities within the typical port system. The following elementary list of tug-ship activities should provide an adequate descriptive basis for the mathematical treatment that follows.

36

(a) A port is visited by a number of ships each year.

(b) There are sailing conditions for ships such as storms, tides, dredged depth of the port, and so forth which must be taken into consideration.

(c) Ships approaching the harbour are aided by various methods of signalling.

1 Entrance lights
2 Luminous buoys for approach
3 Luminous lines
4 Lighthouses (light, radio, foghorn)

(d) When a ship arrives at the inlet of the port, it may require (or may find it mandatory to employ) a pilot as well as tugs to guide it.

(e) The services of pilotage and towage are allocated to ships according to berthing priorities. A pilot and the tug join the ship simultaneously. But, should either be lacking, the ship must queue until both become available.

(f) The time taken by a ship to move between the queuing area and the berth in the centre of the port is chiefly dependent upon ship size, and not upon the power of the tug.

(g) When the ship is berthed, the operation of unloading and loading cargo is performed (independently of what the tug may be doing during this time).

(h) The turnround time for each ship depends upon numerous factors, such as

1 Types of cargo unloaded and loaded
2 Types of ship
3 Types and numbers of handling units available
4 Space in storage for imports and exports

All these factors should be kept in mind, because they exert either direct or indirect influences upon the question of time in relation to the towing system. From the outset, one must remember that the number of pilots and tugs will be limited; and so, a ship to be berthed, even if the berth itself is available, may have to wait in the queuing area until both pilots and tugs become available. Conversely, if a ship has to wait for a berth because of priorities etc., it will remain immobile until one is free, even if pilots and tugs are available.

Throughout most of this chapter, ship service time distribution is assumed for expository purposes to be negative exponential, which means that the model is applicable only to these simple distributions.

The basic reasoning is nonetheless readily applicable to the general case.

Single berth without a tug

This system is easily analysed with the help of elementary queuing theory, provided that ship arrival pattern and service time distribution obey certain probability density functions. For example, if both the ship arrival pattern and the service time follow the Poisson distribution, then the probability of the state that n ships are queuing in the system is given by

$$P_n = \rho^n \cdot P_0 \quad (\rho = \frac{\lambda}{\mu}) \tag{3.1}$$

where λ (ships/day) is the intensity of ship arrival and μ (ships/day) is the ship service rate. The average length of the queue and average waiting time in the queue are given by

$$L_q = \sum_{n=1}^{\infty} (n-1)\, P_n = \frac{\rho^2}{(1-\rho)} \tag{3.2}$$

$$W_q = \frac{L_q}{\lambda} \tag{3.3}$$

Before proceeding to examine the system with tugs included, we might examine ship waiting time for berths without tugs, under the condition of *regular* arrivals and constant services. (The case of *random* arrivals is treated widely already in many published works and need not be reiterated).

Ship waiting time under a 'FIFO' system for regular arrivals and constant services

Let us take as a simple example a port with a FIFO (first in, first out) policy which is able to service ten ships each day. Say that during a period of unusual congestion twelve ships a day are arriving. On the first day the first ten ships will receive immediate service, causing the last two ships to wait one day each. At the end of the fifth day, there will be ten such ships still to be serviced on the following day, all with a waiting time of still only one day. But at the end of the sixth day, with twelve ships remaining unserviced, the last two to

38

arrive will have to wait two days. All ships arriving on the tenth day will have to wait two days uniformly; but the last two arriving on the eleventh day will have to wait three days. And so on. There is thus a series of time intervals, in this example each equal to five days, during which the waiting time for each new arrival in that interval will be uniform. These intervals may be designated by v_p ($v_p = \dfrac{\mu}{\lambda - \mu}$),

where μ is the port handling capacity (ships/day), and λ is the ship arrival rate (ships/day). Figure 3.1 represents the number of ships awaiting services along a time axis in relation to the number of days delay for each. The shaded area below the line $y = (\lambda - \mu)\, x$, which represents the total number of ships waiting for services at time x days, is divided into discrete portions depending upon individual waiting times: those ships in segment 'a' having a one-day delay, 'b' two days, 'c' three days, 'd' four days, and so on. Since the situation is not convergent, the queue will continue to build up either until the traffic level comes down and falls short of the existing handling capacity, or until the port is expanded to contain the traffic level. The resulting

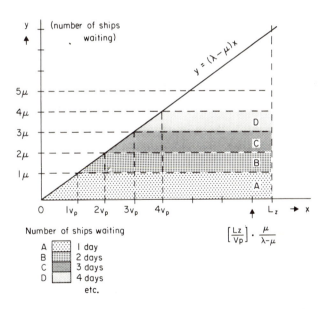

Figure 3.1   Number of ships awaiting services (queue accumulation) with respect to time

39

accumulation of ships in the queue is valid only within the period L_z. The point where $x = L_z$ circumscribes the period of time during which no change is expected, i.e. neither increase nor decrease of the traffic, and neither improvement nor expansion of the existing port capacity.

Ship waiting time (SWT) in terms of ship-days during L_z is calculated from figure 3.1 with the aid of a Gaussian bracket where $[x] = n$ for $n \leqslant x < n + 1$, n: integer.

Example 1

$$L_z = 360 \quad \mu = 200 \quad \lambda = 202$$

$$\text{For } v_p = \frac{200}{202 - 200} = 100, \text{ then } \left[\frac{L_z}{v_p} \right] = 3.$$

$$\text{SWT} = 215,600 \text{ (ship-days)}$$

And proceeding one step further, we can easily determine the average delay per ship $(\bar{D}_{sh})$ in terms of days per ship.

$$\bar{D}_{sh} = \frac{\text{SWT}}{L_z \lambda} = \frac{215600}{360 \times 202} = 2.99 \text{ (days/ship)}$$

Example 2

What happens if the first example is modified by reducing the number of ships per day from $\lambda = 202$ to $\lambda = 201$? In this case where $v_p = 200$, then $\left[\dfrac{L_z}{v_p} \right] = 1.$

$$\text{SWT} = 64,800 \text{ (ship-days)}$$

$$\bar{D}_{sh} = \frac{64800}{360 \times 201} = 0.90 \text{ (days/ship)}$$

Although it was assumed from the outset that the service discipline is FIFO, the resulting average waiting time per ship nonetheless is not very different here from what would be expected in a case where a random service system was in operation. But this may not always hold true.

One must keep in mind that there may be significant differences between (1) the AWT for a ship, which represents an arithmetic average for all ships over a long period of time, (2) the actual waiting time under FIFO conditions for any one ship arriving at a specific point in time which may vary greatly depending on arrival patterns as illustrated in figure 3.1 and (3) the actual waiting time under a system of preferences for service. If the latter system is introduced, giving priority to certain arrivals such as ships carrying capital goods, while assigning low priority to ships with cargo such as iron ore, then the actual waiting time of the low priority ships will increase at a much higher rate.

If any increase in the handling capacity is aimed merely at coping with the traffic volume at that very moment — i.e. $\mu + \Delta\mu = \lambda$ — then this average waiting time is inevitably going to be built into the whole system, thus becoming a chronic profile. In order to escape from this cycle of congestion, port authorities must look ahead of the momentary rate of traffic flow and provide for a handling capacity somewhat in excess of what would suffice for the moment. Otherwise, by the time new facilities were made available, they would not help the state of congestion greatly. The problem is, therefore, within the limits of budgetary, environmental and other constraints — and assuming that there is no decrease in traffic flow — how great the additional handling capacity should be, which is planned at any one time to become fully operative within a specified period.

Single berth with one tug

We may now try to find how the system would work with tug service included.

Assumptions

1　Ship arrivals: Poisson distribution

2　Types and sizes of ships: identical

3　Tug boats sailing (guiding) times:

　　t_1: when guiding the ship from the queuing area to the berth
　　t_2: when proceeding alone from the berth back to the queuing area

4　Service time distribution at the berth: exponential

The fourth assumption is represented by the figure which shows the probability density function of loading/unloading time by $f_{T_s}(t_s)$.

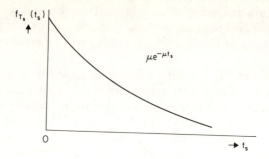

Let us consider the very simple one-berth one-tug system where the port is reasonably busy so that there is always a ship queue of some length or other. There is often

> ... an anchorage area for use while the ship is waiting to proceed to a berth if the port is tidal or subject to congestion, if a ship in ballast arrives before cargo is available or if, for example, there are quarantine conditions or other time-consuming formalities to be satisfied before the ship can proceed inside the harbour limits .... [4]

Take for example the very instant when the berth becomes available. According to the logic of the tug system, the first ship in the queue to be berthed can leave the queue in order to receive servicing only if the tug boat is available. It takes t_1 time for the ship and tug to reach the berth, where it will expect to spend service time t_s. The ship requires the tug for berthing, because of the danger of collisions otherwise; but it may be assumed for simplicity at the beginning of this analysis that the ship can leave the berth under its own steam, thus not requiring the services of a tug after unloading/loading.

Now consider the next ship to be berthed. Normally, t_s will be greater than the tug return-journey time to the queue area t_2; and thus the tug will always be available when the next ship is ready to proceed. But a situation may be imagined in which the distance travelled by the tug is relatively great (or that the tug has other work to do elsewhere along the way), so that when the first ship has finished its servicing, the tug will still be on its way back to the queue and thus not yet available to the next ship in the queue. How can this tricky problem then be analysed? It is worth mentioning here that service time t_s is a random variable, whereas sailing times t_1 and t_2 can be considered as constants.

This system can be treated through some analytical manipulations by introducing the new random variable t_{qd}, which may be called the 'queue interdeparture time'. This is a measure of the space of time beginning with the moment of departure of one ship from the queue and ending with the moment of departure from the queue of the next ship. Queue interdeparture time will in general be simply an extension of service time for any one ship from the viewpoint of the *next* ship in the queue, because only t_{qd} time after the first ship begins to leave the waiting area can the tug begin to guide the next ship towards the berth. Two values may, at this juncture, be assigned to t_{qd}.

1   If $t_s \geqslant t_2$, then the tug will be ready by the time the berth becomes available. Thus we have simply

$$t_{qd} = t_1 + t_s \tag{3.4}$$

One may suspect that the next ship could leave the queue area prior to the first ship's completion of services, and therefore t_{qd} here could be less than $t_1 + t_s$. This complication will be considered below.

2   If $t_s < t_2$, then the tug will not be ready and therefore the next ship will have to wait until the tug returns to the queuing area (even though the berth may be available). In this case

$$t_{qd} = t_1 + t_2 \tag{3.5}$$

From equations 3.4 and 3.5, the expected average of this newly introduced service time can be calculated as follows.

$$
\begin{aligned}
\bar{t}_{qd} = E\left[t_{qd}\right] &= \int_0^\infty t_{qd}\mu e^{-\mu t_s}\, dt_s \\
&= \int_0^{t_2} (t_1 + t_2)\,\mu e^{-\mu t_s}\, dt_s + \int_{t_2}^\infty (t_1 + t_s)\,\mu e^{-\mu t_s}\, dt_s \\
&= t_1 + t_2 + \frac{1}{\mu} e^{-\mu t_2}
\end{aligned}
\tag{3.6}
$$

If a 'no-tug' system is considered, which is equivalent to setting $t_1 = t_2 = 0$, then equation 3.6 is reduced to $\bar{t}_{qd} = \frac{1}{\mu}$. In this simple case, the queue interdeparture time is the inverse of the mean service rate μ, from the fourth assumption.

Suppose that the tug requires t_v time for each linkage (one coupling plus one uncoupling) with the ship. These two actions may be taken as a single unit for convenience, as they must always take place in pairs. It should be noted, moreover, that this t_v time is spent by the tug alone in cases where tugs are abundant, as coupling will take place while the berth is not yet available (thus overlapping with the previous ship's t_s), and also uncoupling can take place while the newly-berthed ship's servicing is already under way (thus overlapping with the latter ship's t_s).

Suppose further that the ship in the queue is allowed to leave the waiting area only t_z time *after* the first ship's service has been completed. This t_z time may be designated as 'quay-clearance manoeuvring' time, and is a measure of the time which the first ship spends in departing from the berth and clearing the quay after its service has been completed.

If the port regulations are such that the second ship can leave the queue immediately the berth becomes available, this would mean that t_z is nil in our model. It may also be questioned here whether t_z could be negative as well as positive. This would mean that the second ship is allowed to leave the queue even before the first ship has finished its servicing. Why not? This is possible when the service time is fixed. If t_s is randomly distributed, however, the service completion time cannot be known a priori.

t_z is included as a factor in tug time (as opposed to ship time) only if the ship requires the assistance of a tug in leaving the berth. If the tug is required, in so far as the fourth assumption holds, then in place of equation 3.6 we get the more generalised equation

$$\bar{t}_{qd} = t_1 + t_2 + t_z + t_v + \frac{1}{\mu} e^{-\mu t_2} \tag{3.7}$$

With these considerations in mind, equations 3.4 and 3.5 should be modified as follows.

$$t_{qd} = t_1 + t_s + t_z \quad \text{if } t_s + t_z \geqslant t_2 + t_v \tag{3.8}$$

$$t_{qd} = t_1 + t_2 + t_v \quad \text{if } t_s + t_z < t_2 + t_v \tag{3.9}$$

If t_z and t_v are constant, equations 3.8 and 3.9 become equivalent to

$$t_{qd} = t_1 + t_s + t_z \quad \text{if } t_s \geqslant t_2 + t_v - t_z \tag{3.10}$$

$$t_{qd} = t_1 + t_2 + t_v \quad \text{if } t_s < t_2 + t_v - t_z \tag{3.11}$$

1 If $t_2 + t_v - t_z < 0$, it should be clear that equation 3.10 holds for every t_s. And therefore $\bar{t}_{qd}$ will be

$$\bar{t}_{qd} = t_1 + t_z + \frac{1}{\mu} \qquad (3.12)$$

Equation 3.12 means that, if the sum of the tug's return journey time plus the tug-ship coupling time is less than the quay-clearance manoeuvring time, then the average quay inter-departure time of this tug-berth system is simply the sum of the tug journey time with a ship, plus the average ship service time, plus the quay-clearance manoeuvring time.

2 If $t_2 + t_v - t_z \geqslant 0$, on the other hand, then either equation 3.10 or equation 3.11 is applicable, depending on the value of t_s. And the expected value of t_{qd} will be expressed as follows.

$$\bar{t}_{qd} = t_1 + t_2 + t_v + \frac{1}{\mu} e^{-\mu(t_2 + t_v - t_z)} \qquad (3.13)$$

Equation 3.13 is the general extension of equation 3.6, and becomes simply $t_1 + t_z + \frac{1}{\mu}$ if $t_2 + t_v - t_z = 0$, which shows that the result of 1 and 2 above coincides if $t_2 + t_v - t_z = 0$.

It may be seen that the average service time of this one-tug one-berth system is constant, so long as $t_2 + t_v \leqslant t_z$; and then it increases exponentially as the value of $t_2 + t_v - t_z$ increases. What is significant in terms of tug-berth service time, given the quay-clearance manoeuvring time t_z, is the critical point $t_2 + t_v = t_z$, beyond which the average waiting time for tug services tends to become large. It suggests that the port should try to reduce the value of $t_2 + t_v - t_z$, while at the same time taking care to reduce t_z as well, since the latter determine the lowest service time possible through the relationship with the base value of $\bar{t}_{qd} = t_1 + t_z + \frac{1}{\mu}$. In other words, the

reduction of $t_2 + t_v - t_z$ should *not* be accomplished by increasing t_z, but by other means. The latter entails the reduction of each value t_1, t_2, t_v, t_z, as well as quay service time t_s, not independently but in co-ordination with particular reference to $t_2 + t_v - t_z$.

It is possible, though by no means easy, to extend this sort of analysis still further to a system of m-tugs and n-berths, with a general form of ship service time distribution other than the Poisson form, which has been assumed here for illustrative purposes. However, from

45

the practical point of view, such a procedure would seem to lead nowhere other than the conclusion naturally extrapolated from the one-tug one-berth system: that more powerful or speedier tugs, or simply a greater number of tugs, should contribute to the reduction of the average tug-berth service time, and also that the marginal rate of reduction per tug is expected to diminish as the number of tugs increases. The latter will be true because many tugs would become redundant at times. Bearing this in mind, let us approach the tug-berth system from the viewpoint of the supplier of the services, in order to derive informative results which will serve more general practical purposes.

Port authorities should provide a suitable number of tugs so that the services to ships are not seriously interrupted by the lack of them. This holds true regardless of whether the tugs are operated by independent firms or controlled by the port authority itself — the choice between which is usually a matter of local custom and convenience. In order to illustrate this problem, a simple case will again be considered.

One-berth system

Let us suppose a ship is guided by a tug from the waiting area in the port to the berth (which requires time t_1 for both ship *and* tug), and that the ship then immediately begins servicing (time t_s for the *ship*) while the tug is uncoupling and then proceeding back to the waiting area (time t_2 for the tug alone). The next ship is allowed to leave the waiting area only t_z time *after* the departure of the former ship from the berth. The time sequence will fall into either one or the other of two categories which can tell us at least a little about the 'sufficient' number of tugs required under this system (which we may here designate as 'N_{sf}').

Category A

If $t_2 + t_v \leqslant t_s + t_z$, (3.14)

then a single tug will suffice to avoid interruptions. And in this case $N_{sf} = 1$.

Category B

If $t_2 + t_v > t_s + t_z$, (3.15)

then either two tugs or more than two tugs will be necessary. Thus $N_{sf} \geqslant 2$, depending on the degree of difference between the two sides of equation 3.15.

An examination of Category A tells us only whether or not a single tug will suffice. A single tug will always be sufficient if the quay inter-departure time is greater than the tug cycle time. This is because the single tug will always arrive back at the waiting area and be ready for guidance in advance of the time when the first ship in the queue is ready to proceed to the berth (i.e. after the ship just completing service has already moved out of the system). In other words, the following must hold true.

If $t_1 + t_2 + t_v \leqslant t_1 + t_s + t_z$, then $N_{sf} = 1$

Category B requires at least two tugs, because the next ship in the queue is ready to move *before* the tug has returned to the waiting area. Thus in order to avoid delay, a second tug will have to guide the waiting ship towards the berth. If $t_2 + t_v$ is *very* much greater than $t_s + t_z$, so that the first tug completes its cycle in excess of the time interval between *two* successive ship departures, then a third tug will be required; and so on for any greater number of tugs.

Multiple-berths system

Thus far we have been examining a system of only a single berth, in order to treat the concept of queue interdeparture time as simply as possible. Since the queue interdeparture time is a random variable, and tug cycle time is considered to be relatively fixed, the difference between them has to be accounted for by a 'slack' period in the available tug time. During this slack time, the tug is alongside the ship in the queue to which it has already coupled, merely waiting for the next berth to become available.

In order to treat a more complex, and the more generally applicable, system in which there are many berths for servicing, we should look at the time intervals between departures from the *berths*. We may now introduce the concept of 'berth interdeparture time', represented by t_{bd}, which is defined as the space of time between the successive departures of ships from the berth (or berths), commencing and ending with the moment that two successive ships begin to move away from the berth (or from different berths). Berth interdeparture time is expected to be a random variable; and a value for t_{bd} may be obtained from the cumulative distribution function for t_{bd} which is in turn obtained from observable data. Though the distribution of t_{bd} is considered to be, either directly or indirectly, related to the number of tugs employed, the analysis will disregard this inter-dependence at first, to avoid complication. But interdependence will be taken up below.

It should be clear that the ultimate criterion for determining the required number of tugs is, in essence, a comparison between tug-cycle time as opposed to berth interdeparture time.

One problem still remains, that the interdeparture times may in actual practice be very close together from time to time, so that an unrealistically large number of tugs would be required if our only purpose were to prevent any ship whatsoever from being delayed merely because there was no tug immediately available to guide it. It will therefore be necessary for us to examine N_{sf} somewhat more closely as a measure of the number of tugs which will represent an *average* level adequate for the port under ordinary circumstances.

Tug employment level as a balance between input and output

Suppose that the port is operating at full capacity and, as is commonly the case, that there is a ship queue in the waiting area. Then the first ship in the queue will be ready for berthing whenever any one of the berths becomes available. In order to avoid loss time, the 'input' of the port (productivity of tugs) should match the 'output' of the port (ship departures). Obviously the output, which is directly related to servicing of the ships, has a definite maximum; and it is this factor which must be treated, rather than ship arrivals.

If we designate tug cycle time as T_{gcy}, then the measure of the productivity of a single tug in terms of ship guidance per unit time will be $\dfrac{1}{T_{gcy}}$. Multiplying this by the number of tugs N_{tg}, we get the input of the system — i.e. the productivity of the whole tug system, which may be expressed as $N_{tg} \cdot \dfrac{1}{T_{gcy}}$. The output of the port, in terms of the number of ships completing servicing per unit time, will be expressed as $\dfrac{1}{t_{bd}}$ where t_{bd} denotes berth interdeparture time.

Combining input with output, one may therefore say that the following should hold true *on average* in the steady-state.

$$N_{tg} \cdot \frac{1}{T_{gcy}} = \frac{1}{t_{bd}} \qquad (3.16)$$

Since half-a-tug or two-thirds of a ship would be a meaningless measurement, equation 3.16 should be relaxed a bit because N_{tg} must be an integer. And therefore, by definition N_{sf} is the minimum integer of N_{tg} which satisfies the inequality relation

$$N_{tg} \cdot \frac{1}{T_{gcy}} \geqslant \frac{1}{t_{bd}} \qquad (3.17)$$

Substituting for T_{gcy} as in the above case:

$$N_{tg} \cdot \frac{1}{t_1 + t_2 + t_v} \geqslant \frac{1}{t_{bd}} \qquad (3.18)$$

In sum, then (using Gaussian brackets):

$$\text{if } t_{bd} \geqslant T_{gcy} \qquad \text{then } N_{sf} = 1 \qquad (3.19)$$

$$\text{if } t_{bd} < T_{gcy} \qquad \text{then } N_{sf} = \left[\frac{T_{gcy}}{t_{bd}}\right] + 1 \qquad (3.20)$$

If t_{bd} is a constant (such a system being called 'deterministic'), then N_{sf} is the upper bound beyond which an increase in the number of tugs will not be necessary.

However, if t_{bd} is not a constant, but randomly distributed (such a system being called 'stochastic'), the notion of N_{sf} requires a little modification. Since N_{sf} will vary depending upon the value of t_{bd}, there can be no unique number N_{sf} as in the above case over the whole range of t_{bd}, which is the sufficient level of tugs to be employed *on average*. In other words, it is expected that at times some tugs will have no work and at others there will be an unavoidable shortage of tugs.

If we know the distribution of $f_{T_{bd}}(t_{bd})$ of berth interdeparture times from recorded data or from reasonable estimations, we are able to measure the 'relatively' sufficient level of tugs ($\bar{N}_{sf}$) which ought to be provided in order to avoid interruption of berthing, at least during most of the year, solely because of a tug shortage. The word 'relatively' is used because, although it may be possible to obtain an 'absolutely' sufficient number of tugs, the decision should be made with economic factors taken into consideration, which consist mostly of the trade-off argument between costs of providing more tugs and benefits from the improved navigation system. This number $\bar{N}_{sf}$ is not

49

an absolute upper bound in this case, because there will be times when traffic will be momentarily heavy and $\bar{N}_{sf}$ tugs will not be entirely adequate. $\bar{N}_{sf}$ could nonetheless be a useful measure for most practical purposes. The expected value of N_{sf} is calculated as follows.

$$
\bar{N}_{sf} = E \ [N_{sf}]
$$

$$
= \int_{0}^{T_{gcy}} \left(\left[\frac{T_{gcy}}{t_{bd}} \right] + 1 \right) f_{T_{bd}}(t_{bd})dt_{bd} + \int_{T_{gcy}}^{\infty} 1 \cdot f_{T_{bd}}(t_{bd})dt_{bd}
$$

$$
(3.21)
$$

The snag in this analytical procedure is that the output productivity may be below the potential capacity for existing facilities purely because of a shortage of tugs at the time when the data are collected. In such a case, t_{bd} will be longer on average than its true potential value. The only possible solution is one of trial-and-error, by increasing the number of tugs up to the first estimation of $\bar{N}_{sf}$ and then collecting further data. If the procedure of matching input and output productivity on the basis of the new data gives a result in which $\bar{N}_{sf} \cdot \dfrac{1}{T_{gcy}} < \dfrac{1}{\bar{t}_{bd}}$, where $\bar{t}_{bd}$ is the mean berth interdeparture time, then the number of tugs should again be increased to the newly estimated $\bar{N}_{sf}$, and further data collected; and so on, until a practically accepted equality is reached. It should be noted that this procedure lends itself readily to the use of computer simulation.

There is no reason to reckon this value $\bar{N}_{sf}$ the most sensible measure of all from an economic point of view, because the determination of the level of employment should be based on the costs (i.e. of providing tugs) versus benefits (i.e. from the reduced interruption of berthing rather than solely on the frequency of interruption). However, the implications of $\bar{N}_{sf}$ in equation 3.21 become practically appropriate where the distribution $f_{T_{bd}}(t_{bd})$ is not sparsely distributed but narrowly shaped. Indeed, if $f_{T_{bd}}(t_{bd})$ is a delta function (i.e. t_{bd} is constant), $\bar{N}_{sf}$ coincides with $\bar{N}_{sf}$ for the deterministic system. And $\bar{N}_{sf}$ is expected to provide a fairly good initial value for the trial-and-error procedure in order to determine the satisfactory number of tugs necessary for achieving the desired berth productivity. Bearing this in mind, three numerical examples are presented below to illustrate the $\bar{N}_{sf}$ calculation.

The formulas for N_{sf} have been derived on the basis of simple systems where the tug merely guides a ship from queue to berth, and then has no further interaction with that ship. If, however, the tug is required to guide some ships (or all ships) away from the berth after servicing, then equation 3.18 where $T_{gcy} = t_1 + t_2 + t_v$ no longer holds true. Two general categories for the latter possibility can be distinguished.

First, if the tug simply waits alongside the ship during servicing, and then spends t_z time towing it away, then tug cycle time will still be $T_{gcy} = t_1 + t_2 + t_v + t_z + t_s$. Second, if the tug has time to return to the queuing area and to guide another ship to berth before the first ship is ready to depart, or if it tows another ship away from its berth in the meantime, or if it does a combination of these, then the value of T_{gcy} will vary considerably, depending on the distances and activities involved. In this second category, the tug cycle for the first ship is 'broken' in the middle, the tug meantime going away to deal with a second ship (which time is counted as part of T_{gcy} for the second ship), and then resuming T_{gcy} for the first ship. One need not attempt a complicated enumeration of such possibilities, since the only factor of ultimate importance is T_{gcy}. And once a value for T_{gcy} is obtained from data collected in the port, equation 3.17 will hold true, regardless of what combination of activities the tug may engage in.

Example 1

$t_{bd} = 1$ hour (regular interval of departure $T_{gcy} = 2$ hrs. 30 mins.

The time sequence is shown in the following figure, which assumes that $t_z = 0$ (i.e. that the next ship in the queue will be allowed to enter the system immediately any berth becomes available). Dotted lines represent tug slack time.

From equation 3.20 we get $N_{sf} = [\frac{2.5}{1}] + 1 = 2 + 1 = 3$. As can

be seen from the figure, it will be necessary to have three tugs in order to avoid any loss time in which a ship in the queue has to wait because a tug is not available.

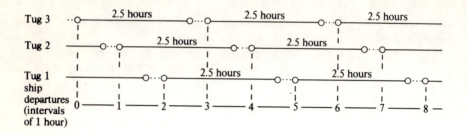

Example 2

The case where berth interdeparture time is uniformly distributed is shown in the following figure, which is based on the assumptions

$$f_{T_{bd}}(t_{bd}) = \frac{1}{7}, \quad 1 \leqslant t_{bd} \leqslant 8, \text{ or otherwise}$$

$$f_{T_{bd}}(t_{bd}) = 0 \qquad\qquad T_{gcy} = 3 \text{ hours}$$

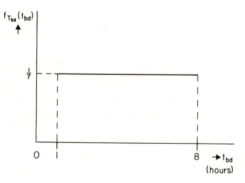

$$E\ [N_{sf}] = 1.36 > 1$$

Thus at least two tugs must be provided in order for our no-delay condition to hold.

Example 3

The berth interdeparture time can also be approximated as having a triangular distribution with a peak (for example) at $t_{bd} = 2$. Also assume that $T_{gcy} = 5$ (hours).

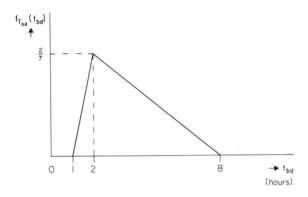

$$E\ [N_{sf}]\ =\ 2.14 > 2$$

As mentioned earlier, these numbers do not give any absolute guarantee. Service interruptions should be expected to occur at times, although the more tugs the less the frequency of such interruptions. This frequency can be estimated by the distribution $f_{T_{bd}}(t_{bd})$ with the number of tugs provided.

Although a triangular distribution function often gives a fairly good approximation in practice, equation 3.21 is not confined within such simple functions as described in the examples. As to the distribution function in general, equation 3.21 can also be easily applied to be calculated by a computer with just one point to be borne in mind. That is, the first part of the integral is stated as starting from nil, which means the berth interdeparture is nil (i.e. ships are departing one after another in a continuous fashion). This is, of course, hardly to be imagined in practice; and the probability that this will happen in reality can be regarded as practically nil. Theoretically speaking, however, such a distribution as a negative exponential, for example $f_{T_{bd}}(t_{bd}) = 1 - e^{-\lambda t_{bd}}$ may be assumed since the steady-state out-

53

put of a queue with a number of channels in parallel, with a Poisson input and parameter λ, and the same exponential service time distribution with parameter μ for each channel, is itself Poisson-distributed (the proof of this fact being due to Burke); and therefore it is in fact an eventual outcome of the Poisson-type queue model of the port to assume this negative exponential distribution for berth interdeparture.

Notes

[1]   *National Ports Council Bulletin*, no.1, Spring 1972, p.33.
[2]   A theoretical treatment of navigation aids in terms of their economic implications is presented by R.O. Goss, *Costs and Benefits of Navigational Aids in Port Approaches*, HMSO, 1971.
[3]   Ministry of Transport, *Report of the Committee of Inquiry into the Major Ports of Great Britain*, p.96.
[4]   UN, *Development of Ports. Improvement of Port Operations and Connected Facilities*, New York 1969, p.7.

4 Analytical approaches to the storage system

Part A: Modelling of the handling system

Basic factors affecting efficiency

In cases where the inflow rate of the system does not match outflow, the slower rate will become dominant in determining the overall productivity. An in-depth consideration of this system, however, necessitates the analysis of the internal structure — although this need not be presented in too complicated a form — focusing upon the capacity of the system. It is not easy to quantify the extent to which facilities need to be overprovided in order to avoid delays at times of peak demand. But it is intuitively clear that some excess berthing capacity is desirable to overcome congestion problems due to factors such as the insufficiency of the handling system, the irregular pattern of ship arrivals, seasonal effects, and bottlenecks caused by poor link-ups.

   General rules for estimating how much slack of excess capacity should be provided for smooth operations seem not yet to have been laid down by ports. Among the considerable number of factors affecting the efficiency of the system, we should take note especially of the following critical ones.

1   Working intensity (effective labour allocation schemes): how many gangs per hatch, how many shifts, how much overtime is possible, etc.

2   Actual productivity of both labour and mechanical equipment (such as cranes, forklift trucks, etc.)

3   Interruptions caused by temporary lack of space for discharging cargo on the quay, mechanical breakdowns, short supply of trucks or trailers, all causing idle time and thus reducing shift output.

One factor that must always be kept in mind is the level of the labour force necessary to meet fluctuations in demand. It would be almost impossible for any port to maintain a labour force capable of handling anything approaching the maximum demand to be expected from time to time, at least not within ordinary working hours. Momentary increases (or decreases) in traffic flow may necessitate corresponding increases in costs due mostly to wages (or losses on rare occasions due to lack of cargo to handle). And because of the necessity of applying overtime wage rates to fill the unusual labour requirement, costs will no longer increase just in simple proportion to time, since: 'in the docks industry there is special cause for overtime deriving in the first place from the need for or desirability of a seven day service and in the second place from *fluctuations in demand*.' [1]

For all practical economic purposes, the labour force ought to be kept near the level necessary to meet the average demand, as otherwise there will be a periodic waste of manpower. In practice it has been found useful to keep the level about 10 per cent above the average. [2] This is just a rule of thumb, however, with no theoretical basis. The optimal level should in general be worked out by balancing the cost of maintaining a higher level and the cost (penalty) of not meeting the demand with a lower level.

Handling system modelling (I): quayside standpoint

Handling capacity of quayside facilities. An analysis of the actual performance of handling facilities has been carried out by the Transportøkonomisk Institutt in Norway for the port of Bergen. Their report includes a proposed formula which can be used for calculating cargo handling rates for container ships. [3] All the constants necessary for this formula establishing the relationship between the quantity of cargo and the handling rate, are determined by regression analysis. The formula may not be entirely applicable to other ports without modifications, because it is determined by the data collected from a specific port. Even within a single port an estimation process of such coefficients, and a curve-fitting examination of various random variables, will have to be carried out from time to time, in order to keep ahead of future traffic trends and structural changes within the port system.

It is easy to imagine that a cargo handling rate will be a random variable rather than a constant, although in some cases it can be considered constant. From the analytical viewpoint, it would be much more tidy if we were to obtain a simple distribution for a handling rate after sorting out data actually collected (such as uniform, negative exponential, Erlang, and so on). Generally speaking, however,

it seems not very often so. And analysis should be carried out carefully, without any presuppositions about such functional forms as
distribution curves offered just for their own attractiveness. In this
sense it would be useful to have an analytical model of the port
system which is presented in the form of fundamental parameters and
is sufficiently flexible to be adjusted and modified whenever necessary.

The efficiency of the system cannot be improved solely by
increasing the handling rate of cranes, since the unloading operation
depends on the space available at quayside at the time of operations.
Needless to say, there is only limited space available for unloading and
for essential manoeuvring required in the transfer operations.

> . . . congestion of quays is a serious difficulty at some ports,
> notably Liverpool, where sheer lack of space combined with
> heavy usage is the main trouble. A contributory factor is the
> practice of sorting and even sampling goods on the quayside.
> . . . every effort should be made to eliminate sorting and samp-
> ling on the quayside, to provide sufficient space for road vehicles
> to have clear access . . . . [4]

Cargo cannot be unloaded if there is no space to discharge it because
of previously unloaded cargo remaining on the quay. Even if some
space is available, cargo is not likely to be unloaded until substantial
clearance is available, in order to avoid confusion between the cargo
from one ship and that from the next.

Thus there has to be co-ordination between loading–unloading
on the one hand, and the transfer operation on the other which is
removing unloaded cargo to the next stages (either to the storage
system or inland transport). The handling rate of this transfer
operation depends on the amount of labour and handling equipment
(number of vehicles etc.) available. Even without the container
revolution, ports could well achieve quicker turnround time just
through systematically organised labour and by using adequate handling equipment. Some fundamental considerations are given here to
clarify the loading–unloading–transfer operations and to suggest ways
of achieving greater efficiency.

For the sake of simplicity, let us take the case of a single ship at
quayside, which is unloading cargo by cranes (in case of liquid
products such as oil, take the pumping rate as its handling rate).

W — units of cargo to be unloaded (which could be defined
in terms of tonnage or in numbers of containers)

r_m — maximum unloading rate of cranes (units/hour)

s_m — maximum transfer rate from quayside (units/hour)

1   If $s_m > r_m$ no hindrance occurs in terms of unloading, assuming that no other bottleneck is found elsewhere. And the shortest unloading time T_s is wholly determined by the handling rate of the cranes, namely

$$T_s = \frac{W}{r_m}$$

(4.1)

In this case, another problem may occur: the under-utilisation of transfer facilities such as forklift trucks.

2   If $s_m = r_m$ (a condition which may be called 'matching co-ordination'), the unloaded cargo can be immediately evacuated by transfer equipment either to sheds or directly to inland transport connections. This unloading time is likewise given by

$$T_s = \frac{W}{r_m} = \frac{W}{s_m}$$

(4.2)

Of the three possibilities here, this would seem to be the simplest choice, [5] since loading–unloading and transfer operations are perfectly matched, and thus no idling of labour or equipment will be found on either side. Thus, space required in practice will be comparatively small.

3   If $s_m < r_m$ the transfer facilities cannot keep up with the speed of cranes operated at their maximum. And therefore cargo will gradually begin to pile up on the quay. For lack of stacking space, the unloading procedure will have to slow down or even halt while waiting for further discharging space to become available.

Denoting here the operating rate of the cargo handling system as r units/hour, and that of the transfer system as s units/hour, where $0 \leqslant r \leqslant r_m$ and $0 \leqslant s \leqslant s_m$, and supposing that the rate of the transfer system is set at its maximum of $s = s_m$, then the accumulation rate of cargo in the stacking area will be $(r - s_m)$ units/hour. For the handling rate r we can exclude the case $0 \leqslant r \leqslant s_m$, since the resulting service time is given by (1) and (2) above. And it has been shown that the shortest unloading operation is achieved at $r = s_m$, as given in equation 4.2. We therefore need consider only the case for $s_m < r \leqslant r_m$.

First, however, let us introduce the concept of the 'space factor'. Cargo which is very dense, having a low cubic measure per ton, and certain other cargoes which may be structurally strong enough for stacking to a high level, will occupy fewer square metres of space on the quay than will cargoes which may be less dense, more fragile, or otherwise unsuited to stacking. A 'space factor' peculiar to each type of cargo, or to the type of packaging used (if not standard containers), must therefore be taken into account in order to provide a ratio between total cubic measure of cargo volume and the total square metres of quayside space. Multiplying the space factor by the total space at quayside, one can derive the maximum capacity at quayside (designated by G) for that particular type of cargo, given in terms of units (either numbers of containers or tons).

$$G = \text{quayside space (m}^2\text{)} \times \text{space factor} \left[\frac{m^3}{m^2} \text{ or } \frac{ton}{m^2} \text{ or } \frac{\text{number of containers}}{m^2} \right]$$

N.B. Take the available tank storage capacity for G as regards liquid products like oil.

A   If $(r - s_m) \cdot \dfrac{W}{r} \leqslant G$, there is no need to slow down or stop

the crane operation in order to adjust the procedure to the space restriction. The crane can proceed to handle the cargo at speed r units per hour without hindrance, because the transfer system is simultaneously evacuating the quay at a rate such that there is always some space available for unloading.

B   If $(r - s_m) \cdot \dfrac{W}{r} > G$, the unloading operation should be

controlled while keeping the transfer operation at its maximum rate. The question in respect to condition (B) is how to control the handling speed in order to achieve the shortest unloading operation. From a practical viewpoint, it would be unrealistic to control the crane speed continuously because of the nature of the work. Therefore let us suppose here a discrete control only.

Turnround time under admissible handling rate controls. There are four basic ways in which cranes can be utilised. The simplest case is that in which the handling rate of the crane r in unloading cargo from the ship is exactly equal to the transfer rate s_m of evacuation away from the quay to storage or to inland transport terminals. It is often thought, perhaps erroneously so in many cases, that this model is the most logical and best possible to adopt. But it will be shown that the length of time in which the cranes are in operation can be considerably shortened by adopting one of the other three possibilities; and that the costs of one of the more complex systems may be much less.

The time sequence of the movement of cargo is shown in figure 4.1. Time T_0 represents the moment unloading operations commence, and time T_{tr_f} the time at which all the cargo has reached its immediate destination (storage or inland terminal). T_{tr0} is the point at which the transfer system begins to move cargo away from the quay; and this point may be considered, for most practical purposes, as nearly identical to T_0. Unloading is completed at point T_s, whereas transfer of cargo from the quay continues until point T_{ef} when the entire quay has been evacuated of cargo from that particular ship. It should be noted that the *immediate* destination of the cargo may be some distance away, and that the point of 'quay evacuation' T_{ef} is not necessarily the same as the point T_{tr_f} at which 'cargo transfer' is finally completed.

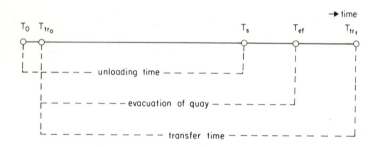

Figure 4.1 Time sequence for unloading and transfer of cargo

Now let us consider graphically the four general ways in which the operating rates may be reduced or otherwise modified to fit the evacuation rate and quayside space restrictions. The analysis presented here is based upon the total space G available at quayside for a particular type of cargo, as explained above. The shaded areas in the following group of figures indicate the accumulation of cargo on the quay, with the maximum permissible level at point G. Crane operations at whatever rate (including nil, when the cranes cease to operate) are indicated by thick lines. If the unloading rate is greater than the transfer rate away from the quay, cargo will begin to accumulate on the quay; and once the total accumulation reaches point G (as shown in figures 4.2b, 4.2c, 4.2d), then the unloading rate will have to be reduced.

Admissible control 1: matching rate type

In this case the handling and transfer rates are set equal to each other. Cargo is thus evacuated at exactly the same rate as it is deposited on the quay, and therefore never accumulates to any significant level. By the assumption $s_m < r \leqslant r_m$, it is clear that $s_m < r_m$ in this case, which means the crane is working consistently at a rate lower than its maximum.

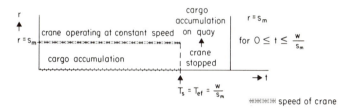

Figure 4.2a   Matching rate handling control

Admissible control 2: dual rate type

The handling rate here is maintained at its maximum until no further space is available at quayside. The rate is then reduced to match the evacuation rate until all cargo has been unloaded.

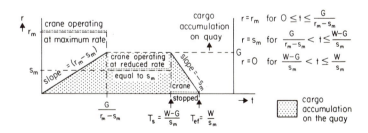

Figure 4.2b   Dual rate handling control

61

Admissible control 3: stop–go type

Here the handling rate is maintained at its maximum for the entire time that it is in operation. When the cargo accumulation at quayside reaches its maximum, unloading then ceases entirely until the quay is evacuated. When all, or most, of the cargo has been removed, the unloading operation commences again at its maximum rate. And so on, until all cargo is unloaded. Figure 4.2c shows the case where all cargo is unloaded during the second 'go' phase of unloading, following the first 'stop'. If cargo accumulation were to reach point G again before the ship were entirely unloaded, then there would have to be a second 'stop' while the quay is evacuated, and yet a third 'go' phase of unloading would have to follow. And so on, until all cargo is unloaded.

$$r = r_m \text{ for } 0 < t \leqslant \frac{G}{r_m - s_m}$$

$$r = 0 \quad \text{for } \frac{G}{r_m - s_m} < t \leqslant \frac{G}{r_m - s_m} + \frac{G}{s_m}$$

$$r = r_m \text{ for } \frac{G}{r_m - s_m} + \frac{G}{s_m} < t \leqslant \frac{G}{s_m} + \frac{W}{r_m}$$

$$r = 0 \quad \text{for } \frac{G}{s_m} + \frac{W}{r_m} < t \leqslant \frac{W}{s_m}$$

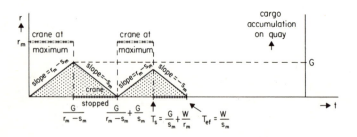

Figure 4.2c   Stop–go handling control

Admissible control 4: convergent rates type

In this case the handling rate is set such that the unloading of cargo is completed at the very moment that the accumulation of cargo on the quay reaches its maximum permissible level.

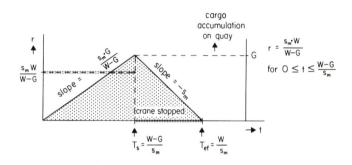

Figure 4.2d   Convergent rates handling control

Quay evacuation time fluctuation. It has been shown that the unloading time for W units of cargo is given by a simple formula, if the handling facilities are used systematically, taking into account various factors such as available space, amount of cargo, handling rates of cranes and so on. However, the completion time even for a single ship may fluctuate if the service time of handling equipment plus labour vary in a stochastic sense. For instance, if the quay evacuation rate s has a certain distribution because of machine breakdown, unavailability of vehicles, labour problems (e.g. vehicle drivers), and so forth, then obviously this would be reflected in the service time fluctuation through the form of $t_{ef} = \dfrac{W}{s}$.

Examples of quay evacuation time fluctuation

1   *Uniform transfer rate distribution.* The probability density function $f_s(s)$ is:

$$f_s(s) = \frac{1}{s_2 - s_1}, \text{ for } s_1 \leqslant s \leqslant s_2. \text{ Otherwise, } f_s(s) = 0$$

(4.3)

63

Therefore, the completion time distribution is given by the following probability density function $f_{T_{ef}}(t_{ef})$.

$$f_{T_{ef}}(t_{ef}) = \frac{W}{s_2 - s_1} \cdot \frac{1}{t_{ef}^2} \text{ for } \frac{W}{s_2} \leqslant t_{ef} \leqslant \frac{W}{s_1} \qquad (4.4)$$

Given the probability distribution function as in equation 4.4, some basic values such as mean and variance for the quay evacuation completion time are easily calculated.

$$E[T_{ef}] = \frac{W}{s_2 - s_1} \cdot \ln \frac{s_2}{s_1} \qquad (4.5)$$

$$\text{Var}[T_{ef}] = \frac{W^2}{s_1 s_2} - \left(\frac{W}{s_2 - s_1} \cdot \ln \frac{s_2}{s_1}\right)^2 \qquad (4.6)$$

2   *Negative exponential transfer rate distribution.* The probability density function $f_S(s)$ is

$$f_S(s) = \mu_r e^{-\mu_r s} \text{ for } \mu_r > 0, \text{ otherwise } f_S(s) = 0 \qquad (4.7)$$

Here μ_r is a constant, and is actually the mean transfer rate. Now the probability density function $f_{T_{ef}}(t_{ef})$ is

$$f_{T_{ef}}(t_{ef}) = \mu_r W \cdot \frac{1}{t_{ef}^2} \cdot e^{-\frac{\mu_r W}{t_{ef}}} \text{ for } 0 \leqslant t_{ef} \qquad (4.8)$$

With respect to fluctuation in ship size (or to be more precise, the amount of cargo to discharge) the derivation of these statistical figures is much more straightforward when other factors can be assumed constant. If an annual report reveals that the frequency distribution curve of cargo unloaded by each ship could well be fitted to such familiar distributions as pseudo-normal, exponential or others, then the average completion time of ships throughout the year is easily estimated.

Operation cost comparison among admissible controls. Besides ship turnround time, operation cost is now to be considered. Since the handling rate of cargo transfer from the quayside is fixed for the moment, consideration is given here to the cost of unloading operations from the ship, along with comparisons for the operational costs of Controls 2 and 4. The cost of the unloading operation depends on fixed costs (i.e. capital cost and its depreciation), overhead cost, wages for labour, fuel consumption and so on. Here C_{cop} will represent the cost of crane operations (£/hour). K_{cop} (2) and K_{cop} (4) are operating costs for the completion of unloading W tons of cargo by Control Modes 2 and 4, respectively.

Case 1: Cost curve linear against the handling rate

$C_{cop} = a_1 \cdot r + a_2$, where a_1, a_2 are constants

$$K_{cop}(2) = \left[a_1 \cdot r_m + a_2\right] \frac{G}{r_m - s_m} + \left[a_1 \cdot s_m + a_2\right] \frac{W - \dfrac{r_m G}{r_m - s_m}}{s_m}$$

$$= a_1 \cdot W + a_2 \cdot \frac{W - G}{s_m} \tag{4.9}$$

$$K_{cop}(4) = \left[a_1 \cdot \frac{s_m W}{W - G} + a_2\right] \frac{W - G}{s_m} = a_1 \cdot W + a_2 \cdot \frac{W - G}{s_m} \tag{4.10}$$

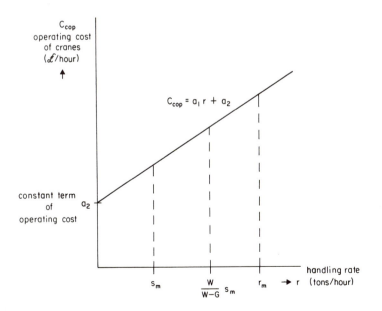

Figure 4.3 Operating cost of cranes versus handling rate: linear case

Therefore no difference in terms of operation cost is seen in this linear case between Control 2 and Control 4.

Case 2: Cost curve non-linear against the handling rate

$C_{cop} = C_{cop}(r)$, where $C_{cop}(r)$ is a non-linear function of r.

$$K_{cop}(2) = C_{cop}(r_m) \cdot \frac{G}{r_m - s_m} + C_{cop}(s_m) \cdot \frac{W - \frac{r_m G}{r_m - s_m}}{s_m}$$

$$K_{cop}(4) = C_{cop}\left[\frac{s_m W}{W-G}\right] \cdot \frac{W-G}{s_m}$$

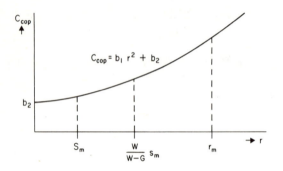

Figure 4.4   Operating cost of cranes versus handling rate: non-linear case

Example

Assume that $C_{cop} = b_1 \cdot r^2 + b_2$ (quadratic form with b_1, b_2 as constants).

$$K_{cop}(2) = b_1 \cdot (s_m W + r_m G) + b_2 \cdot \frac{W-G}{s_m} \tag{4.11}$$

$$K_{cop}(4) = b_1 \cdot \left[\frac{s_m W^2}{W-G}\right] + b_2 \cdot \frac{W-G}{s_m} \tag{4.12}$$

The comparison of operating costs of these two controls now depends on the value of $b_1(s_m W + r_m G)$ and $b_1 \left[\frac{s_m W^2}{W-G}\right]$, namely

66

$$K_{cop}(2) \gtrless K_{cop}(4) \text{ depending on } b_1 \cdot (s_m W + r_m G) \gtrless b_1 \left[\frac{s_m W^2}{W - G} \right]$$

However, it can be shown particularly in this case that only one possibility holds: $K_{cop}(2) > K_{cop}(4)$.

Conclusions concerning admissible controls. Among the four admissible controls, 2 and 3 are 'switching' controls, while 1 and 4 require no switching. As far as the completion time is concerned, there is no difference at all among them, since each gives $T_{ef} = \frac{W}{s_m}$. However, from the viewpoint of ship turnround time, 1 is at least desirable because this control does not make use of the space available at quayside, and hence needs longer time to complete the unloading operation. Between 2 and 3 there is only a fractional difference in this respect. But 3 is a rather inefficient means of handling cargo in comparison with 2, because 3 always requires a greater turnround time than 2 — or at best an equal amount of time. Moreover, this 'stop–go' type of control is, practically speaking, no better than the 'smooth' types such as 1 and 4. No stand-by is required once the necessary work force is allotted for the smooth type, whereas the 'stop–go' work force should be set at the maximum required level, thus incurring potential redundancies.

With respect to ship turnround time, 2 and 4 are equivalent, with $T_s = \frac{W - G}{s_m}$, where T_s is ship turnround time. The justification of these criteria remains yet to be seen, because it depends on the intensity of ship arrivals as well as on the operating cost profile. For instance, if ship arrivals are comparatively sparse, the residual pile of cargo after the departure of one ship does not cause any problems. However, if arrivals are dense, then residual cargo should be evacuated to serve the next ship as soon as possible.

Controls 2 and 4 are equal in terms of total length of time actually spent by the cranes in unloading operations. Control 1 requires the longest time of all. And Control 3 requires the shortest. It should be noted, however, that overall time, beyond which unloading from a particular ship ceases, is shortest for Controls 2 and 4, since Control 3 is of the stop–go type, with an interval for quay evacuation during which the unloading equipment remains idle for a time before resuming again at the maximum unloading rate.

1   From the viewpoint of actual control, the 'switching' control is less desirable than the continuous control, because facilities might not be fully utilised in this case. If, on the other hand, the handling rate is constant, and thus no stand-by labour is necessary, then the labour force may be spared and allotted to other jobs.

2   As far as the quay evacuation time is concerned (the period from T_{tr_o} to T_{tr_f}), there is no difference at all among the various admissible controls.

3   For the sake of shorter ship turnround time, Controls 2 and 4 are preferable to Controls 1 and 3.

4   In terms of operation cost consideration, Control 2 is equivalent to Control 4, if the cost function is linear against the handling rate. And in this case, Control 4 is a better one. Control 4 provides for the unloading equipment as well as the unloading labour units to complete the work on that particular ship at the earliest possible point in time, thus freeing them to go elsewhere.

5   If the cost function is non-linear, then the superiority of Controls 2 and 4 depends upon the operation cost function. And the cost of Control 4 is smaller than that of Control 2 in the case of a quadratic relationship.

6   Since this unloading operation plus the transfer operation should be considered in relation to the other subsystems (e.g. storage and inland transport), the problem of allocating facilities to achieve the overall optimum for all systems taken together still remains to be analysed.

Handling system modelling (II): shipside standpoint

Individual ship service time. In examining the service times for individual ships, let us take as an example a particular ship with W units of cargo to unload, and estimate the average service time to be expected for this ship, given a discharging space of G units where the unloading rate r and the evacuation rate s are independently distributed random variables. The time for completing the unloading operation is given by

$$t_s = \frac{W}{r} \text{ if } W \leqslant \frac{r}{r-s} \cdot G \text{ or equivalently } r \leqslant \frac{W \cdot s}{W-G}$$

$$t_s = \frac{W-G}{s} \text{ if } W > \frac{r}{r-s} \cdot G \text{ or equivalently } r > \frac{W \cdot s}{W-G}$$

Here t_s represents a random variable of the state variable T_s.

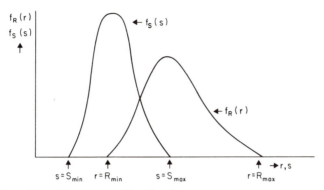

Figure 4.5   Handling rates distribution

The probability that the unloading rate and the evacuating rate lie in the region (r, r + dr) and (s, s + ds), respectively, is simply $f_R(r)f_S(s)drds$ since these two random variables are independently distributed. Therefore the expected value of T_s (average unloading time) for the ship, which may be designated as $\overline{T}_s$, will be

$$\int_{S_{min}}^{S_{max}} \int_{R_{min}}^{R_{max}} t_s f_R(r)f_s(s)drds$$

If $\frac{WS_{max}}{W-G} \leqslant R_{min}$, then $\overline{T}_s$ simply becomes the following.

$$\overline{T}_s = (W-G) \int_{S_{min}}^{S_{max}} \frac{f_S(s)}{s} \, ds$$

(4.13)

And especially when $f_S(s) = \delta\,(s-s_0)$, which means s is constant, where $\frac{Ws_0}{W-G} \leqslant R_{min}$, then we get: $\overline{T}_s = \frac{W-G}{s_0}$

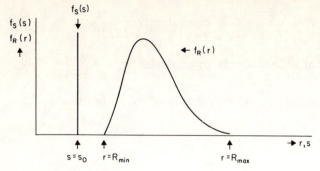

Figure 4.6   Unloading rate distribution with constant
transfer rate

As shown in figure 4.6, s_0 here is a constant value for s (i.e. the evacuation rate does not fluctuate).

If $\dfrac{WS_{min}}{W-G} \geqslant R_{max}$, then T_s can be rewritten as follows.

$$\overline{T}_s = W \int_{R_{min}}^{R_{max}} \frac{f_R(r)}{r}\, dr$$

$$(4.14)$$

And again, especially when $f_R(r) = \delta\,(r - r_a)$, which would mean r is constant, $\dfrac{WS_{min}}{W-G} \geqslant r_a$, then $\overline{T}_s = \dfrac{W}{r_a}$

This result together with the first one above can be reckoned as the extension of the particular cases which have already been analysed under the headings of constant handling rates. This individual-ship aspect of unloading operations deals with an average expected value of unloading time for a particular ship carrying certain units of cargo.

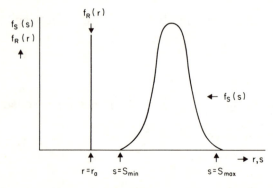

Figure 4.7   Transfer rate distribution with unloading rate constant

70

Variation of intrinsic transfer capacity with immobilisation time

A certain relationship exists between the intrinsic transfer capacity of load-carriers and such determining factors as the number of vehicles employed, the handling capacity of each vehicle, the distance of transfer, the speed of vehicles, the amount of time needed for loading and unloading, and so forth. This will hold true for whatever type of load-carriers are installed — transfer trucks, forklift trucks, straddle carriers — for the transfer of cargo between the quay area and storage, or between the quay area and the inland transport terminals. It is not difficult to formulate this relationship into a simple equation, provided that the whole situation is simplified: all vehicles running at the same speed (v_f), carrying the same amount of cargo (w_f), transferring it a specified distance (D_{tr}), and requiring a constant time to unload (T_{cd}). The intrinsic transfer capacity C_f is given as follows.

$$C_f = \frac{\rho_{tr} \cdot n_{tr} \cdot w_f}{T_{cd} + \frac{2D_{tr}}{v_f}}$$

(4.15)

where ρ_{tr} is the utilisation factor of the vehicles, and n_{tr} is the number of vehicles employed. From the equation one readily finds that C_f varies in accordance with the inverse of immobilisation time T_{cd}, and also obviously increases proportionately to the increase of the number of vehicles actually employed (or, more precisely, to the increases in $\rho_{tr} n_{tr}$). Nonetheless, this formula needs some modification in order to account for the fact that vehicle speed will not be independent of the number of vehicles.

Vehicles within the manoeuvring area will have to be gradually slowed down as the number of vehicles increases. This is simply because the space used by the vehicles is physically somewhat limited. Taking an extreme case, it would obviously become impossible beyond a certain high value of n_{tr} for any vehicle to move at all, because the whole passage would then be jammed with vehicles. The maximum value at such an immobilisation point is denoted by n_{trm}.

Vehicle behaviour may be visually illustrated by figure 4.8 where L_f is the length of a vehicle plus the minimum clearance between two vehicles, and v_{fm} is the maximum speed of a single vehicle. It would not be so unreasonable to suppose a gradual decrease of vehicle speed between points A and B. The precise shape of curve $\widehat{AB}$ will, of

71

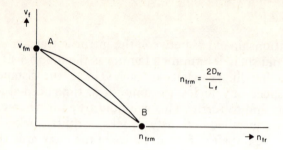

Figure 4.8   Vehicle speed versus number of vehicles
             employed

course, depend upon many factors: road surface conditions, driving
skill, types of vehicle, and so on. But what is important here is to
realise that some pressure restraining the speed of vehicles will occur
as the number increases. An attempt is made by the Road Research
Laboratory to establish how the average journey speed is related to
the flow and composition of traffic and to the width and layout
characteristics of the road. [6]   Although it might be felt too daring
to make a direct analogy from this report, a similar approach is
possible in respect to traffic planning within the port manoeuvring area.
    Taking the simplest case, suppose that the speed decreases linearly
in proportion to the number of vehicles. Then

$$v_f = -\frac{v_{fm}}{n_{trm}-1} \cdot (n_{tr}-n_{trm}) \qquad v_f = v_{fm} \text{ at } n_{tr} = 1$$

$$v_f = 0 \text{ at } \quad n_{tr} = n_{trm}$$

We assume also $v_f = v_{fm}$ at $n_{tr} = 0$

$$v_f = -\frac{v_{fm} \cdot n_{tr}}{n_{trm}-1} + \frac{v_{fm} \cdot n_{trm}}{n_{trm}-1} \tag{4.16}$$

Combining equations 4.15 and 4.16, we get

$$C_f = \frac{\rho_{tr} \cdot w_f \cdot n_{tr}}{T_{cd} + \dfrac{2D_{tr}}{-\dfrac{v_{fm} \cdot n_{tr}}{n_{trm}-1} + \dfrac{v_{fm} \cdot n_{trm}}{n_{trm}-1}}} \tag{4.17}$$

And by making the following substitutions, we can get the simplified formula of equation 4.18.

$$A = \frac{v_{fm} \cdot T_{cd}}{n_{trm} - 1} \qquad\qquad C = \frac{\rho_{tr} \cdot w_f \cdot v_{fm}}{n_{trm} - 1}$$

$$B = \frac{v_{fm} \cdot n_{trm} \cdot T_{cd}}{n_{trm} - 1} + 2D_{tr} \qquad D = \frac{\rho_{tr} \cdot w_f \cdot v_{fm} \cdot n_{trm}}{n_{trm} - 1}$$

$$C_f = \frac{- C \cdot n_{tr}^2 + D \cdot n_{tr}}{- A \cdot n_{tr} + B}$$

$$(4.18)$$

In order to find the maximum value of C_f, we simply differentiate equation 4.18 with respect to n_{tr} and find the number n_{tr}^* which gives the maximum of C_f where $0 \leqslant n_{tr}^* \leqslant n_{trm}$.

It can be shown that C_f attains its maximum at n_{tr}^* where

$$n_{tr}^* = \frac{B}{A} - \sqrt{\frac{B}{A}^2 - \frac{BD}{AC}}$$

$$(4.19)$$

Example

Forklift trucks with a manoeuvring length of about 10 metres each (including the minimum clearance) for carrying containers may require one or two minutes time to pick up and set down one container. Suppose the travelling speed is 360 m/min., load capacity is 25 tons, and the vehicle has to transfer containers a distance of 500 metres.

ρ_{tr} = 1 (supposing that every vehicle is in use at any moment)

T_{cd} = 3 minutes (or 0.05 hours, unloading and loading each requiring 1.5 minutes on average)

w_f = 25 tons

v_{fm} = 360 m/min. = 21.6 km/hr.

D_{tr} = 500m = 0.5 km

$n_{trm} = \frac{2D_{tr}}{L_f} = \frac{2 \times 0.5}{0.01} = 100$

73

Substituting these values into the above formulas:

$$A = \frac{21.6 \ (km/hr) \times 0.05 \ (hr)}{100 - 1} = 0.0109 \ (km)$$

$$B = \frac{21.6 \ (km/hr) \times 100 \times 0.05 \ (hr)}{100 - 1} + 2 \times 0.5 \ (km) = 2.0909 \ (km)$$

$$C = \frac{1 \times 25 \ (tons) \times 21.6 \ (km/hr)}{100 - 1} = 5.4545 \ (ton\text{-}km/hr)$$

$$D = \frac{1 \times 25 \ (tons) \times 21.6 \ (km/hr) \times 100}{100 - 1} = 545.45 \ (ton\text{-}km/hr)$$

Table 4.1
Vehicle number versus vehicle productivity

n_{tr} number of vehicles	v_f vehicle speed (m/min)	$\dfrac{n_{tr}}{T_{cd} + \dfrac{2D_{tr}}{v_f}}$ (1/minutes)	$\dfrac{w_f \cdot n_{tr}}{T_{cd} + \dfrac{2D_{tr}}{v_f}}$ vehicle productivity (tons/hour)
51	178.2	5.92	8880
52	174.5	5.96	8940
53	170.9	5.99	8985
54	167.3	6.01	9015
55	163.6	6.04	9060
56	160.0	6.05	9075
57	156.4	6.06	9090
58	152.7	6.075	9113
59	149.1	6.078	9117 ← Maximum
60	145.5	6.076	9114

Therefore, from equation 4.19 C_f attains its maximum at

$$n_{tr} = n_{tr}^* = 191.83 - \sqrt{36797.1 - 19182.7} = 59.1 \ (\text{number of forklift trucks})$$

Comparing with n_{trm} we get

$$59.1 = n^*_{tr} < n_{trm} = \frac{2D_{tr}}{L_f} = \frac{1000}{10} = 100 \text{ (number of trucks)}$$

This value of n_{tr} shows that the intrinsic capacity will be limited by this number of forklift trucks — i.e. fewer than 100 for maximal use. The iterative calculation in table 4.1 tells us that it is, in fact, at $n_{tr} = 59$. And here, if 59 vehicles are fully and efficiently utilised ($\rho_{tr} = 1$), the maximum C^*_f will be

$$C^*_f = \rho_{tr}w_f \frac{n_{tr}}{T_{cd} + \dfrac{2D_{tr}}{v_f}} = 25 \times 6.078 \text{ (ton/min)} = 9117 \text{ (ton/hr)}$$

It is worth noting that the intrinsic capacity could be wrongly over-estimated if the speed of vehicles were considered to be a completely independent variable. In the above case, C^*_f would then be estimated at

$$C^*_f = 1 \times 25 \times \frac{59}{3 + \dfrac{2 \times 500}{360}} \times 60 = 15318 \text{ (ton/hr)}$$

which would be a full 68 per cent beyond the estimated intrinsic capacity.

Optimal number of vehicles

It would be useful at this juncture to translate the figure and calculations given above into a method for determining the optimal number of vehicles in terms of the intrinsic capacity of the transfer vehicles. The optimal number will vary according to the shape of the vehicle speed function in terms of the number of vehicles, as shown by curves E_1, E_2, E_3 in figure 4.9. The only way to find the optimal solution is to replace the straight line by the actual curve constructed from data gathered in the port, and simply carry on the same calculations as presented above. The resulting C_f – n_{tr} curves may then appear somewhat like F_1, F_2, F_3 (corresponding to E_1, E_2, E_3, respectively), as shown in figure 4.9.

The E_3 curve is the extreme case, which assumes (rather unrealistically, that an unlimited increase in the number of vehicles will produce no decrease in vehicle speed. Thus the corresponding F_3 curve assumes an indefinite increase of capacity in proportion to continual increases in numbers of vehicles.

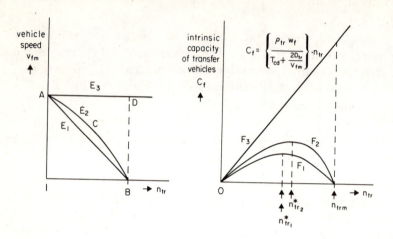

Figure 4.9 Vehicle speed and intrinsic capacity with respect
to vehicle number

A more realistic curve would be E_1, which provides a fair
approximation to the general case, although curve E_2 is the general
form which one is most likely to encounter. The corresponding
curves F_1 and F_2 share various features in common. And it is clear
that the maximum point of either curve can be precisely determined
in order to find the exact values of $n^*_{tr_1}$ or $n^*_{tr_2}$, respectively.

The optimal number of vehicles, *in its true economic sense*, however, should of course remain to be soundly determined on the
trade-off basis between the cost of providing vehicles and the benefit
accruing from the resultant intrinsic capacity to be obtained.

76

Part B: Labour and resource allocation

Labour allocation for higher operational efficiency

Thus far we have investigated the overall efficiency of the cargo handling system by describing the simplified input-output model constructed in the section on handling capacity. From a practical viewpoint the productivity of the handling system depends on various factors — in short, on the handling rate of mechanical equipment, the volition of the ship operator in favour of faster ship turnround time even at higher costs, the port policy with respect to gang allocations and so on. It would seem worthwhile here to shed light on the labour allocation problem. This is of considerable importance in terms of operational efficiency given the physical restrictions: e.g. the number of gangs available, possible use of lighters for working overside, and the hatch pattern of vessels. Such restrictions may be compounded by port regulations, such as the widespread rule against allowing more than two gangs to work on a single hatch at any one time. A brief survey of actual operating conditions at a number of ports throughout the world is given below, in order to illustrate some of the problems which may be encountered in this respect.

Operating conditions at various ports worldwide:

Port of Bergen, Norway

1   The shift system for gangs may have a great influence on the waiting time for ships. [7]

2   'In the Port of Bergen export cargo arrives to the sheds during the last four days before the ship's arrival. Import cargo will stay in the sheds up to 3 weeks, mostly less than one week and only 4 per cent more than two weeks.' [8]

Port of Karachi, Pakistan [9]

1   Once a gang is allocated to a ship, it will continue to work that ship until there is no work left for it.

2   Once recruited, the gang is paid for the full shift, whether it works or not.

3   Gang sizes are usually the same for any cargo. That is, there are 7 men for discharging and 11 men for loading in a hatch, with 8 men on the quay for shed transfer and 6 for wagons.

4   Acceptance of ships is based on the first-come first-served

rule, with some exceptions.

5   Prior to discharge on the quay, the agent says whether the cargo is destined for open storage or for sheds.

Port of La Valletta, Malta [10]

1   At the request of the shipping agents, gangs are allocated, according to the number available, in proportion to the amount of cargo in the commanding hatch and the cargo distribution among the hatches.

2   Gang sizes on the deepwater quay tend to be constant. A typical gang consists of 26 people, of whom 10 work on the ship, 5 are lightermen who work under the hook, and 11 work in the transit sheds and open stacking areas.

3   Berthing priority may depend on conditions in the sheds.

4   Unhooking is done by lightermen putting the cargo into the lighter.

5   Special treatment is given to perishable goods (such as meat and cheese).

6   About 80 per cent of the incoming traffic goes into sheds. About 20 per cent is either put on open storage areas, or else goes directly onto road vehicles.

Port Louis, Mauritius [11]

1   Port Louis handled about 1,434,000 tons of cargo of all types in 1970, with exports of sugar and molasses accounting for nearly 50 per cent of this total. The other main commodities handled at the port were imports of rice flour, petroleum products and general cargo.

2   Nearly all cargoes are loaded or discharged into lighters working between the ships and the quays.

3   Three stevedoring companies in Port Louis are responsible to the shipping companies for the loading and unloading of cargo from their ships.

4   The stevedoring companies employ among them a total of 38 gangs of stevedores, consisting of between 12 and 16 men each.

Port of Pusan, Korea [12]

At Pusan wheat is discharged mainly at anchorage into

lighters at a rate of about 1,200 tons each day. The lighters are brought ashore and discharged, where the wheat is then either bagged and taken by truck to a warehouse, or hauled by trucks in bulk to the mills.

Port of Valparaiso, Chile [13]

1   Shipping agents give notice to the port authority of the ship's expected time of arrival, and provide the port with a cargo list which gives the distribution of tonnage in each hatch.

2   Apart from ships carrying more than 50 passengers (which have priority), ships are berthed on a first-come first-served basis.

3   Shipping companies occasionally use barges as a means of increasing the rate of discharge.

4   Almost all transfer on the quays is carried out by means of forklift trucks.

Determination of optimal hatch pattern

The percentage of each cargo class moving on the quay by each mode — (a) transfer to transit shed, (b) transfer to open storage, (c) discharge overside, or (d) direct delivery to rail, road or barge — can be calculated from observed data. If this modal split is fixed for each hatch (independently of ship class), then the problem which arises is to find the optimal hatch pattern of cargo mix so that a certain objective is fulfilled. Let us examine a simple example of the operational aspects of cargo handling for a ship with a number of hatches.

Hatches are numbered 1, 2, . . . , L, and any one of these hatches at any one time may be designated by i. Similarly, the various kinds of cargo are numbered 1, 2, . . . , M, and any one of these kinds at any one time may be designated by j. The fraction of W (total amount of cargo for the entire ship) which is of j-class in hatch i is designated by y_{ij}. The handling capacity for this j-class cargo at hatch i is designated by μ_{ij}. And by definition of course the summation of all these fractions is equal to unity.

$$\sum_{i=1}^{L} \sum_{j=1}^{M} y_{ij} = 1$$

(4.20)

If we designate $\sum_{i=1}^{L} y_{ij} = a_j$, then from equation 4.20 we get

$$\sum_{j=1}^{M} a_j = 1 \tag{4.21}$$

Using the above fractions, the actual *amount* of class-j cargo in hatch i is $W \cdot y_{ij}$. And unloading time for this cargo will be

$$t_{f_{ij}} = \frac{W \cdot y_{ij}}{\mu_{ij}} \tag{4.22}$$

The slowest completion time (which gives final completion time) for hatch i is

$$t_{f_i} = \text{Max} \ \frac{W \cdot y_{ij}}{\mu_{ij}} \quad \text{for } j = 1, 2, \ldots, M \tag{4.23}$$

Overall completion time for this ship with W tons of cargo mix is therefore

$$t_f = \text{Max} \ t_{f_i} \quad \text{for } 1 \leqslant i \leqslant L \tag{4.24}$$

This is a different way of looking at the unloading operation; and we can suppose the following objective with respect to ship turnround time. That is, determine the fraction-matrix y_{ij} so as to minimise this t_f given the handling rate matrix μ_{ij} inherent in the existing facilities. For simplicity, let us consider the following example of a single-commodity case ($j = 1$).

W = total amount of cargo y_i = fraction matrix μ_i = handling matrix.

Since there is only one commodity, the fraction-matrix becomes $(L \cdot 1)$, so that y_{ij} and μ_{ij} can be expressed as this one dimensional matrix. The problem then is to determine Minimax $\dfrac{W \cdot y_i}{\mu_i}$ subject to

$\sum_{i=1}^{L} y_i = 1$ for $1 \leqslant i \leqslant L$.

In this particular case the optimum solution is given as follows.

$$y_1 = \frac{\mu_1}{\mu_1 + \mu + \ldots + \mu_L}, \ y_2 = \frac{\mu_2}{\mu_1 + \mu_2 + \ldots + \mu_L}, \ldots, y_L = \frac{\mu_L}{\mu_1 + \mu_2 + \ldots + \mu_L}$$

$$\tag{4.25}$$

Now, returning to the general problem where we consider mixed cargo (j=1,2, ... , M), this argument can be applied without any significant modification. Since the handling system for each cargo is independent at each hatch — and we are concerned not with the local Minimax problem, but with the overall Minimax problem for the ship — the optimal fraction-matrix y_{ij} (i=1,2, ... , L and j=1,2, ... , M) is given by

$$y_{ij} = \frac{a_j \cdot \mu_{ij}}{\mu_{1j} + \mu_{2j} + \ldots + \mu_{Lj}} \quad \text{for } \begin{matrix} i=1,2, \ldots , L \\ j=1,2, \ldots , M \end{matrix} \tag{4.26}$$

Since $\dfrac{W \cdot y_{ij}}{\mu_{ij}}$ gives the unloading time for cargo of class j at hatch i, this time is given by $\dfrac{a_j \cdot W}{\mu_{1j} + \mu_{2j} + \ldots + \mu_{Lj}}$. And given the values of a_j and $\{\mu_{ij}\}$, the dominant unloading time for the ship will thus be

$$t_f = \text{Max} \frac{a_j \cdot W}{\mu_{1j} + \mu_{2j} + \ldots + \mu_{Lj}} \quad \text{for } 1 \leqslant j \leqslant M \tag{4.27}$$

Example

Cargo mix consisting of two bagged and bulk commodities

W = 1000 tons   i = 1,2,3,4 (hatch numbers)

a_1 = 0.4 (j=1 for bagged cargo) a_2 = 0.6 (j=2 for bulk cargo)

Hatch	tons/hour for j=1	for j=2
1	$\mu_{11} = 30$	$\mu_{12} = 40$
2	$\mu_{21} = 25$	$\mu_{22} = 60$
3	$\mu_{31} = 25$	$\mu_{32} = 60$
4	$\mu_{41} = 20$	$\mu_{42} = 40$

Handling rates (tons per gang hour at each hatch) are given in the above matrix. By use of the formula given above, the optimal distribution of cargo among hatches is:

81

$$y_{11} = 0.12 \, , \; y_{12} = 0.12$$
$$y_{21} = 0.1 \quad , \; y_{22} = 0.18$$
$$y_{31} = 0.1 \quad , \; y_{32} = 0.18$$
$$y_{41} = 0.08 \, , \; y_{42} = 0.12$$

In this case the minimum ship turnround time is $t_f = 4$ hours

Hatch	Completion time (hours)	
	for j=1	for j=2
1	4.0	3.0
2	4.0	3.0
3	4.0	3.0
4	4.0	3.0

In order to make a comparison with random allocation, consider the following fraction-matrices.

1   Instead of the optimal fraction among hatches with reference to class-1 cargo (which is 0.3-0.25-0.25-0.2), here we take 0.4-0.4-0.1-0.1 to make a comparison, while leaving the fraction with respect to class-2 cargo as before. For the matrix $y_{11} = 0.4 \times 0.4$, $y_{21} = 0.4 \times 0.4$, $y_{31} = 0.4 \times 0.1$, $y_{41} = 0.4 \times 0.1$ one gets the following results.

Hatch	Completion time (hours)	
	for j=1	for j=2
1	5.3	3.0
2	→ 6.04	3.0
3	1.6	3.0
4	2.0	3.0

$$t_{f_{11}} = 5.3$$
$$t_{f_{21}} = 6.04$$
$$t_{f_{31}} = 1.6$$
$$t_{f_{41}} = 2.0$$

$$t_f = 6.04 \text{ hours}$$

The ship's turnround time will not be affected by those hatches where the unloading time for a particular cargo is very much shortened but by the commanding hatch (in this case Hatch 2) which requires the longest completion time.

2   On the other hand, if we take the following fraction for class-2 cargo, instead of the value taken above, the result for the matrix $y_{12} = 0.6 \times 0.5$, $y_{22} = 0.6 \times 0.1$,

82

$$y_{32} = 0.6 \times 0.3, \quad y_{42} = 0.6 \times 0.1 \quad \text{will be}$$

		Completion time (hours)	
	Hatch	for j=1	for j=2
$tf_{12} = 7.5$	1	4.0	7.5
$tf_{22} = 1.0$	2	4.0	1.0
$tf_{32} = 3.0$	3	4.0	3.0
$tf_{42} = 1.5$	4	4.0	1.5

$$t_f = 7.5 \text{ hours}$$

3   It would also be interesting to see the outcome in terms of completion time for a ship whose distribution fraction-matrix is determined at random for both classes of cargo simultaneously, in comparison with the optimal allocation, by use of the method presented. This gives $t_f = 7.5$ hours, whereas the method outlined above gives an optimal completion time of $t_f = 4$ hours.

	Completion time (hours)	
Hatch	for j=1	for j=2
1	5.3	7.5
2	6.04	1.0
3	1.6	3.0
4	2.0	1.5

$$t_f = 7.5 \text{ hours}$$

Hatch capacity limit

In order to complete the construction of an effective hatch distribution formula, one must ensure that the inherent physical limitation of the ship — hatch capacity itself — is not exceeded. If C_{hi} represents the accommodating capacity of hatch i, then the following restriction is imperative.

$$\sum_{j=1}^{M} Wy_{ij} \leqslant C_{hi} \tag{4.28}$$

Optimal allocations can be achieved only by solutions which satisfy this condition. Let us reconsider the above example with this condition taken into account.

First allocation

tons

Hatch	for j=1	for j=2	total	C_{hi}	slack excess capacity	C_{sei}	admissible excess capacity	C_{aei}
1	120	120	240	300	+ 60		+ 40	
2	100	180	280	250	− 30			
3	100	180	280	200	− 80			
4	80	120	200	300	+100		+ 40	

N.B. In the first allocation $y_{11}W = 0.12 \times 1000 = 120$ tons. This is the value of row 1 column 1 of the table. Other values are worked out in the same way.

As regards Hatch 1, for example, the amount of cargo of class j=2 in Hatch 1 can be increased up to $t_f \cdot \mu_{12} = 4 \times 40 = 160$ tons without any effect on the overall minimum time required for the completion of service. In this case, 160-120 (row 1, column 2) = 40 tons is the admissible excess capacity. Admissible excess capacity cannot be calculated for Hatch 2 or Hatch 3, which already have an overflow. This necessitates a shift of excess cargo from these two hatches to the remaining hatches where excess space is available. By this operation we know that the ship turnround time will have to be extended beyond the minimum value $t_f = 4$ hours. The problem is to keep this increment as slight as possible.

As far as the ship turnround time is concerned, what really matters is the longest time required by any single hatch. Since the minimum time required in case of no capacity constraint (in this case $t_f = 4$) cannot be improved, one should shift only the types of cargo which require the least time to complete servicing. In our example this is bulk cargo (j=2) whose completion time is $t_{f_2} = 3$ hours (in contrast to $t_{f_1} = 4$ hours). Shifting may be carried out up to (but not surpassing) the point where t_{f_2} reaches the minimum overall value $t_f = 4$.

First, take 40 tons from row 3 column 2, and allocate it to row 4 column 2. Second, take 30 tons from row 2 column 2, and allocate it to row 1 column 2. This stage is illustrated by the table for the second allocation.

84

Second allocation

t o n s

Hatch	for j=1	for j=2	total	C_{hi}	C_{sei}	C_{aei}
1	120	150	270	300	+ 30	10
2	100	150	250	250	0	
3	100	140	240	200	− 40	
4	80	160	240	300	+ 60	0

Third, since an overflow still remains in Hatch 3, take 10 tons from row 3 column 2 and allocate it to row 1 column 2, which gives the third allocation.

Third allocation

t o n s

Hatch	for j=1	for j=2	total	C_{hi}	C_{sei}	C_{aei}
1	120	160	280	300	+ 20	0
2	100	150	250	250	0	
3	100	130	230	200	− 30	
4	80	160	240	300	+ 60	0

The completion time matrix t_{ij} at this stage, without considering the hatch capacity restraint, is the following.

Hatch	Completion time (hours)	
	for j=1	for j=2
1	4	4
2	4	2.5
3	4	2.17
4	4	4

t_f is still 4 hours; but we have to move 30 tons from Hatch 3 in such a way as to produce the least additional increment in turnround time.

Hatch	Marginal increment (hours/ton)	
	for j=1	for j=2
1	$\frac{1}{30}$	$\frac{1}{40}$
2	$\frac{1}{25}$	$\frac{1}{60}$
3	$\frac{1}{25}$	$\frac{1}{60}$
4	$\frac{1}{20}$	$\frac{1}{40}$

Let us examine the marginal increment of time per unit transfer of cargo at each cell of the matrix. We cannot transfer any cargo to Hatch 2 because it is already full. It is demanded that distributing the 30 tons of excess cargo among available hatches would lead to the least possible increment of time. But how? Cargo should be distributed in proportion to the marginal rate given to each cell (i, j). Suppose x tons of class-1 is to be taken from row 3 column 1 of the third allocation, and y tons of class-2 is to be taken from row 3 column 2. Then

Constraint 1) $x + y = 30$

$$\Delta W_{11} = \frac{3x}{5}$$

$$\Delta W_{41} = \frac{2x}{5}$$

$$\Delta W_{12} = \frac{y}{2}$$

$$\Delta W_{42} = \frac{y}{2}$$

Constraint 2) $\Delta W_{11} + \Delta W_{12} \leqslant 20$

$$\Delta W_{41} + \Delta W_{42} \leqslant 60$$

Distribute the excess in porportion to the handling rate of each hatch, to produce equal increments of completion time, since what determines the overall efficiency is not the shortest but the longest of the completion times of all the hatches.

Combining these two constraints, we get $-450 \leqslant x \leqslant 50$.

Positive increment of
completion time matrix
(Δt_{ij})

Hatch	for j=1	for j=2
1	$\dfrac{3x}{5} \cdot \dfrac{1}{30}$	$\dfrac{y}{2} \cdot \dfrac{1}{40}$
2		
3		
4	$\dfrac{2x}{5} \cdot \dfrac{1}{20}$	$\dfrac{y}{2} \cdot \dfrac{1}{40}$

The amount of cargo to be transferred is 30 tons from Hatch 3; and this is within the limit of constraint 2. Because the capacity of constraint 2 does not hinder any transfer insofar as constraint 1 is maintained, the optimal allocation is therefore

$$\frac{3x}{5} \cdot \frac{1}{30} = \frac{y}{2} \cdot \frac{1}{40} \qquad x = \frac{150}{13} \qquad y = \frac{240}{13}$$

Final allocation

Hatch	tons for j=1	tons for j=2	total	C_i	C_{sei}		Completion time (hours) for j=1	for j=2
1	126.9	169.25	296.15	300	+ 3.85	→	4.23	4.23 ←
2	100	150	250	250	0		4.0	4.0
3	88.5	111.5	200	200	0		3.54	1.86
4	84.6	169.25	253.85	300	+46.15	→	4.23	4.23 ←

The overall optimal completion time taking capacity restraint into account is thus $t_f = 4.23$ hours.

This result can be compared with the following alternative calculated intuitively. Suppose that 80 tons of class-2 had been moved from Hatch 3 to Hatch 4, and 30 tons of class-2 into Hatch 1. Such a straightforward choice would have ended in a completion time $t_5 = 5$ hours, which is of course greater than the value determined by the method above by about 18 per cent.

Intuitive allocation

Hatch	for j=1	for j=2	total	C_i	C_{sei}	for j=1	for j=2
			t o n s			Completion time (hours)	
1	120	150	270	300	+ 30	4.0	3.75
2	100	150	250	250	0	4.0	2.5
3	100	100	200	200	0	4.0	1.67
4	80	200	280	300	+ 20	4.0	5.0 ←

*General rules for allocating cargo among hatches
under capacity restraint*

Step 1. Determine the fraction-matrix y_{ij} in such a way that y_{ij} is proportionately distributed according to the handling rate for the cargo of class j at hatch i.

$$y_{ij} = \frac{a_j \cdot \mu_{ij}}{\mu_{1j} + \mu_{2j} + \cdots + \mu_{Lj}} \quad \text{for } j = 1, 2, \ldots, M$$

Step 2. Allocate the cargo among hatches according to this matrix, and obtain the cargo distribution matrix W_{ij}.

$$W_{ij} = W \cdot y_{ij} \quad \text{for } i = 1, 2, \ldots, L \text{ and } j = 1, 2, \ldots, M$$

Step 3. If the capacity restriction condition $\sum_{j=1}^{M} W_{ij} \leqslant C_{hi}$ is met for all i, the optimal distribution is given by Step 2, and the service completion time is

$$t_f = \text{Max}\left\{ \frac{a_j \cdot W}{\mu_{1j} + \mu_{2j} + \cdots + \mu_{Lj}} \right\} \quad \text{for } 1 \leqslant j \leqslant M$$

Step 4. If the capacity restriction does not hold for all i, then all the excess cargo should be shifted to where space is available. Mark all of those rows in the table where

$$\text{Sign} \left[C_{hi} - \sum_{j=1}^{M} W_{ij} \right] \quad \text{becomes negative.}$$

Step 5. Transfer excess cargo of class *j* for which the completion time is less than the overall service completion time t_f (and allocated to the hatches where this sign is negative) to other hatches where it is positive, while observing the following conditions.

Step 5a. This transfer should not increase the handling time for the hatch beyond t_f.

Step 5b. The amount of this transfer should not exceed the slack capacity of the hatch to which it is transferred.

Only the smaller possible amount of cargo restricted by these two conditions can be transferred. This operation should be continued until no excess cargo remains at all. If this is done and all the excess capacity is absorbed by other available hatches, the solution is reached at that point. It should be remembered that there may not be a unique solution; but all possible solutions should yield the same completion time.

Step 6. If after Step 5 some excess cargo still remains to be transferred, it should be distributed among available hatches so as to minimise the maximum of the eventual increase of completion time of those hatches. Select the hatches which are still over-saturated at this stage. Suppose that we partition the total excess cargo still remaining into M portions by allocating x_{k_1} to class 1, x_{k_2} to class 2, x_{k_3} to class 3, and so on. Naturally $\sum_{j=1}^{M} x_{k_j} = 1$. The distribution of excess cargo among available hatches should be the same as before, namely in proportion to the handling rate at each hatch. Again, we end with the capacity restraint with respect to each hatch; and these constraints may limit the amount of cargo to be transferred determined by equating the time increment due to the transfer of cargo at each hatch. But even by transferring the maximum possible amount of cargo, the problem will either solve itself immediately, or re-pose itself until it ultimately does so.

Gang allocation among ships

We have considered the problem of achieving greater efficiency by distributing cargo among hatches given the existing facilities at quayside. The natural extension of this is the parallel question of allocating labour as well as machine equipment efficiently to achieve the same objective. The formulation of this problem needs certain modifications, because it is to allocate the port facilities among hatches of various ships (given the distribution of cargo for each one) in order to reduce the average service time of all taken together. In this case it is insufficient to consider each ship alone and independently, because one ship will certainly be affected by another in terms of labour as well as handling equipment available to it. Therefore, it is necessary to take into account all ships which are to receive services at any one time.

The distribution of labour among hatches is one of the important factors which affect turnround time even when sufficient labour (gangs per shift) is available.

> It is a commonplace that in every industry machines are re-placing human labour as a source of power. This process has certainly been at work in the docks. . . . Output per man has increased (in the United Kingdom) from 723 tons per annum in 1948 to 1,419 in 1962 and we attribute this in the main to mechanisation. . . . In the docks, where so much of the work is done in gangs, economy of labour can be achieved only by a reduction in the size of the gang. [14]

This statement is certainly true if the system is optimally organised; yet there is usually room for an increase of labour productivity through better systematic allotment. In order to get a clear view of the problem, let us represent every hatch on a particular ship by a number which will show the amount of work to be done, measured in terms of gang-shifts. And, as is usually the case, suppose one hatch can be worked by no more than one gang at a time.

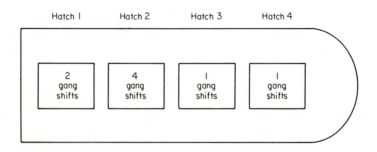

Figure 4.10   Distribution of amounts of work among hatches

If the objective is to complete the work as quickly as possible, it is the principal hatch that determines the shortest possible service time — four shifts in the case shown in figure 4.10. There are several possible ways of allocating labour among the hatches to achieve this objective. For example, one can employ four gangs in the first shift, two gangs in the second shift, one in the third and one in the fourth, or alternatively use two gangs in the first, two in the second, two in the third and two in the fourth (the latter case utilising a constant flow of work pattern). In any event, the shortest possible turnround time is determined by the commanding hatch (Hatch 2 in this example) and the amount of work required in it. The average number of gangs allocated per shift (N_g) will be

$$N_g = \frac{\text{Total amount of work}}{\text{Amount of work in the commanding hatch}}$$

Example 1 (total work = 8 gangs)

N.B. + sign represents one gang working one shift.

	Case A				Case B			
Original distribution of cargo (gang-shifts)	2	4	1	1	2	4	1	1
First shift (4/2 gangs)	+	+	+	+	+	+		
cargo remaining	1	3	0	0	1	3	1	1
Second shift (2/2 gangs)	+	+			+	+		
cargo remaining	0	2	0	0	0	2	1	1
Third shift (1/2 gangs)		+				+		+
cargo remaining	0	1	0	0	0	1	1	0
Fourth shift (1/2 gangs)		+				+	+	
cargo remaining	0	0	0	0	0	0	0	0

$$N_g = \frac{8}{4} = 2 \qquad N_g = \frac{8}{4} = 2$$

Example 2 (total work = 8 gangs)

	Hatch				
	1	2	3	4	
Original distribution of cargo (gang-shifts)	2	2	2	2	$N_g = \frac{8}{2} = 4$
First shift (4 gangs)	+	+	+	+	
cargo remaining	1	1	1	1	
Second shift (4 gangs)	+	+	+	+	
cargo remaining	0	0	0	0	

Example 2 shows the case of balanced distribution of cargo among hatches. Aside from the number of gangs required per shift, the ship turnround time in Example 2 can be shortened from four shifts to two shifts by allocating four gangs in the first shift and four again in the second. If other things are equal, therefore, an equal distribution seems preferable to an imbalance of cargo among hatches. However, the problem is not so simple. For example, pressure on shed space may be vital; and a ship may have no choice but to wait to discharge cargo until it becomes available. Also there will normally be several ships awaiting service, perhaps each with a different pattern of distribution. The supply of labour, moreover, is not unlimited. Consider the following example and suppose that only three gangs are available per shift.

Example 3

	Ship A				Ship B		
	Hatch				Hatch		
	1	2	3	4	1	2	3
Original distribution of cargo (gang-shifts)	2	4	1	1	1	1	2
	(total = 8)				(total = 4)		

There is a considerable number of ways of allocating labour between these two ships in order to complete the total work to be done. We should concern ourselves with the problem of minimising the *average* turnround time per ship under the given labour constraint.

Allocation 1
    First shift : 3 to A
    Second shift : 3 to A
    Third shift : 1 to A, 2 to B
    Fourth shift : 1 to A, 2 to B
    Total : A:4 shifts
            B:4 shifts
    AST (average shift time) = 4

Allocation 2
    First shift : 3 to B
    Second shift : 1 to B, 2 to A
    Third shift : 3 to A
    Fourth shift : 3 to A
    Total : A:4 shifts
            B:2 shifts
    AST = 3

92

This example implies that, from the viewpoint of aggregate ship servicing, priority in allocating labour should be given to the ship with the shortest potential shift time. (This is not necessarily in direct proportion to total cargo to be unloaded.) Once the shortest possible shift time (SPST) has been calculated for each ship, it cannot, by definition, be shortened. As exemplified above, any ship with a longer SPST will simply have to await the servicing of one with a shorter SPST.

The method presented here does not always necessarily give the shortest AST. But, it can be expected to produce a close enough approximation to the most efficient allocation.

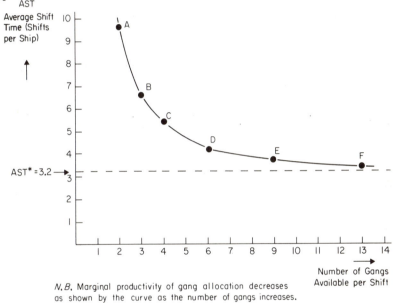

Figure 4.11 Average shift time versus number of gangs available

Rules for allocating labour among ships

Step 1. Number the ships waiting for service according to the amount of work in the commanding hatch of each ship.

Step 2. If the amount of work required by the commanding hatch happens to be equal for more than two ships, the ship with the least amount of cargo in total, and/or with the fewest hatches, should be serviced first, because the maximum possible discharging rates of such ships are comparatively less flexible. This may be explained as follows.

The reason why one ship carrying more cargo than another should be assigned lower priority may not seem so unreasonable when one takes into account the possibility that the former may require longer shift times given the limited supply of labour, thus making the AST longer. As regards the number of hatches, take the following possibility where the total gang shifts and the amounts of work in the principal hatches are equal for two ships, although the numbers of hatches (hence the distributions) are different. Not more than two gangs can be assigned to Ship B at one time, while four gangs can work on Ship A (provided they are available). Therefore, depending upon the availability of labour, there are more ways of allocating labour to Ship A than to Ship B. Suppose now that there is only one gang available for the first and second shifts, but four from the third shift onward. Ship A can thus complete its unloading in three shifts by allocating 1, 1, and 4 gangs respectively, while Ship B (carrying the same amount of cargo but with fewer hatches) would require at least 4 shifts from the same gangs (i.e. 1, 1, 2, 2). This means Ship A has more capacity for self-compensation in the earlier stage than Ship B, and therefore could be serviced later; but not vice-versa.

	gang-shift distribution			
Ship A (6 gang-shifts)	1	3	1	1
Ship B (6 gang-shifts)	3	3	—	—

Step 3. When gangs are allocated to each ship, they should be distributed in such a way that the principal hatch to be worked has first priority.

Let us now see how this will work in practice. In the example below, ship E is designated as 'Ship 1' and it is assumed that only three gangs are available per shift.

Example:

Ship	Total gang-shifts required	Principal Hatch index (PHI)	Number of hatches	Ships numbered in order of the PHI
A	8	3	5	→ → 3
B	8	4	3	→ → 4
C	4	3	2	→ → 2
D	10	4	5	→ → 5
E	5	2	3	→ → 1

After allocating three gangs to Ship 1, the number of non-zero hatches is two. And since after the two gang allotment to Ship 1 there are no non-zero hatches, the service is thus completed for Ship 1 within two shifts.

Now one gang becomes available in the second shift; and since this is fewer than the number of hatches of Ship 2 (Ship C), one gang is allocated to Ship 2. After this shift, the number of non-zero hatches of Ship 2 is still two, so that two gangs are allocated to this ship in the third shift. The available number of gangs in the third shift is one; and this is allocated to Ship 3. After the third shift, Ship 3 has five non-zero hatches, while Ship 2 has one hatch yet to be finished; so one gang is allocated to Ship 2 in the fourth shift, leaving two gangs available for Ship 3. And thus, in the fourth shift, two gangs are allocated to Ship 3. And so on, until all the work is completed.

Now we should examine the effects of an increasing number of gangs available per shift on the average shift time. For comparison, we will examine six situations, with between 2 and 13 gangs available in each, to serve the same five ships as in the above example. These results are plotted in figure 4.11 which shows that an increase in the number of gangs available per shift results in a decrease of AST, but only up to a certain point AST*, where the curve flattens out. And any further increase in the number of gangs will have no result other than the production of idle gangs.

In this case AST* may be found by adding together all the PHIs, which gives the minimum total gang shifts, and dividing this number by the number of ships. Thus $AST^* = \frac{16}{5} = 3.2$.

Resource allocation : lighters

Lighters can be used in a number of ways to facilitate the unloading of cargo from ships. They can sometimes relieve pressure on quayside space by receiving directly part of the cargo unloaded from a berthed ship, and transferring it either to an inland transport terminal (if adjacent to the port waterway system) or else directly to barges for shipment along the inland waterway system. In some cases lighters may be used for unloading part, or all, of the cargo from ships at anchor outside the port, thus helping effectively to relieve pressure on the berths themselves.

> . . . by the standards prevailing in the Eastern Mediterranean, ports in Morocco and Tunisia are relatively uncongested. The use of more container units at Morocco's big ports, particularly Casablanca, and of *lighter barges to facilitate unloading* have helped the country to absorb a big rise in imports. [15]

95

In some cases lighters might be especially helpful in reducing the waiting time of a ship that has only a small quantity of cargo to unload in a particular port. As a short-cut circumventing the berths, the use of lighters in Western European ports, as suggested in the following report, seems to vary in proportion to the importance of the inland waterways system.

> In London and to a lesser extent some other ports (e.g. Liverpool and Hull) loading and unloading of ships from and to barges and lighters is a most important part of the port's activity, particularly as far as certain cargoes, e.g. timber, are concerned. . . . In many of the large Continental ports, however, lighterage is far more common because of the volume of tonnage due onward shipment by the inland waterways which are much more extensive and can take much bigger vessels than our own. . . . Lighters may be ordered either by the ship or by the shipper or receiver in accordance with the custom of the port. [16]

The importance of lighters to ports such as Bangkok is raised in another context elsewhere. [17]

In dealing with a lighter service system, the problem is to allocate a limited number of lighters to each ship according to a specified performance index, such as minimisation of average service time, given the number of lighters, the number of ships, and their sizes. Let us denote the following variables.

m_0 = number of lighters

T_r = turnround time of lighters (hours)

w_a = cargo capacity of lighters (tons)

n_{hi} = number of hatches

W = cargo capacity of the ship (tons)

And suppose the cargoes are distributed evenly among the hatches.

One ship for servicing. If just one ship is to be served in this berth system, then obviously the minimum time for service is given by the following.

For $m_o \geqslant n_{h_o}$ use n_{h_o} numbers of lighter simultaneously.

For $m_o < n_{h_o}$ use m_o number of lighters simultaneously.

In sum, the optimal solution will be to use Min $\{m_o, n_{h_o}\}$ number of lighters simultaneously. Therefore, minimum service time T_{sm} for

96

this ship is given by

$$T_{sm} = T_r \cdot \left\{ \left[\frac{W}{w_a \cdot \text{Min} \{m_o, n_{ho}\}} \right] + 1 \right\} \tag{4.29}$$

However, if $\dfrac{W}{w_a \cdot \text{Min} \{m_o, n_{ho}\}}$ is an integer, then in place of

the Gaussian brackets we can substitute

$$T_{sm} = T_r \cdot \left[\frac{W}{w_a \cdot \text{Min} \{m_o, n_{ho}\}} \right] \tag{4.30}$$

Two ships for servicing. Suppose that m_o lighters are available. Then the problem is how to allocate them to each ship, m_1 to ship 1 and m_2 to ship 2, so that the average turnround time will be minimised.

	Ship 1	Ship 2
Cargo (tons)	w_1	w_2
Number of hatches	n_{h1}	n_{h2}

where $m_1 + m_2 \leqslant m_o$; m_1, m_2 must be positive integers

$$\sum_{i=1}^{2} T_{sm_i} = T_{sm_1} + T_{sm_2}$$

$$\text{Average } T_{sm} = \bar{T}_{sm} = \frac{T_{sm_1} + T_{sm_2}}{2} \tag{4.31}$$

Example 1
m_o = 5 (lighters available)
w_a = 70 tons (lighter cargo capacity)
Ship 1 — W_1 = 500 tons, n_{h_1} = 3
Ship 2 — W_2 = 1000 tons, n_{h_2} = 4

Arranging the five lighters in all possible combinations for the two ships, we can compute the following possible minimum service times.

	m_1	m_2	$\dfrac{T_{sm_1}}{T_r}$	$\dfrac{T_{sm_2}}{T_r}$	$\dfrac{\Sigma T_{sm_i}}{T_r}$	$\dfrac{\overline{T}_{sm}}{T_r}$
	$m_1 \leqslant 3$	$m_2 \leqslant 4$				
Case A	3	2	3	8	11	5.5
Case B	2	3	4	5	9	4.5 ←
Case C	1	4	8	4	12	6.0

For this example the optimal allocation is two lighters to Ship 1 and three lighters to Ship 2. If $n_{h_1} + n_{h_2} \leqslant m_o$, then obviously the optimal allocation is n_{h_1} lighters to Ship 1 and n_{h_2} lighters to Ship 2.

Three ships for servicing. Similar arguments stand for this case; and another example is given below for illustration.

Example 2

m_o = 7 (lighters available)

w_a = 50 tons (lighter cargo capacity)

Ship 1 — W_1 = 300 tons, n_{h_1} = 2 hatches

Ship 2 — W_2 = 700 tons, n_{h_2} = 3 hatches

Ship 3 — W_3 = 1000 tons, n_{h_3} = 4 hatches

From the table it can be seen that the optimal allocation is two lighters for Ship 1, two lighters for Ship 2, and three lighters for Ship 3. It is clear that service time distribution of a lighter service system can be derived by this method if one is given the actual cargo capacity and the number of hatches of each ship.

	m_1	m_2	m_3	$\dfrac{T_{sm_1}}{T_r}$	$\dfrac{T_{sm_2}}{T_r}$	$\dfrac{T_{sm_3}}{T_r}$	$\dfrac{\Sigma T_{sm_i}}{T_r}$	$\dfrac{\overline{T}_{sm}}{T_r}$
Case A	2	3	2	3	5	10	18	6.0
Case B	1	3	3	6	5	7	18	6.0
Case C	2	2	3	3	7	7	17	5.7 ←
Case D	2	1	4	3	14	5	22	7.3
Case E	1	2	4	6	7	5	18	6.0

Let us now see what happens if we assume further that lighters can be allocated to work on other ships immediately after they complete servicing of one ship, a situation which is very likely to arise when the port is congested. For purposes of comparison, let us consider three alternatives for Example 1 above, given the flexibility that any lighter once free can be switched to serve another ship without delay.

By use of the same algorithm, the shortest turnround time $\dfrac{T_{sm}}{T_r}$

is 4 for Example 1 and 5 for Example 2.

Under a situation where there is flexibility with respect to lighters, the average service time can be reduced further than it could be in a situation without such flexibility. The optimal allocation scheme is easily found by the procedure given in the illustrative examples above. However efficiently the lighters are allocated, nonetheless, the minimum average ship service time, for k number of ships to be considered, cannot be reduced to a value less than

$$\frac{\overline{T}_{sm}}{T_r} = \left(\frac{\left[\dfrac{W_1}{w_a{}^n h_1} \right] + \left[\dfrac{W_2}{w_a{}^n h_2} \right] + \ldots + \left[\dfrac{W_k}{w_a{}^n h_k} \right]}{k} \right) + 1$$

(4.32)

Notes

[1]   Lord Devlin, *Final Report of the Committee of Inquiry under the Rt. Hon. Lord Devlin into Certain Matters concerning the Port Transport Industry*, HMSO, 1965; reprinted 1966, p.24 (italics added).
[2]   Ibid.
[3]   Odd Gulbrandsen and Frode Eidem, *Port Development Planning,* Transportøkonomisk Institutt, Oslo, 1973, pp 19-22.
[4]   *Report of the Committee of Inquiry into the Major Ports of Great Britain,* p.95.
[5]   It is not necessarily an *efficient* choice, however. See also the concluding section on admissible handling rate controls.
[6]   *Road Research Laboratory Leaflet*, May 1970. For another treatment of limitations on numbers of vehicles for a given urban area, see Hajime Nishimura, 'Ji Do Sha Yu So No Technology Assessment', 'Technology Assessment of Motor Transport', *Ko Gai Kenkyu*, 'Research on Pollution', IV/1, July 1974, pp 48-59
[7]   Gulbrandsen and Eidem, *Port Development Planning*, p.69.

[8]   Ibid., p.27.
[9]   UNCTAD, *Berth Throughput. Systematic Methods for Improving General Cargo Operations*, New York, 1973, p.39.
[10]   Ibid., pp 44-5.
[11]   Government of Mauritius, *Mauritius Port Study*, London 1973, pp 4, 10, 12.
[12]   Lyon Associates (Consulting Engineers), *Korea Port Development Study. Draft Final Report. Determination of Port Development Priorities*, Government of Korea and International Bank for Reconstruction and Development, *ca.* 1971, p.52.
[13]   UNCTAD, *Berth Throughput*, p.42.
[14]   Lord Devlin, *Final Report of the Committee of Inquiry*, p.21.
[15]   *The Financial Times*, 16 February 1976, italics added.
[16]   Ministry of Transport, *Report of the Committee of Inquiry into the Major Ports of Great Britain*, p.32.
[17]   See *infra*, pp 179-80.

5 Analytical approaches to the storage system

System identification and description

The basic functions of the storage system of a port are to keep cargo for certain formalities such as customs clearance and to accommodate cargo for varying periods of time, providing a flexible period for shippers to adjust to delivery requirements. The system can therefore be said to function in various respects as a 'buffer' between the maritime and overland inflow-outflow of cargo.

There are a number of factors within the port system which can impede smooth operations and thus retard the level of throughput. Some examples include the efficiency of handling equipment at berths, the number of forklift trucks available for cargo carriage service, the degree of sophistication in the overall information system, the reliability of the decision tree of the management on stacking locations, restacking and consolidation, and relations with labour organisations. But one of the main determinants of berth throughput under normal circumstances is the capacity of the storage system. Taking into account the facts that the amount of storage space available in a port is usually quite limited and that any expansion scheme (including land reclamation) would involve a substantial reshaping of the port layout and thus require considerable capital investment, it is not difficult to imagine the critical importance of this particular subsystem, especially in view of the danger of its becoming the most greatly constricted bottleneck of the total system.

The capacity of a storage system cannot be defined for general purposes in any way other than in terms of space (cubic feet or metres) per cargo unit (e.g. ton or containers or individual items). The following basic terms must also be defined. (1) *Holding capacity*. This is the static amount of space in the storage system, measured by specified units and clearly fixed at any one point in time. (2) *Intrinsic capacity*. This is a measurement of the effective capacity in terms of operations, which takes into account the dynamics of the movements of cargo through the storage system. It may be defined as follows.

intrinsic capacity = holding capacity x number of times the
(per year/month/   cargo turns over
week/day)   (per year/month/
                                         week/day)

Given a particular set of facilities, the simplest means of increasing its intrinsic capacity will be to reduce the transit time the cargo spends in the storage system, thereby increasing the annual turnover rate. Nonetheless, a consideration of mere average transit time is not sufficient for the purpose of obtaining a precise profile of the storage system. Instead, one must investigate the distribution of the transit time thoroughly.

One reason for shortages in capacity may be simply that existing facilities are not large enough to absorb future as well as current traffic. This situation is well illustrated by the ever-increasing congestion problems faced by ports in Middle Eastern countries due to the rapid expansion programmes of trade volume made possible by the flood of oil-dollars into these countries. Another reason may be the inefficiency or inadequacy of the operational aspects of the storage system, which might be improved in numerous ways : through a systematic layout with clearly defined bays and gangways, through efficient arrangements for stacking in stores, along with good handling and stacking equipment operated by an adequate labour force, through rapid customs clearance, and so forth. A critical factor, which overlaps in some respects with operational management, is that very few importers or exporters are themselves concerned directly with the final delivery of their goods to customers; and as a result they often fail, consciously or unconsciously, to meet fixed delivery dates. Some do not bother at all with cargoes once they have been offloaded, treating the port storage system as a cheap warehouse facility. Although this is not the case in general as is illustrated by the following quotation:

> Goods destined for Nepal pay port rent not because it is cheaper but because there is no possibility of storing the goods elsewhere. The shortage of railwagons prevents the rapid onward movement of goods and storage is inevitable.
> . . . Nepalese goods therefore become liable to port rent for reasons which are outside Nepalese control. [1]

Where storage space is in short supply, charges should be applied for storage so as to ration the limited supply of services sensibly.

By increasing the intrinsic capacity of storage facilities in order to accommodate more traffic, one can also reduce the ship turnround time either directly or indirectly through faster handling operations at quayside. The accompanying advantages to the firms concerned are numerous. For example, the door-to-door movement of cargo will be faster. The shorter the time between the firm's receipt of an order and its fulfilment, the lower the level of stock the firm needs to hold in order to provide a given service due to less uncertainty. If the delay

102

time of this kind is reduced, the prediction of the demand will become less uncertain. To take the extreme case, if there is no delay between the order and the receipt of cargo, the firm knows exactly what amount it needs; and therefore the stock requirement can be kept minimal. While if the delay is expected to be a few months, the firm has to face the difficult task of predicting the demand level a few months ahead, during which interval considerable fluctuation is likely to take place. The savings in interest on cargo can be significant, especially in the case of high-value cargo. Faster transit may also affect insurance costs by reducing the levels of damage and theft.

Faster transit may nonetheless be regarded as a positive disadvantage by certain firms which appreciate the free, short period of warehousing provided by the port. This is applicable mainly to agricultural goods, which are harvested or produced sometime before the overseas markets require them. In such cases, the port storage at both export and import stages may help to provide a kind of fine tuning for their delivery schedules.

Throughout the following discussion, one should also bear in mind the custom of the 'free period', which is the length of time cargo may be stored without having any storage charge imposed on it.

> Most ports have a short period, frequently a week, during which no storage charges are payable. After expiry of this free period, a storage charge is made and in some ports the weekly charge increases for each additional week that cargo is left in store. One reason why receivers fail to collect promptly is that the charge for storage in the port is sometimes less than receivers would have to pay elsewhere. [2]

In most of the cases studied, the free period during which no charge is made for transit storage begins at the end of discharging operations (in the case of imports) or at the time of deposit in the storage area (in the case of exports). [3] After the free period has expired, the cargo is shifted out of the transit area, and the tariff for warehousing is then usually applied to it. A customarily accepted limit for free period is three days; but the time may vary widely from port to port. Singapore, for instance, follows the three-day rule. The port of Mombasa in Kenya allows four days for imports without specifying an exact limit for exports. Halifax in Canada generally allows five days, although a limit of eight days is permitted if gauging or inspection are required. Southampton Docks have a limit of seven days. [4] Sheds in the United States generally permit five days of free period for accumulating outbound cargo, and ten days for inbound tonnage. Cargo to be held beyond the ten-day free period is usually conveyed to a warehouse elsewhere, but reasonably close to the transit shed. About 2.5 to 5 per cent of all general cargo handled in the United States passes to a warehouse either from or through a transit shed, and of this amount about 10 to 20 per cent will be warehoused on the waterfront for about three months. [5]

Estimation of expected throughput level

While the volume of traffic passing through a port requires something more than static measurements in order to assess its dynamic nature, it is necessary to use observed data in order to forecast future trends. One could simply extrapolate past figures into the future, or else make use of much more sophisticated stochastic methods such as time series analysis. Presented below is one example of a useful formula which provides a crude estimation of the annual throughput by collecting data on the amount of cargo each ship discharges, with the provision that ships arrive at random (i.e. fit the Poisson arrival model) with a constant intensity. If we get the mean value of the amount of cargo each ship discharges, and the mean of the square of it, then the mean and the variance of the throughput during the specified period are at hand.

It is often the case that ship arrivals for a certain port obey the Poisson distribution type with intensity v (ships/day) and that the ship arriving at time t_n carries w_n amount of cargo. Supposing the amount of cargo to be unloaded at this port is a random variable of independent distribution, then it would be essential to know $X(t)$, the total amount of cargo unloaded in the time period from 0 to t, in order to determine how large the size of the intrinsic capacity of the warehouse (or open storage) during this period should be.

This compound Poisson process $\{X(t), t \geq 0\}$ has stationary independent increments, and characteristic function, for any $t \geq 0$,

$$\phi_{X(t)}(u) = e^{vt \{\phi_w(u) - 1\}} \tag{5.1}$$

where $\phi_w(u)$ is the common characteristic function of the independent identically distributed random variable w_n, and v is the mean rate of ship arrivals at this port. Since $E[W^2] < \infty$, then $X(t)$ has finite second moments given by

$$\begin{aligned} E[X(t)] &= vt\,E[W] \\ \mathrm{Var}[X(t)] &= vt\,E[W^2] \end{aligned} \tag{5.2}$$

We should estimate such moments as E [W], Var [W²] to get the mean and the variance of the total amount of cargo to be unloaded during the time period (0, t) at this port.

Equation 5.2 suggests that if the ship arrivals are considered to obey a Poisson process, and if the amount of cargo each ship carries is independent of other ships, then the mean level of the aggregate cargo traffic through this port will simply be: the mean value of the amount of cargo, which is determined independently of the pattern of traffic, times the expected number of ships of call during the specified period. Moreover, the *variance*, which is of considerable concern in terms of storage capacity requirement, is given by the mean of the square of the amount of cargo each ship discharges, times the expected number of ship arrivals during this period. The second half of equation 5.2 shows that the variance will increase in proportion to the length of the specified period if the distribution of the amount of cargo each ship discharges is not expected to change greatly.

Effects of storage tariff change on cargo transit time

One of the major factors affecting the intrinsic capacity of the port storage system is the length of cargo stay (transit time). If cargo stays in a storage system with a holding capacity of 5,000 tons for an average of 10 days, then the annual turnover of the system is 36.5 times a year; and therefore the intrinsic capacity of this system is 5000 x 36.5 = 182,500 tons per annum. A closer investigation of this system necessitates further considerations of the transit time distribution, a typical pattern of which is given in figure 5.1

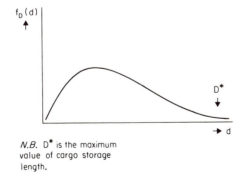

N.B. D^* is the maximum value of cargo storage length.

Figure 5.1 Typical transit time distribution

If the port storage system proves to be an impediment to a higher

105

throughput, there are basically two ways of tackling the problem: either to improve the storage holding capacity by expansion, more systematic storage layout, improved management, a better information system, and so on, or else to reduce the transit time spent by cargo in the system. As the former is discussed elsewhere, let us consider the latter along here for a moment.

Progressive tariff for long-staying cargo:
A justifiable position?

It is often suggested that what needs to be critically examined is that cargo which stays in the system over a long period, which is said to impair the potential capacity for storage.

> In 22 per cent of cases, the storage charge per unit of time remains constant, regardless of how long cargo remains in storage after the free period. However, in many cases, the charge per unit of time increases with the length of time spent in storage in order to discourage any *abusive prolongation* of storage. [6]

Another United Nations report points out that

> It is the slow-moving consignments . . . that particularly need to be looked at. . . . After expiry of this free period a storage charge is made and in some ports the weekly charge increases for each additional week that cargo is left in store. . . . Cargoes which are not delivered promptly effectively reduce the capacity of the store for dealing with the cargoes of later ships. [7]

Both reports emphasise that some measures should be taken to discourage long-staying cargo, in order to increase the intrinsic capacity of the storage system, and thus to increase throughput. This proposal does not, on the surface of it, seem unreasonable, if one looks solely at the question of throughput *per se.* Indeed, every day by which the average number of days stay in storage is shortened will help to increase capacity. One may also argue that this will be beneficial to the port in more general terms, as an increase in throughput may be of regional importance, and it will tend also to bring in more revenues from dues on a larger quantity of goods and on more ships. Since port revenue consists of fixed dues (cargo dues per ton basis, or vessel dues per register ton), which do not vary with regard to the length of cargo stay in the port system, and variable dues, which do depend on the length of cargo stay, it is easy to suppose that the port prefers a shorter staying cargo to a longer staying one. The reason is that the former

106

provides a higher rate of revenue per ton per day.

If we consider one ton of cargo going through this port using the storage system, the tariff of which being k_s (£/ton/day), with d_1 days stay, and another one ton with d_2 days ($d_1 < d_2$), then roughly speaking, the former pays p_d (£) for cargo dues plus the variable charge, in this case $k_s (d_1 - d_0)$, while the latter pays p_d plus $k_s (d_2 - d_0)$, where d_0 represents the number of days free period. In terms of the port revenue per ton per day, the former gives a higher rate since

$$\frac{p_d + k_s (d_1 - d_0)}{d_1} > \frac{p_d + k_s (d_2 - d_0)}{d_2} .$$

From the viewpoint of operating cost alone, on the other hand, the longer staying cargo may even be preferable, simply because 100 tons once stored require no further handling, while 100 tons stored daily would require an equivalent daily handling operation (hence operating costs). And further, if the chief reason for the longer average length of cargo stay is the inefficiency or the inadequacy of the paperwork involved (customs checks, exchanges of documents, submissions, etc.), then the solution to the storage congestion problem will certainly have to be sought elsewhere than in an increase in storage charges.

Beyond the undoubted aspect of increasing port revenues, however, one may seriously question the overall advisability of instituting such a scheme as a progressive tariff. For, regardless of the type of scheme, if higher charges are fixed per diem for cargo staying beyond certain arbitrarily fixed cut-off points, then the port is discriminating against long-staying cargo in favour of short-staying cargo. According to the United Nations reports cited above, most of the ports investigated by UNCTAD had already adopted some sort of progressive scheme. But is this necessarily desirable? And does long-staying cargo really 'abuse' the port storage system, as is so often claimed?

There are various arguments which tend to support a total rejection of progressive tariff notions. Firstly, cargo which is long-staying occupies no greater amount of space than would the short-staying cargo intended to replace it; and a progressive tariff merely distorts, in this respect, the more efficient usage of the facilities by the former. A progressive scheme could be economically justified only if the tariff imposed actually reflected the costs incurred by the port. For example, if longer stay means that cargo becomes 'buried' in the system, and thus greater retrieval costs are involved because of having to shift other cargo from on top of or in front of it, and if greater costs are incurred because the probability of loss or damage is greater, then the port is justified in imposing a higher rate — but only to cover such

107

retrieval and compensatory costs. It would seem justifiable to impose here a flat-rate increase over which additional costs are to be incurred, rather than a progressive increase, unless the additional cost itself is progressive. It is not conceivable, moreover, that this flat-rate, once-and-for-all jump will add any particularly large percentage in comparison with the initial charge.

A second major argument against progressive schemes is that, although widely applied, they tend to ignore the viewpoint of the users. The argument that long-stay users 'abuse' the port system is to be deprecated, as it hinges upon the dubious assumption that long-staying cargo remains in the port simply because users find port storage cheaper than warehousing elsewhere. What else is one to expect! Users are generally cost-conscious; and indeed they do have their own reasons, dictated by their business strategies, for leaving their cargoes in port storage. They do so simply because all other alternatives are more costly, or at least less desirable for some reason or other. And if this argument were pushed to its logical extension, even short-staying cargo could be said to 'abuse' port storage because it, too, enjoys the relatively cheap rates. If the port authorities impose a higher charge on cargo which, because of the particular requirements of the user, has to remain in storage longer than some arbitrarily set time, then the port may in fact be upsetting the entire strategy and pricing system of the user, and even ultimately the market demand for the commodity itself, by imposing a kind of 'surcharge' or penalty for staying 'too long'. The danger exists in extreme cases then, that the port may in fact be squeezing some marginal enterprises and commodities entirely out of the market, leaving them with no commercially viable alternative transport route, while at the same time letting short-staying cargo enjoy cheaper rates.

It may be questioned whether the port should have any right to exercise such a prerogative at all. Doubtless it is not any of the port authority's business to meddle in the internal affairs of a particular user's strategy. The port is a service to industry, and should behave accordingly. One cannot justify discriminatory policies which run counter to the interests of the users, if they are imposed for no reason other than to boost the port's own revenues or throughput.

This line of reasoning assumes that ports are a national industry, as they tend to be, and service (rather than profit) orientated. It will not hold entirely true for privately owned ports, as the latter certainly must consider their own financial positions and profits along with everything else. (For general port financial objects, in this respect, see chapter 8). It should also be pointed out that there are, of course, exceptions to the 'strategy' argument outlined above. For example,

> Gulf Port Management Services . . . found, when it started to work last October (1975), large tonnages of cargo which had been sitting on the quayside for several months. Many of the receivers claimed not to have been told of its arrival, an omission of which in some cases was almost certainly due to the problems of communication to the area but also to a lack of thoroughness on the part of those shipping the cargo. [8]

In such cases, improvements are to be sought in the sphere of management — not in raising the tariff.

Rationing of the port storage system

It has been suggested that the most sensible alternative to a progressive tariff scheme would be a flat-rate scheme, in so far as this represents actual cost profiles. Whatever scheme is selected, some sort of rationing policy will probably have to be adopted, given the limited supply of service facilities. Where this differs from ordinary 'rationing', in which there is just a change in the quantity of commodities available, is that the demand could change either in the form of through traffic (tons) or in the form of storage length (days). The response of the users to the tariff change is thus two-dimensional. Apart from the convenience, customary usage, and other reasons usually given for using the storage system in preference to alternative routes, what makes the port storage system so attractive in relation to other commercially viable warehouses elsewhere are: (i) the free period provided by the port and (ii) the relatively low port storage rate. There seems to exist no clear economic justification for the so-called 'free period'. There is in fact no thorough economic study of the entire question of such practice, although the wide range of free days allowed by ports throughout the world would seem to justify a careful analysis into the efficacy of these policies, and even possibly the question of the need for any free period at all.

With reference to the question of port storage charges being 'too low' and thus more desirable for users relative to the alternatives, it is shown in chapters 7 and 8 that the port tariff (especially port storage charges) should be appraised from the viewpoint of the cost structure of the whole transport system open to cargo, all the way from the port system up until final delivery, with particular reference to the domestic depot warehouses. The port tariff should ideally be based upon marginal cost pricing, where the tariff charge imposed reflects the price to cover the marginal usage at the demand level. It is often difficult, however, to implement such a policy, either because of the indivisibility of the facilities or administration complication.

Storage tariff elasticity of demand

From all the preceding considerations, it would seem that the storage charge should be a flat rate, rather than a progressive one, insofar as there is no difference in cost terms (cost per day) as regards storing cargo for differing lengths of time. The 'rationing' policy should, accordingly, be a flat rate increase also — one which is uniform over the whole range of the length of cargo stay. Suppose that, before the port charge increase, the transit time distribution looks like curve A_1 in figure 5.2. What happens, after the increase, is that the cargo storage length tends to be reduced, the extent of the shift of the curve being dependent on the rate of the charge increase. For instance, if the rate of increase is not big enough to induce some cargo to find a cheaper alternative, no shift at all would occur. The port would then enjoy a revenue increase — although no improvement of its storage throughput. If, on the other hand, the increase was too big, so that, for most cargo, the port storage was no longer cheaper to use, in spite of the free period benefits, then one would expect to see not only a shift of the distribution curve, but also a considerable drop in the traffic entering the system. And the latter would mean simply that the direct route will become unusually congested, while the storage system remains far from saturated.

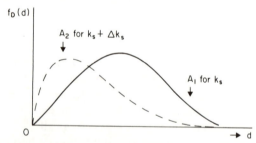

N.B. The shift could be towards the right as well as the left, depending on the total transport cost structure.

Figure 5.2   Effect of flat-rate storage charge increase on transit time distribution profile

Although it is often claimed that total port traffic is rather inelastic to tariff change, this does not imply that the *distribution* of the traffic through the available routes (direct or indirect) will also be inelastic. This sort of switch-over from one route to the other could be expected especially when the cargo in question is relatively cheap, making transport cost in proportion to its market price relatively large; and also true in cases where the profit margin is not very large.

It may well be argued that the tariff change would induce some — but by no means all — of the users to reduce the length of cargo stay; but their changes at any rate would depend on the type of cargo, their ability to pay, the destination (final market), the cost structure of the alternative routes, and so on. It seems therefore almost impossible to predict with any precision the resulting shape of the transit time distribution. And if the resulting shape of the distribution curve cannot be estimated for a particular price change, how can the port management work out an appropriate tariff increase to achieve a desired storage throughput?

The tariff scheme with respect to the storage system should be given special consideration because of the peculiar nature of the services of this system. Simply put, charges are usually based on the traffic volume as well as on the length of stay of cargo. Both these considerations make it difficult to appraise the effect of price change on the volume of cargo using the system; but they must nonetheless be examined if an adequate appraisal of the storage system is to be made.

The concept of price elasticity of demand is quite clear in the case of commodities (as a measure of responsiveness of quantity-bought to changes-in-price). However, it does not seem so straightforward a matter to extend this concept to the demand for the storage system, because of the latter's two-dimensional nature, in which users express their demand in terms of both length of storage and volume. As is tacitly accepted, demand for ports is reckoned to be rather inelastic as a whole. Yet it is reasonable to expect at least some sort of responsiveness on the part of users to a particular tariff change in the storage charges, especially if there are alternatives available to them (e.g. the direct route instead of the indirect one). 'Quantity bought' in this case is neither the length of stay nor the tonnage handled through the storage system, but seems rather to be the multiple of the two.

Since the storage tariff is mostly levied on a per-unit-ton and a per-unit-time basis, the revenue from warehousing for the port (or, from the shippers' viewpoint, the storage cost) is, roughly speaking, the storage charging rate k_s, in the case of a flat rate scheme, multiplied by the average length of stay of cargo in storage ($\bar{d}$), multiplied by the

111

annual throughput via the storage system (ϕ_{as} tons per annum).
With the distribution function for the length of stay of cargo in the
storage, $\phi_{as} \cdot f_X(x)$ dx tons of cargo spends x and x + dx days, and
thus pays $k_s \cdot x$ (£/ton). Therefore, the total revenue for the port,
from the storage, will be expressed as:

$$R_{ps} = \int_0^{D^*} \phi_{as} k_s x f_X(x)\, dx = \phi_{as} k_s \int_0^{D^*} x f_X(x)\, dx$$

$$= \phi_{as}\, k_s\, \bar{d}\ \ (\text{£/year}) \tag{5.3}$$

The tariff change to be considered, and the demand response to it,
seem even harder to quantify when one considers that the demand for
the storage system is affected not solely by the storage system charging
rate, but more widely by the *sum* of the port dues to be added (i.e.
port dues plus other handling charges), which are fixed per ton basis.
As a result of a port storage charge increase, the traffic proceeding by
way of storage may decrease, even though the transit distribution
remains intact, or the distribution may shift leftwards as in figure 5.2,
even though total through traffic remains unchanged; or a combination
of these two basic changes may occur.

One thing, however, is certain: the multiple of the storage through
traffic ϕ_{as} and the average length of cargo stay $\bar{d}$ will be reduced. And
whatever may be the shape of the distribution curve, the following
relation should hold true on average.

$$V_s = \frac{\phi_{as} \cdot \bar{d}}{L_a}$$

$$\tag{5.4}$$

where L_a denotes the effective working days per year, ϕ_{as} the annual
storage throughput, and V_s the working level of the storage. This
relation suggests that the responsiveness of the users to the tariff
change could be measured and interpreted not especially in terms of
the throughput alone or the shape of the distribution curve, but rather
in terms of the *working level* of the storage. One should not, of
course, attempt to deduce too much from this measure, since the
index by itself is one-dimensional whereas the nature of the problem is
two-dimensional. Nonetheless, this can serve as a useful measure for
judging the users' responses.

Let ϵ_p be the tariff elasticity of storage demand with respect to its
charging rate k_s (£/ton/day). Assuming constant elasticity for ϵ_p over

112

a reasonably narrow region of k_s, the working level of the storage can be expressed as

$$V_s = A \cdot k_s^{-\epsilon_p} \tag{5.5}$$

where A is a constant. That is, an increase of k_s from k_{s_1} to k_{s_2} (insofar as this change does not violate the assumption of constant elasticity) will cause a decrease of the working level of the storage from V_{s_1} to V_{s_2}, where

$$\frac{V_{s_1}}{V_{s_2}} = \left(\frac{k_{s_1}}{k_{s_2}} \right)^{-\epsilon_p} \tag{5.6}$$

Example

Suppose that the working level of the storage system is approaching the holding capacity C_s, and therefore is causing inefficient handling due to congestion. If the elasticity of the storage demand in terms of the working level around the existing charging rate k_{s_1} is

considered to be constant (say, $\epsilon_p = 0.5$), and if the port authority tries to relieve the congestion by increasing this rate to a working level of, say, 90 per cent of the holding capacity, then the new charging rate k_{s_2} should be (from equation 5.6, and by setting $V_{s_1} = C_s$, $V_{s_2} = 0.9\,C_s$, and $\epsilon_p = 0.5$:

$$\frac{k_{s_2}}{k_{s_1}} = \left(\frac{C_s}{0.9 C_s} \right)^{\frac{1}{0.5}} = 1.23.$$

This means the storage charging rate should be increased by about 23 per cent in order to achieve a reduction of 10 per cent in the storage working level.

Central warehouse system versus a system of back-up sheds adjoining each berth

Two basic components comprise the port storage service: a number of relatively independent back-up sheds adjoining each of the berths, and/or a central warehouse serving essentially the same purpose but used by all the berths. It can be shown that traffic fluctuations affecting each of the berths would be effectively flattened out by introducing a central warehouse instead of using back-up sheds; and operating costs might become smaller in the case of a large warehouse, due to the wider possibilities for mechanisation.

Supposing a port must absorb a certain volume of traffic, regardless of which system is adopted, then the central warehouse capacity requirement will be less than the aggregate of the combined sheds, because the amplitude of the fluctuation of the combined system will most likely be less than the sum of the individual sheds, which are all fluctuating at rates independent of each other. On the other hand, average transfer distance may have to be sacrificed in the case of central warehousing, because it seems unlikely for a port to have a large central warehouse directly in the middle of the port manoeuvring area, as that might make every sort of handling operation inefficient. In examining the two systems from a comparative point of view, therefore, one must focus attention upon the trade-off between, first, the fixed cost saving gained by a lower capacity requirement for the central warehouse system and, second, the expected increase of the variable cost due to the increase of the average transfer distance from the quay to the warehouse and from there to the inland transport access.

There are various advantages, respectively to both the back-up shed system and the central warehouse system. In the back-up shed system there is usually less mixing up of cargo of different types, assuming each berth is servicing different types of cargo, and thus less confusion to be expected in classification within the storage system. The back-up shed sometimes involves less transfer distance, although on this point one cannot be precise. If, for example, lorries have immediate access to the back-up sheds, then transfer distance for the port transfer equipment is reduced to a minimum — merely the distance from the quay to the shed. But, depending on the physical arrangement of port facilities, the back-up sheds can also be at a great distance from the inland transport terminus, whether for road, rail, or inland waterway.

Perhaps the foremost advantage of the central warehouse system is that under this system it is less likely that cargo will begin to pile up at quayside than would be the case where a back-up shed is used, assuming that there is no delay in transfer services. Transfer distances can be fixed so that the site chosen for the warehouse is an optimal one for all of the berths it serves, taking into account all transfer costs and the problem of manoeuvring efficiency. A warehouse can also function as the back-up storage for longer-standing cargo, which tends to require excessive use of transit shed space.

Notes

[1]   Simon Thomas, 'India-Nepal Transit System', unpublished

paper, Transport Studies Unit, University of Oxford, 1976, pp 15 and 43.

[2]   UNCTAD, *Berth Throughput*, p.20.
[3]   UNCTAD, *Port Pricing*, New York 1975, pp 20-1.
[4]   I.G. Heggie, 'Charging for Port Facilities', *Journal of Transport Economics and Policy*, VIII/1, January 1974, pp 4-5.
[5]   Maurice Grusky, 'Harbor Engineering', in R.W. Abbett (ed.), *American Civil Engineering Practice*, New York, 1956, II, pp 78-81.
[6]   UNCTAD, *Port Pricing*, p.21, italics added.
[7]   UNCTAD, *Berth Throughput*, pp 20-21.
[8]   *The Financial Times*, 28 July 1976.

6 Co-ordination of port and inland transport systems

Inland transport connections

Some analysis in regard to the basic factors relating to the operational structure of the port has been made in other chapters. The factor which is usually beyond the control of the port authority — the inland transport system — has yet to be scrutinised. It is not the purpose of this work, however, to deal with anything further than the limitations imposed upon the speedy removal of cargo from the port, because the operation of the inland transport sector itself does not fall within the scope of this work.

It is a truism that port development cannot meet any expected targets without a corresponding improvement in the efficiency of the inland transport system linked with the port. One outstanding example stressing the need for such co-ordination is a port planned more than a decade ago for a site lacking adequate inland transport connections.

> . . . in southeast Iran a new deep-water port near Bandar Abbas has been designed costing approximately 20 million dollars. For this port to be utilized at a level justifying the port investment, a road system connecting the port with the hinterland will simultaneously have to be constructed at a cost of at least *again* the order of magnitude of the port itself. [1]

This problem is common among developing countries. And it has been a major factor in the one-port economies of some countries of Africa and Asia where for economic, and occasionally political, reasons the governments have hindered the growth of port facilities merely by withholding from one potential port area or another the transport links necessary to connect the site with the interior.

Variegated external factors, unrelated to the interests of shippers or of the port itself, have often acted as deterrents to port development. One case in point is the port of Bangkok where, until quite recently, ships of any but light draught could not cross the bar at the mouth of the river for much of the year; and thus large cargo vessels had to anchor in the lee of Sichang Island in the gulf. Lighters were thus used to transfer cargo from the Bangkok docks some 90 kilometres downriver and out to the island. As a result of the booming export trade (especially in bulk products such as rice and teakwood), by the turn of the twentieth century the lighterage industry in Bangkok came to be one of the largest of its kind in the world. A simple cut in the sandy bar, with regular dredging, would have facilitated shipping and port operations immeasurably. But, this was not done. Not wishing to see any measures taken which would render their fleet of lighters largely useless, the owners (most German companies) exerted pressure on the government. The government itself, wary of gunboat attacks (from French Indochina), did not wish, for defence reasons, to facilitate the passage of large vessels. In addition, it was feared that, until a metropolitan waterworks was completed, as an alternative to using river water, any cut in the bar might cause the river at Bangkok to become brackish. [2] It was not until 1953 that the first phase of the Bangkok deep-sea port was finally completed, allowing deep-water ships to enter. But even today, the port of Bangkok is hardly adequate to meet demands. The old lighterage industry still exists, but in greatly reduced form. There is still opposition, as there has always been, against any alternative site for a deep-water port around the gulf coast (including the proposed adoption of the Satahip naval base, or the development of the natural harbour at Chanthaburi near the Cambodian frontier), emanating from external factors — vested business interests in Bangkok and the multitude of bureaucrats who control the lucrative Customs department, to name but two. One has to consider also the sensitive question of a suitable transportation network for the hinterlands, which are divided among four nations. The principal routes were surveyed and planned across the borders of Thailand, Cambodia, Laos and Vietnam more than three-quarters of a century ago. But, there has never been a suitable opportunity for the prerequisite political negotiations among the nations involved, as a prelude to the type of international co-operation scheme which would be necessary in order to make any port development projects economically justifiable. Regional politics have thus acted as a barrier to regional development from the point of view of seaports.

Goods are transported away from the port by basically three modes — road, rail or barge. Clearly enough, the reliability of the delivery system greatly depends on the operating efficiency of the vehicles (lorries, railway wagons and barges) available for the port. If, for instance, there is a definite shortage of railway wagons serving the port, goods will be forced to wait until a substantial number of wagons become available. More commonly, goods simply have to wait until a freight train with adequate space arrives in port and also, of course, is bound for the correct destination. It might seem a quite

117

simple solution merely to increase the number of wagons in the event of shortage, since it would appear at first glance that the larger the number of wagons travelling along the railway routes, the greater the capacity of the system. But the problem is not that simple. Sheer increases in the numbers of wagons may lead to nothing more than idle capacity, without improving the operating efficiency of the system at all.

Movement restriction of cargo is a common occurrence at ports. This is usually because there is a lack of facilities sufficient to handle the cargo. However, it is very often not at all apparent whether the problem is caused by inadequate conveyance equipment (e.g. a shortage of railway wagons) or by delays at the several transhipment points involved. A good case in point is the routing of imports through India.

> The transit system begins at the Port of Calcutta through which all goods destined for Nepal have to be imported. . . . If the freight is dispatched by rail it has to be transhipped at the Gahara Marshalling yards (near Barauni) . . . . At the Indian border point of Raxaul almost all goods . . . are again transhipped.
> . . . It is not completely clear whether the major problems are caused by the shortage of wagons (as such) or as a result of congestion at the transhipment point. . . . If the problem was simply lack of wagons, changing the gauge to the border would have beneficial effects and would ease the problem of wagon availability by reducing turnaround times, but this would be only a partial solution. If the problem is at the transhipment point, then provision of more wagons would lead to almost no benefits, for it would not remove the bottleneck of the system and only provide idle capacity. [3]

This study has identified the germane points; but owing to the unavailability of sufficient data and analytical methods, it is unable to proceed systematically towards a definitive solution. The analysis presented below provides one method of identifying such problems, as well as a means of dealing with them.

Single transhipment transport model [4]

For a simple system in which only a single transhipment (junction) point is involved, one should establish the relationship between the transporting capacity and the efficiency of transhipment operations. Rail transport is taken here as a representative of the three basic inland transport facilities, since it is not the purpose of this book to present a collection of various workable models for each transport mode. Each mode, of course, requires an extensive investigation for itself and it is almost impossible to work out a generally applicable model. Hence emphasis is placed on the essence of the methodology. This by no means indicates that other modes are more difficult to tackle.

In case of inland waterways, for example, it costs both time and money for barges to clear locks which exist in their transporting routes. This lock effect could be regarded as a potential bottleneck to the efficient transport voyage of barges as if they were the transhipment points. By considering this lock effect, a formula to derive barge freight cost can be easily estimated. Although this freight cost model is not included in the text in order to avoid unnecessary complications, it may be interesting to note that the freight cost could be formulated as the linear combination of the transport distance and the number of locks to negotiate. It imples that each additional lock is equivalent to a constant addition of voyage distance to the total transport distance with respect to the freight cost. This result is obtained from the assumptions that both the fixed and the operating costs of barges are proportionately split among all the possible round trips and also no difference is made among the characteristics of the locks. Nonetheless, it proves to give a fair approximation in practice and serves as a useful tool for the appraisal of the respective advantage of mutually competing ports with the same hinterland, in terms of the inland transport cost. Such models could be varied and more sophisticated, of course, depending upon the nature of the problems to be considered.

Coming back to our rail transport model, initially we should make the following assumptions.

1   There are no breakdowns as regards rail wagons.

2   Every freight train consists of equal numbers of wagons.

3   The time required for the transhipment of cargo at the terminal is given in such a way that whenever operations on one train are completed, the next can commence immediately.

4   The time required for loading and unloading depends on the type of cargo as well as the size (carrying capacity) of the train.

The cycle time of a train may be defined as that time spent by the train (1) during its transhipping operations at Terminal 0 (the port terminus), plus (2) the journey time to Terminal 1, plus (3) its transhipment time at Terminal 1, plus (4) the return journey time to

119

Terminal 0 (see figure 6.1). To calculate this, let us make the following designations.

T_{η_0}, T_{η_1} = transhipment times at Terminals 0 and 1, respectively

d_{01} = distance between Terminals 0 and 1

u_1 = speed of a train between Terminals 0 and 1, when fully laden

v_1 = speed of a train between Terminals 0 and 1, when *empty*

m_{fr_1} = number of freight trains operating between Terminals 0 and 1

w_{fr_1} = capacity of a freight train (tons/train) operating between Terminals 0 and 1

w_{fr_1} = $w_{wg_1} \cdot n_{wg_1}$ where w_{wg_1} = capacity of a wagon (tons/wagon); n_{wg_1} = number of wagons per train

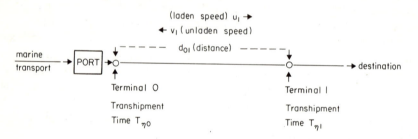

Figure 6.1   Time sequence for single transhipment model

For figure 6.1, the cycle time T_{ω_1} will be

$$T_{\omega_1} = T_{\eta_0} + T_{\eta_1} + d_{01} \left(\frac{1}{u_1} + \frac{1}{v_1} \right)$$

(6.1)

If all trains are available for use at any time, theoretically speaking they are phased with an equal time interval of T_{ξ_1} :

$$T_{\xi_1} = \frac{T_{\omega_1}}{m_{fr_1}}$$

(6.2)

120

To clarify a minor point, we are considering relatively long distances; and therefore the length of the freight train itself is of no consequence. Also, equation 6.2 presumes a regular service with respect to the amount of cargo transported over a period of time, so that there should occur no discontinuity of train services.

Now let us suppose that the transhipment at Terminal 1 takes a longer time than that at Terminal 0. Thus $T_{\eta_1} > T_{\eta_0}$. (The opposite case where $T_{\eta_0} \geqslant T_{\eta_1}$ is covered by exactly the same argument).

Such transhipment times have no effect whatsoever on the running operations of the trains, if the number of trains is small enough so that the time spacing between the arrivals of any two trains is wide enough to be greater than the greater of the two transhipment times. In this case, it is simply necessary that $T_{\xi_1} \geqslant T_{\eta_1}$. In other words, no train should arrive at Terminal 1 until after the departure of its predecessor. So far as this remains the case, the capacity of the railway transport increases proportionately to the increase in the number of trains employed.

If the number of trains becomes so large that the theoretical time interval T_{ξ_1} is reduced to the point where $T_{\xi_1} < T_{\eta_1}$, then the above situation ceases to hold true. Let us see what will then take place at Terminal 1. A train arrives, but finished its operation after time T_{η_1}.

Another train has therefore arrived before the completion time, and thus must wait. Only after the departure of the first can the second begin its operation. This necessitates a longer transhipment time for the second train; and so on and so forth for a third, a fourth and all subsequent trains arriving at the terminal.

One result of this should be clear. Regardless of the times of arrival or the delays encountered, the trains leaving Terminal 1 will eventually become phased out with a new equal time interval of T_{η_1}.

And since at Terminal 0, from the assumption $T_{\eta_1} > T_{\eta_0}$, there occurs no interruption due to the transhipment time, at the steady state all the trains will thus become timed with equal intervals of T_{η_1}.

Under these circumstances, any increase in the number of vehicles beyond $\widetilde{m}_{fr_1}$, where $\widetilde{m}_{fr_1} = \left[\dfrac{T_{\omega 1}}{\text{Max}\,(T_{\eta_0},\, T_{\eta_1})} \right]$, will not lead to any further improvement in transporting capacity. (See Point R in figure 6.2) To the contrary, it will only result in idle capacity. This

121

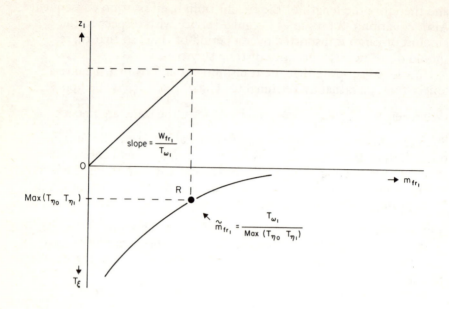

Figure 6.2 Productivity of transport system versus number of vehicles

'idle capacity', which may be designated as m_{z_1}, is calculated (using Gaussian brackets) as

$$m_{z_1} = m_{fr_1} - \tilde{m}_{fr_1} \tag{6.3}$$

In sum, the 'transport' rate z_1 of the rail system may be given as follows.

$$z_1 = \frac{W_{fr_1}}{T_{\omega_1}} \cdot m_{fr_1} \quad \text{for } m_{fr_1} \leqslant \tilde{m}_{fr_1}$$

$$z_1 = \frac{W_{fr_1}}{T_{\omega_1}} \cdot \tilde{m}_{fr_1} \quad \text{for } m_{fr_1} > \tilde{m}_{fr_1} \tag{6.4}$$

These results may be illustrated as shown in figure 6.2. The point at which the plateau is reached is the point beyond which any increase in vehicle numbers, within the existing network, will result largely in an increase in idle capacity and no increase in carrying capacity. It is thus the transport rate z_1 that is of significance — rather than the nominal rate, which is simply the unit vehicle productivity times the number of vehicles employed. In considering the co-ordination between the port's handling capacity (intake to and offtake from the port) and that of the inland transport, it is clear that the efficiency of the transhipment operations plays a significant role in terms of over-all marine-port-inland transport productivity.

Two transhipments transport model

It would obviously be far more efficient for cargo to proceed directly from the port itself (Terminal 0) to its inland destination, as each transhipment point along the inland route is a source of extra costs and loss of time. Nonetheless, the passage of freight inland, whether by road, rail or barge, often involves several unavoidable tranship-ments for a variety of reasons — sometimes for geographical reasons due to natural obstacles such as rivers, straits or mountains, and some-times for historical and political reasons, due to lack of co-ordination and planning in the development of the internal and international links between different segments of the roads and railways networks.

A comprehensive example of these difficulties is the landlocked kingdom of Nepal, whose potential supply routes are determined by the encircling Himalaya mountains in the first instance, and seriously limited even further by the situation in neighbouring India (the only practicable route to the sea). India permits Nepal the use of the port of Calcutta alone (one of the least efficient in the world), and can offer at best an inland transport route across a patchwork rail system built at various times with various gauges and never standardised (each segment necessitating transhipment at its terminals).

To expand our simple model above one step further in the direction of such complicated systems as the Calcutta-Nepal route, it may be interesting to consider the following case where cargo has to undergo an additional journey from Terminal 1 to Terminal 2 en route to its destination, as shown in figure 6.3. Transhipment time at the inter-mediary Terminal 1 is now divided into two parts $T_{\eta_{11}}$ and $T_{\eta_{12}}$, applying to Systems 1 and 2, respectively, since the two trains of the two systems may have differing specifications. As in the previous case, the cycle times for the first and the second rail systems (d_{01}, d_{12}) will be calculated as

$$T_{\omega_1} = T_{\eta_0} + T_{\eta_{11}} + d_{01} \left[\frac{1}{u_1} + \frac{1}{v_1} \right]$$

$$(6.5)$$

$$T_{\omega_2} = T_{\eta_{12}} + T_{\eta_2} + d_{12} \left[\frac{1}{u_2} + \frac{1}{v_2} \right]$$

$$(6.6)$$

These results may be illustrated as in figure 6.4.

Let us consider a system in which goods at the port have to be loaded onto rail wagons at Terminal 0, and travel up to Terminal 1, where all the goods are unloaded onto the platform (or into temporary storage facilities), and then loaded again onto the other wagons to be transported to Terminal 2. At Terminal 2 all goods are unloaded for final delivery.

Alternatively, the goods could be unloaded directly from the wagons at Terminal 1 and placed into other wagons straight away. The basic arguments apply equally to this case, although some modification of the model would be required.

An example of a particular case is given in table 6.1, summarising all relevant variables for calculations to be made along the lines outlined above. A graphical representation of the systems from table 6.1 is given in figure 6.4. Line z_1 reaches its plateau at $\widetilde{m}_{fr_1}$ = 4.5 and

thus, as one can have only whole numbers of trains operating simultaneously in one system, the maximum capacity of System 1 (i.e. rail transport between Terminals 0 and 1) marked by point P_1 on the graph, will be the 20 tons/hour provided by allotting four trains to this system. (All points beyond point E to the right on curve 1 representing 5 or more trains for System 1 will indeed give a higher absolute maximum capacity at 22.5 tons/hour; but these are not considered as they are all on the plateau and thus represent idle capacity in part.) With the three trains allotted in the case to System 2 (transport between Terminals 1 and 2), the latter's maximum capacity will then be 11.8 tons/hour (marked by point Q_1 on the graph). Therefore, the maximum handling rate of the aggregate system will be bound by the maximum operating capacity of System 2.

Transhipment time depends on the capacity of trains and the type of cargo, as well as the handling facilities and labour productivity. In the case given in table 6.1 it is assumed that the number of wagons per train is determined by technical design of the trains (e.g. power) and railway conditions.

As can be readily seen from the graph, the gap can be narrowed by increasing the number of trains for System 2. An increase of a single train would result in a new maximum capacity of 15.8 tons/hour (a

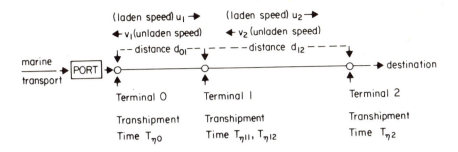

Figure 6.3   Time sequence for a two-transhipments model

Table 6.1
Example of specifications for two connected rail systems

	System 1 Terminals $0 \rightarrow 1$	System 2 Terminals $0 \rightarrow 1$
capacity of a wagon	w_{wg_1} = 10 tons	w_{wg_2} = 15 tons
number of wagons per train	n_{fr_1} = 9	n_{fr_2} = 10
maximum capacity of train	w_{fr_1} = 90 tons/train	w_{fr_2} = 150 tons/train
number of trains running	m_{fr_1} = 4 trains	m_{fr_2} = 3 trains
speed of train	u_1 = 50 km/hour v_1 = 60 km/hour	u_2 = 40 km/hour v_2 = 50 km/hour
distance	d_{01} = 300 km	d_{12} = 600 km
transhipment times	T_{η_0} = 3 hours $T_{\eta_{11}}$ = 4 hours	$T_{\eta_{12}}$ = 6 hours T_{η_2} = 5 hours
maximum transhipment time of the system	Max. = 4 hours	Max. = 6 hours
cycle time	T_{ω_1} = 3 + 6 + 4 + 5 = 18 hours	T_{ω_2} = 6 + 15 + 5 + 12 = 38 hours
cycle time / maximum transhipment time	$\tilde{m}_{fr_1}$ = 18/4 = 4.5	$\tilde{m}_{fr_2}$ = 38/6 = 6.3

125

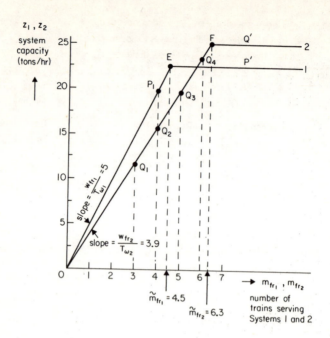

N.B. The values of m_{fr_1} and m_{fr_2} which give the kinked points on each curve m_{fr_1} and m_{fr_2} are determined by the train cycle time divided by the maximum transhipment time in each system.

Figure 6.4   System capacity of the inland transport link versus number of trains in service involving transhipment operations

shift from point Q_1 to Q_2), assuming no change in System 1. The bottleneck in this example represented by the imbalance between points P_1 and Q_1 is clearly the shortage of rail wagons for System 2. If a total of five trains are allotted to System 2 (a shift from point Q_1 to Q_3), the system will, theoretically speaking, provide its maximum handling rate of 19.7 tons/hour.

Let us see what happens beyond this allottment Q_3. With 6 trains operating in System 2, the capacity of System 2 (Q_4 = 23.7 tons/hour) will exceed that for System 1 (P_1 = 20 tons/hour), bringing the idle capacity factor into play even before the plateau is reached, since the plateau of System 1 is at 22.5 tons/hour). All subsequent points Q' could provide an absolute maximum of 25.0 tons/hour, but would be on the plateau.

If either point P or Q is shifted upward along their respective straight lines $\overline{OE}$ and $\overline{OF}$, so that it reaches the plateau, the sheer increase of trains would thereupon result in nothing further than idle capacity, with no improvement as regards the productivity. In such a case, the bottleneck can be identified as the transhipment operation rather than the shortage of rail wagons. Measures must then be taken to reduce cycle time.

Transhipment times might be lessened by means of better organisation of labour, an overtime or overwork scheme, replacement of inefficient operations by efficient ones, the introduction of mechanised facilities and so forth. The operations for System 1 at Terminal 1 ($T_{\eta_{11}}$) might, for example, be reduced from 4 hours to 3 hours, and those for System 2 at the same terminal ($T_{\eta_{12}}$) from 6 to 5 hours. Cycle time T_{ω_1} would then be reduced from 18 hours to 17 hours, while T_{ω_2} would be reduced from 38 hours to 37 hours. $\tilde{m}_{fr_1}$ would then become 5.7 instead of 4.5, and $\tilde{m}_{fr_2}$ would become 7.4 instead of 6.3. Thus, with no change in the number of wagons for System 1, its maximum output could reach 21.2 tons/hour. System 2 will benefit from this improvement, providing a maximum of 12.2 tons/hour with 3 trains and 20.3 tons/hour with 5 trains.

These changes are summarised in table 6.2, which is the same example given in table 6.1 except for the stated modifications. The improvement in the transhipment phase is represented in figure 6.5, which shows not only that the maximum capacity will be greater, in comparison to figure 6.4, for either system for a given number of trains, but also that both plateaux have shifted so that each system can now add one additional train beyond the maximum of the original case without becoming involved in idle capacity.

In figure 6.5 the maximum capacity of System 1 before reaching the plateau (represented by point P_2 for 5 trains) is now 26.5 tons/hour, and for System 2 (point Q_5 for 7 trains) is 28.4 tons/hour. With the improvement in transhipment there is now some room for greater productivity; and 6 trains operating in System 1 plus 8 trains in System 2 will enable the aggregate system to handle an absolute maximum on the plateau of 30 tons/hour (compared with 22.5 tons previously for 5 trains in System 1 and 6 trains in System 2), beyond which an increase in trains will produce no increase in capacity.

Table 6.2
Policy comparison with and without transhipment operations improvements

Existing system 1 — Point P_1 (with 4 trains)
Existing system 2 — Point Q_1 (with 3 trains)

Situation to be considered : 3 additional trains for system 2		Initial system capacity	Improved system capacity	Percentage improvement
Policy 1	no improvements in transhipment operations	11.8 tons/ hour	$Q_1 \rightarrow Q_4$ in figure 6.4 20.0 tons/ hour	+ 69.5%
Policy 2	with improvements in transhipment operations	11.8 tons/ hour	$Q_1 \rightarrow Q_4$ in figure 6.5 21.2 tons/ hour	+ 80.0%

$T_{\eta_{11}}$: 4 → 3 hours
T_{ω_1} : 18 → 17 hours
  5.6% reduction in cycle time for System 1

$T_{\eta_{12}}$: 6 → 5 hours
T_{ω_2} : 38 → 37 hours
  2.6% reduction in cycle time for System 2

Thus the handling efficiency of the whole system is shown to be dependent on two basic factors: 1) the level of employment of vehicles, and 2) the efficiency of the transhipment operations. As shown in table 6.2, two policies may be adopted, the second providing an improvement in transhipment operations and the first none. Under Policy 2, with improvements, a 5.6 and a 2.6 per cent improvement, roughly speaking, in the cycle times of Systems 1 and 2, respectively, could, alone, contribute to a 10 per cent increase in the aggregate system capacity.

Although this result may not be striking, what is really of significance is that the improvement in transhipment operations, as mentioned earlier, when it is critical, will make room for the possibility of increasing the maximum handling capacity of the aggregate system. This is clearly shown by the fact that the maximum handling capacity of the whole system under Policy 1 is bound by the

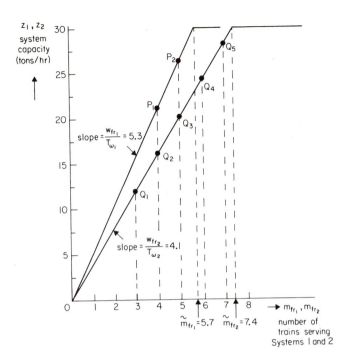

Figure 6.5 Effects of transhipment improvements on handling efficiency

plateau of 22.5 tons/hour, irrespective of the level of vehicle employment, while that of the system under Policy 2 is increased to 30 tons/hour — i.e. about 33 per cent upwards in this simple case.

The preceding line of argument can be similarly extended to a three-system (or other multi-system) model where the terminals are all in series along a single route, or where the route branches in two or more directions at one of the transhipment points.

Conclusion

An attempt has been made to clarify the interrelation between the efficiency of inland transport facilities and the level of employment of vehicles. And this has been done here with particular reference to the railway system. The model, although simplified, provides a point of departure of considerable significance for any further analysis of a more complex nature, and may be recapitulated as follows.

1   Assume that the rate of cargo outflow from the port is liable to be dictated by the adequacy of the available inland transport facilities, in a sense that the maximum handling capacity of the inland transport system may not be increased to absorb the expected demand for cargo transport through the port.

2   Assume also that the improvement of either the level of employment of vehicles or the transhipment operations at the terminal(s) is not entirely satisfactory, so that a mere increase in the number of vehicles will probably result in nothing but idle capacity, especially if the system itself has already reached a 'plateau' state.

If such is the case, a substantial reduction in the transhipment operation times then becomes the first task to be undertaken in order to improve the efficiency of the transport system.

The transport models considered in this chapter are perhaps open to the criticism that, in reality, one cannot expect to encounter such simple systems. This may be true in some respects, particularly where there are huge terminals servicing simultaneously tens of trains. One also has to take into account such facts as trains having to undergo maintenance operations from time to time, having to carry cargo on return journeys whenever possible in order to avoid idle runs, and so on and so forth. It is possible to construct theoretical models to represent these far more complicated systems; but it is obviously impossible to lay down any general rule which would cover every conceivable combination.

What seems important, however, is not the construction of a complicated model for its own sake, but rather the clear exemplification of fundamental problems by a simple, yet reasonably realistic, model in order to show what is indeed the bottleneck that is blocking the betterment of the system, and thus point the way towards how it can best be tackled. This should help, in good measure, anyone concerned with understanding the essential state of the system to come to grips with the task of improving the system, and therefore it should be made easy for such people to apply the essence of the methodology to a particular problem which they have encountered.

In sum, there are three basic elements requiring consideration: (a) the vehicle cycle time, (b) the time spacing among vehicles (including the numbers of vehicles), and (c) the transhipment time(s) at the terminal(s). If the co-ordination between the port system and the inland transport system is in question, the capacity of the former can be estimated, given the existing facilities, by use of such analytical methods as presented in chapters 3 to 6 above, whereas that of the latter should be estimated with the level of vehicle employment and transhipment operations under consideration as shown in this chapter. Whichever gives the lower transport capacity will pinpoint the bottleneck; and the relief of the bottleneck problem can then be worked out straight away. These two rates are subject to mutual influences, of course. And the efficiency of the transhipment operations at the interface (port and inland transport access) exerts an influence on both.

Notes

[1]   J. Kaufman, 'Planning for Transport Investment in the Development of Iran', *The American Economic Review, Papers and Proceedings*, LII, 1962, p.400, italics added.
[2]   Despatch 14, Stringer to Salisbury, 26 February 1900, in the Public Record Office, London, Foreign Office Series 69, volume 209. I am grateful to a colleague in St Antony's College for supplying me with a copy of this document.
[3]   Simon Thomas, 'India-Nepal Transit System', unpublished paper, Transport Studies Unit, University of Oxford, 1976, pp 9 and 24.
[4]   Single, double and triple transhipments models here refer only to *intermediary* transhipments, not to the port itself or the destination.

7 The integrated system

Introduction

In the preceding chapters all the essential subsystems have been examined separately. Important though these individual system analyses may be, a chief interest of the present work is the analysis of the integrated port system, where each subsystem can be shown to have a causal relationship with the others, and to function as a part of the overall organic system.

One cannot hope to reach any final conclusion about the productivity of a port without talking first about the efficiency of the various connecting transport systems. In general, the level of vehicle employment within a port is relatively easy to adjust to the traffic demand, if only to absorb minor fluctuations by employing a relatively minor amount of capital. This will not be true of a more dramatic reshaping of the whole port system in line with dynamic growth of the traffic level, regional development planning, the change of trade patterns reflecting the transition of domestic economy, and so on. The latter case may require far more substantial capital for extensive dredging of the harbour, massive construction of new berths, reclamation of land to create space and so on. The magnitude of this sort of port development is exemplified by the following case.

> The value of the work to be undertaken by Balfour Beatty Construction on the new harbour complex at Jebel Ali near Dubai will be in excess of £100 million . . . . The work covers the erection of one and a half kilometres of break-waters to protect an artificial creek and lagoon and also includes the construction of berths and wharfage to a total of 10 to 12 kilometres.
>   . . . the Government unveiled its plans to construct a massive 74-berth port costing over 3 billion Dirhams (£428 million). [1]

Another contemporaneous example for the same region suggests equally high costs.

> Contracts for the expansion of Aqaba Port where four new berths will be built at an estimated cost of . . . (about £24 million) are likely to be awarded to a British company . . . . [2]

These two examples suggest a figure of roughly £6 million per berth, which contrasts enormously with the few hundred thousands of pounds probably sufficient to reinforce a vehicle force in general.

As regards the inland transport system, the case is similar, but not exactly the same. It is plausible to adjust its capacity to the emerging state of traffic, if this is minor, by an increase in the number of rail wagons. But if the necessary improvement is persistent or drastic in nature, the requirement would be very large indeed, in terms of both capital outlay involved and time for completion, involving construction of new roads or overall reinforcement of the railway lines. One of the notable characteristics of such investment is 'indivisibility'. For example, a single additional vehicle may contribute to a noticeable improvement in port internal manoeuvring, while two and a half cranes would be unrealistic to imagine. The inland transport system generally requires a large sum of capital simply because the construction of a mere ten metres of roads, say, would not likely, of itself, be of much significance, unless the construction leads to an improvement of the transport services between the two sites concerned. In our examination of the integrated system here we should bear such limitations in mind.

The pattern of charges for different kinds of freight should be related to the pattern of costs of servicing the cargoes, although this is commonly not the case.

> In most developing countries, governments do not charge the users of roads, ports, airports, etc. adequately for the cost of these services through fuel taxes, licence fees, tolls or other charges. As in the case of subsidized tariffs, this is likely to lead to distortions between different transport modes, over-investment in transport as a whole, inefficient location of new industries. [3]

The costs consist, broadly speaking, of two main elements: the loading-unloading operations, and the provision of space for each item. If costs-related charges are not imposed, a situation may result in which there is a cross-subsidisation of some items by others; and this will naturally have long-run effects upon the pattern of those economic activities which are dependent upon the port. What may be required to stimulate greater use of the excess capacity of port facilities is a lower level of fares and charges, at least at certain times. On the other hand, though, what may be required to solve congestion problems is a higher level of dues. Both requirements must be taken into consideration and balanced one against the other, lest a headlong rush towards expansion be overtaken by a swamping of port facilities through uncontrolled usage.

133

Cargo split among alternative routes

The relative transport costs of three alternative routes are examined in this chapter. In the *PSS* (Port Storage System) *Route* cargo follows the indirect route within the port area itself and thus makes use of the port storage system. It is stored there for the variable period d_a days, of which d_0 is provided free (free period). The cargo is then transported by inland transport to the final destination. The PSS route is thus the combination of the port's internal indirect route and its connecting inland transport routes. (see figure 7.1).

In the *DDW* (Domestic Depot Warehouse) *Route* cargo follows the port's internal direct route (which by-passes the storage system) to the inland transport terminus. It is then conveyed to a commercial domestic depot warehouse, where it is stored for its variable period d_a, with no free period being provided. From there it is taken by inland transport to its destination.

The *CPD* (Combination of PSS and DDW) *Route* is a category for the various alternative routes deviating from the two basic ones outlined above. Cargo follows the port's internal indirect route, but makes use of the port storage system *only* for the free period, and then follows the inland transport route to domestic depot warehousing, where it remains for the rest of its total requirement of d_a days. And from there it is taken to its destination by inland transport.

In order to consider the relative costs for cargo routing, a simplified case will be investigated here. The assumptions, which it is to be hoped will shed some light on the behaviour of users in relation to charges, will be based on the following conditions.

a) The cargo is homogeneous.

b) The length of cargo stay in the storage system before delivery to the final market is, for various reasons, predetermined at d_a days by the traders.

c) The cargo has to pay both a handling operations charge and a storage charge.

d) The choice among the routes usually depends on economic considerations (relative cost-cheapness), convenience, avoidance of temporary congestion, and customary tradition (historical reasons).

Let us now make the following designations.

Handling operations charges

h_s = port storage (£/ton for transfer and loading-unloading operations)

h_{dr} = direct route transfer (£/ton for transfer and loading-unloading)

h_{dw} = domestic inland depot warehousing (£/ton for transfer and loading-unloading)

Freight charges

z_s = freight cost of the PSS Route (£/ton)

z_d = freight cost of the DDW Route (£/ton)

Storage charges

k_s = transit shed in the port (£/ton/day)

k_{dw} = domestic inland depot warehousing (£/ton/day)

β_{tr} = difference of transport operations cost (£/ton) between the DDW and the PSS routes. That is, $\beta_{tr} = z_d - z_s$; β_{tr} could be negative as well as positive.

β_{hd} = difference between handling costs: i.e. $\beta_{hd} = h_{dr} + h_{dw} - h_s$

Consideration will be given here only to the differences between two alternatives, PSS and DDW, available for the transport of cargo from the quay to the final market.

Subtracting the transport costs common to the alternative routes, the remaining charges which cargo has to pay for each unit (ton) of cargo are as follows.

PSS Route: $h_s + z_s + k_s (d_a - d_0)$

DDW Route: $h_{dr} + h_{dw} + z_d + k_{dw} \cdot d_a$

If shippers are very cost-conscious, one would expect them to select the cheaper of the two routes, all other things being equal. Quite often, when the shippers reckon the port storage system to be a relatively cheap 'warehousing' facility, then the PSS route becomes preferable to the DDW route; and consequently the port transit shed becomes congested. Such a situation implies, using the notations above for the difference in costs, that

$$k_s (d_a - d_0) \leqslant (\beta_{hd} + \beta_{tr}) + k_{dw} \cdot d_a \qquad (7.1)$$

For $d_a < d_0$, k_s is set at $k_s = 0$. As the port provides a free period of

135

d_0 days, whereas domestic depot warehousing usually does not, d_0 can therefore be deducted from d_a on the left-hand side of this inequality. This factor may be of critical significance in making a decision between the alternatives, as will be seen.

One may substitute γ_d, which is the ratio of the free period to the chargeable period, for the radio d_0/d_a, i.e. $\gamma_d = \dfrac{d_0}{d_a}$ with the

assumption that $d_a > d_0$. To begin with, we assume that $0 < \gamma_d < 1$ because this case is the most important, and is thus given substantial treatment first. In prosaic terms, every cargo needs storage for more than the d_0 free period given by the port storage scheme. The inequality then becomes

$$k_s \leqslant \frac{k_{dw}}{1-\gamma_d} + \frac{\gamma_d \, (\beta_{hd} + \beta_{tr})}{(1-\gamma_d) \, d_0} \qquad (7.2)$$

which gives the limit of the port storage charge beyond which the route using DDW becomes cheaper than PSS, in terms of k_s in relation to k_{dw}. For expository purposes, the ratio of k_s to k_{dw} may now be

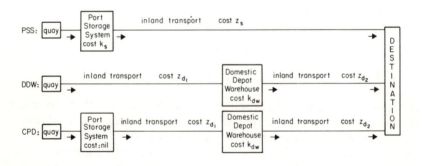

Figure 7.1   PSS, DDW and CPD routes

expressed by $g_p = k_s/k_{dw}$. The inequality is violated if k_s is greater that $\hat{g}_p \cdot k_{dw}$ where

$$\hat{g}_p = \frac{1}{1-\gamma_d} + \frac{\gamma_d\,(\beta_{hd}+\beta_{tr})}{(1-\gamma_d)\cdot d_0 \cdot k_{dw}} \qquad (7.3)$$

Here $\hat{g}_p$ is the value of g_p obtained by equalising both sides of equation 7.2 using the definition of $g_p = k_s/k_{dw}$.

A high positive value for $\hat{g}_p$ would mean that the port storage rate k_s could be comparatively large to make PSS attractive in relation to the domestic depot rate, whereas a negative value for $\hat{g}_p$ would mean that a port storage rate even cheaper than that of DDW is not attractive enough for the port users to induce them to select the PSS route in preference to DDW. In order to elucidate the ambiguities inherent in this statement, let us examine the implications of the above analysis with the help of a graphical presentation. Given the length of the free period d_0, a different γ_d means of course a different d_a. Therefore, the selection of the cargo route in terms of relative cheapness is interpreted from the angle of the length of cargo storage d_a.

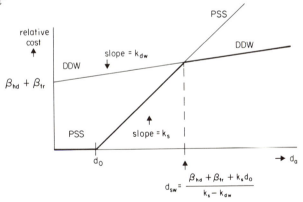

1    $\beta_{hd} + \beta_{tr} \geqslant 0$. If $k_s \leqslant k_{dw}$, PSS is cheaper than DDW no matter how long cargo requires to be kept in the storage system before delivery to the final market. If $k_s > k_{dw}$ PSS is cheaper than DDW for cargo requiring fewer than d_{sw} days, but is expensive for cargo requiring more days.

$$2 \quad \beta_{hd} + \beta_{tr} < 0 \text{ where } d_1 = -\frac{\beta_{hd} + \beta_{tr}}{k_{dw}} \geq d_0$$

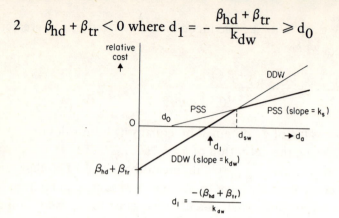

If $k_s < k_{dw}$, PSS is cheaper than DDW for cargo requiring more than d_{sw} days storage. Otherwise DDW is cheaper. If $k_s \geq k_{dw}$, DDW is cheaper for cargo requiring any length of storage whatever, where $d_1 = -\frac{\beta_{hd} + \beta_{tr}}{k_{dw}} < d_0$

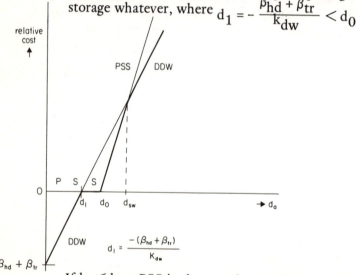

If $k_s \leq k_{dw}$ PSS is cheaper than DDW for cargo requiring more than d_1 days. If $k_s > k_{dw}$ PSS is cheaper for cargo requiring more than d_1 days but fewer than d_{sw} days. Otherwise, DDW is cheaper.

Consideration of the third alternative

The arguments so far have dealt with the case where there are only two alternatives: PSS and DDW. However, another alternative is readily conceivable — as might naturally be expected, a combination of the two, using the port storage system for as long as cargo is allowed to stay free, and then making use of domestic depot warehousing. This combination of PSS and DDW is the CPD Route. The cost of using this route for $0 < \gamma_d < 1$, subtracting as before the costs common to the alternative routes, will be $h_s + h_{dw} + z_d + k_{dw}(d_a - d_0)$. The cheapest route will then depend on the relative magnitude of PSS-DDW-CPD costs.

In order to investigate $\gamma_d \geqslant 1$, we have to keep in mind that the $k_s (d_a - d_0)$ term disappears from the value of the PSS Route cost, and also the $k_s (d_a - d_0)$ term disappears from the CPD Route cost value. (N.B. here $\gamma_d = 1$ means $d = d_0$.) The same arguments outlined above will then be applicable in a similar manner.

For expository comparison, cases in which there is no free period allowed at all in the transit shed should be mentioned also. In this situation, our equations and values for relative costs outlined above will be modified by setting d_0 equal to zero.

Throughput increase under direct/indirect route saturation

Congestion caused by 'incompetence' in the capacity of handling facilities may occur when traffic increases to such an extent that the level of commodity flow eventually becomes oversaturated. It may also occur when a certain kind of deterioration takes place on the handling side, including the possible disruption of the efficiency of the system taken in the widest sense. Qualitatively speaking, the handling capacity on the quayside is, by and large, dictated by the successive subsystems — that is, those involved in both the direct and the indirect transfer routes. And if the storage system (or alternatively the direct route system) becomes saturated, cargo cannot be transferred away from the quay unless some sort of measure is taken to create space (or alternatively provide greater handling capacity) for it.

Direct route saturation : increased throughput via storage

When the direct route is saturated, one might suppose that a diversion of the excess traffic to storage would be the first logical step to be considered. But if the excess traffic is not satisfied with such a diversion, and would rather wait until the direct route transfer facilities become available, then the storage system will not work satisfactorily as a temporary substitute, unless some means are taken to make the indirect route through the port more attractive. It will be shown here that, if the direct route handling system cannot be improved beyond s_d tons/day, and if cargo is to go through the indirect route (provided that it can be induced to accept the latter in preference to waiting on the quay), then the average cargo stay d will play a significant role in terms of congestion.

Let us suppose that cargo spends $\bar{d}$ days on average in the storage system. For simplicity, one may assume that the daily outflow from storage to the inland sector (as well as the inflow to the port) does not vary very much so that the level of stock in storage at any one time remains nearly constant. In other words, there is little daily fluctuation away from the $\bar{d}$ days average. Within such a steady-state, where $\bar{V}_s$ represents the working level of storage, cargo will therefore be taken away from the quay into the storage section at the rate of $\dfrac{\bar{V}_s}{\bar{d}}$ tons per day. ($\bar{V}_s$ depends on the nature of the commodity fluctuation and is, at most, equal to the holding capacity C_s of the storage system.) If, in addition, the direct route is functioning at an offtake rate of s_d tons per day (maximum), this port is providing in sum a mean service rate μ_s (which will be assumed constant in this case) of

$$\mu_s = \frac{\bar{V}_s}{\bar{d}} + s_d \text{ (tons/day)} \tag{7.4}$$

In order to make the case easier to examine, let us assume that the ship arrival pattern follows the Poisson distribution pattern, with a mean arrival rate of λ ships per day, each unloading $\bar{W}$ tons of cargo on average. Then μ (or 'mean ship service rate') becomes

$$\mu = \frac{\mu_s}{\bar{W}} \text{ (ships/day)} \tag{7.5}$$

Now, divide this mean arrival rate λ by the mean service rate μ and express the ratio by ρ.

$$\rho = \frac{\lambda}{\mu} = \frac{\lambda \cdot \bar{W}}{\dfrac{\bar{V}_s}{\bar{d}} + s_d} \tag{7.6}$$

140

where $0 \leqslant \bar{V}_s \leqslant C_s$. By use of the analogy of this simple port system to a fundamental Poisson-input-constant-service type of queue model, the average waiting time T_q for any ship will be given as follows.

$$T_q = \frac{L_q}{2\lambda} = \frac{1}{2\lambda} \cdot \frac{\rho^2}{1-\rho} \quad \text{(days/ship)} \tag{7.7}$$

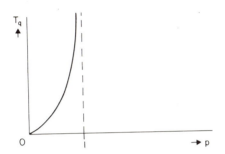

Figure 7.2   Average ship waiting time versus the utilisation factor

Taking the formula for the slope of the T_q-ρ curve

$$\frac{dT_q}{d\rho} = \frac{1}{2\lambda} \cdot \frac{2\rho - \rho^2}{(1-\rho)^2} \tag{7.8}$$

we can plot T_q against ρ as in figure 7.2. One can see instantly from the figure, as well as from equation 7.7, that T_q approaches infinity as ρ approaches unity.

This ρ is usually called the utilisation factor of the system, since the value of $(1-\rho)$ measures the fraction of time during which the service facilities are free. In the case where ρ is larger than, or equal to, unity, there can be no steady-state solution, because in such a case the queue should diverge, with an ever-increasing number of ships awaiting service.

If $\lambda > \frac{s_d}{\overline{W}}$ then it is equation 7.6 which reveals the 'critical value' for $\bar{d}$, which may be designated as $\bar{d}_{cr}$. This is calculated by equating ρ to unity in equation 7.6 (given the rate of ship arrivals, the storage capacity and the handling capacity of the direct route).

$$1 = \frac{\lambda \cdot \overline{W}}{\frac{\overline{V}_s}{\overline{d}_{cr}} + s_d} \quad \text{and thus} \quad \overline{d}_{cr} = \frac{\overline{V}_s}{\lambda \overline{W} - s_d}$$

$$(7.9)$$

This means that the queue will begin to diverge if the average length of stay of cargo in storage becomes larger than $\overline{d}_{cr}$ with the working level at $\overline{V}_s$ and other things being equal. It should be noted that if $\lambda < \frac{s_d}{\overline{W}}$ then ρ will always be less than unity. If $\lambda = \frac{s_d}{\overline{W}}$ the queue will always converge unless the working level of storage is nil. (That is, $\overline{V}_s = 0$ would mean the closure of the indirect route altogether.)

Having denoted the maximum handling rate of the direct transfer route by s_d, equation 7.9 suggests, in general, that the maximum limit of the average length of cargo stay in the storage system, before a divergent ship queue is encountered, will be given by

$$\overline{d}_{cr} = \frac{C_s}{\phi_d - s_d}$$

$$(7.10)$$

where ϕ_d is the average daily throughput for the port. Equation 7.10 implies that, as the traffic level increases, the critical length of the average cargo stay will decrease. Though equation 7.9 is derived from the assumption of random arrivals, and constant services, equation 7.10 is expected to give a fair measure of the critical value $\overline{d}_{cr}$ since, insofar as the utilisation factor is less than unity, the queue is, over a fairly long time span, expected to converge in general.

Direct route saturation: increased throughput via direct route

It has so far been assumed that the direct route is the one saturated; and the analysis of the length of cargo stay in relation to congestion has implied that the traffic increase might be absorbed solely by modifications in the storage system. This assumption will be sensible only where there is no strong objection to routing excess cargo by way of the storage system. Otherwise, if the direct route through the port becomes saturated while the storage system itself remains unsaturated, then the direct route is the one in most prominent demand. Thus, why not switch some of the transfer vehicles used by the indirect route over to the direct route system, to help increase the handling capacity of the latter?

142

One objection to this solution may be that it is sometimes not possible to make such 'switch use' of handling equipment, either because of limitations on vehicle functions or because differences in the type of handling operations make it impractical. Moreover, if the cargo needs proper protection, and cannot simply be left at the sidings, then the only alternative would be to use the storage system route.

It might also be argued that a scheme to expand the storage system may be easier to undertake than one which would modify the direct route system. And this expansion could take any of several forms: through the reconstruction of the inland transport terminals into more extensive, efficient ones accommodating more rail wagons etc. to transport goods; through more semi-protected stacking space for goods; or through the reshaping of the port internal road system, to enable more vehicles to operate between the quay and the terminal. Even if the direct route is already jammed with transfer vehicles, and there is therefore no possibility of 'switch use' of vehicles, it may still be found sensible to transfer cargo away from the quay towards the indirect route. This will avoid putting into storage any cargo which prefers the direct route in the first place. And by shifting it at least as far as the inland transport terminal an increase in the aggregate through traffic as demanded can be realised.

Storage system saturation

From an overall point of view, it might seem more plausible to assume that the storage system (rather than the direct route) is saturated. This is true because the service provided by the storage system cannot be replaced by any other means within the port system. Unless the storage system is expanded, some measure will have to be designed to increase the handling rate of the direct route in order to absorb the excess through traffic. But, if the increase of the direct route capacity is supposed to be achieved simply by a reinforcement in transfer vehicles, or some similar means, how can this really be accomplished in terms of the handling rates of the two routes?

Let us describe the system at the steady state, supposing an increase in traffic to a level which is expected to continue for a long period ahead — a trend which therefore must be absorbed by some appropriate action. Suppose further that the storage system in the steady-state has been operating at full capacity C_s, and that no further accommodation of traffic by way of the indirect route is possible. (Or, this could be described in another way: the former state may have had some slack capacity in both direct and indirect routes, but the traffic increase was absorbed up to the point where the storage system became saturated, and now there is leeway for further accommodation only by way of the direct route.) From this point on, any further increase in throughput can only be absorbed by increasing the capacity of the direct route. For simplicity, no change in tariff is to be considered.

Since all the resulting properties of a Poisson process are determined by the utilisation factor ρ, we have only to specify the value of ρ (say, ρ_s) for the steady-state level of services in terms of average ship waiting time. The system factors before and after the counteracting measure may be denoted as λ, $\overline{W}$, C_s, $\overline{d}$, s_d and $\lambda + \Delta\lambda$, $\overline{W}$, C_s, $\overline{d}$, $s_d + \Delta s_d$, respectively.

If the policy is *not to maintain* the previous level of services, but rather to reduce the congestion to a certain extent, which is in turn interpreted in terms of the utilisation factor (say from ρ_{s_1} to ρ_{s_2}, where $\rho_{s_1} > \rho_{s_2}$), then the necessary increase of the direct route capacity s_d is

$$\Delta s_d = \frac{\Delta\lambda \cdot \overline{W}}{\rho_{s_2}} + \left(\frac{C_s}{\overline{d}} + s_d \right) \left(\frac{\rho_{s_1}}{\rho_{s_2}} - 1 \right)$$

(7.11)

Here $\frac{C_s}{\overline{d}} + s_d$ is considered to be the expected aggregate handling rate of the port system.

If, on the other hand, the policy is *to maintain* the previous level of services in terms of average ship waiting time, then the necessary increase Δs_d is found by equating ρ_{s_2} equal to ρ_{s_1} (say, $\rho_{s_1} = \rho_{s_2} = \rho_s$) in equation 7.11.

$$\Delta s_d = \frac{\Delta\lambda \cdot \overline{W}}{\rho_s} = \frac{\Delta\phi_d}{\rho_s}$$

(7.12)

where ϕ_d is the daily traffic level.

Saturation of the aggregate system

Finally, it goes without saying that, if the aggregate transport offtake rate is already saturated, then there is no point in increasing the working capacity of either the direct or the indirect route through the port.

Throughput capacity of the integrated system

With the capacities of all the subsystems at hand, the problem is now to analyse the interrelationships among them and to estimate the throughput of the integrated system with reference to this relationship. Once the capacity of each subsystem has been clearly determined, then the following analysis shows how to identify the bottleneck from the broadest viewpoint of the integrated system, and suggests what measures might be taken to solve the problem.

Let us denote the quay handling rate by x tons/day, the transfer rate by the indirect system by y_a, the transport offtake rate with access to the indirect route by z_a, the transfer rate by the direct route system (i.e. to the inland transport terminal directly) by y_b, and the inland transport offtake rate with access to the direct route by z_b. Generally speaking, each rate in practice has its maximum at

$$0 \leqslant x \leqslant x_M \tag{7.13a}$$
$$0 \leqslant y_a \leqslant y_{a_M} \tag{7.13b}$$
$$0 \leqslant y_b \leqslant y_{b_M} \tag{7.13c}$$
$$0 \leqslant z_a \leqslant z_{a_M} \tag{7.13d}$$
$$0 \leqslant z_b \leqslant z_{b_M} \tag{7.13e}$$

In case the transfer vehicles are switchable between the direct and indirect routes, then equations 7.13b and 7.13c may be relaxed as

$$0 \leqslant y_a + y_b \leqslant y_M \tag{7.14}$$

where y_M represents the total transfer vehicle force. And similarly, if some of the inland transport vehicles (rail wagons, trucks, lorries, barges) are switchable between z_a and z_b, then equations 7.13d and 7.13e may be relaxed as

$$0 \leqslant z_a + z_b \leqslant z_M \tag{7.15}$$

(For simplicity, workshifts are not considered.) No matter how vast the port storage may be, the upper limit of this port system is bound by $z_a + z_b$; and any speed-up of the unloading operation beyond this limit, unless complemented by some improvement in terms of inland transport, will produce no practical results.

This need not always be true, however. For example, the traffic may fluctuate rather strongly, sometimes with a rash of vessel arrivals and spasmodic ones at other times. And the quay space may be substantial enough to allow faster cargo handling at quayside. If the nature of ship arrivals is such that the short-term (e.g. daily) average of cargo unloading does not greatly exceed the transfer rate maximum $y_a + y_b = y_M$, then the maximum of the handling rate (crane speed) could temporarily be greater than $z_a + z_b$, so long as the quayside space remains sufficient not to hinder unloading operations. (See chapter 4 on this point).

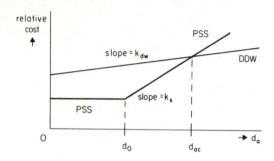

Figure 7.3   PSS/DDW routes cost comparison

Let us examine the behaviour of traffic through the port by use of a simple model, especially the modal choice among the alternative routes, with the transport cost structure given. If the relative transport cost looks like figure 7.3, cargo requiring less than d_{ac} days finds the PSS route cheaper. Given the cost structure of the two basic alternatives within the port, the way in which cargo becomes split between them, if shippers are all cost-conscious, is induced by the length of the aggregate storage requirement of the cargo *after* its landing and *up until* its final delivery. This 'aggregate storage requirement' may be designated by d_a (days), and should be distinguished from the d days spent in the port storage system alone (the latter forming only a portion of, or at most being equal to, the aggregate d_a).

Suppose that the cargo traffic using this port has, for strategical reasons or because of market conditions, a certain distribution for the aggregate storage requirement as shown in figure 7.4. In practice we cannot expect such a clear-cut split between the two routes. Yet if the relative cost is clearly worked out as in figure 7.3, there is reasonable ground to expect a profile similar to this one. However, an examination of 'indifference curves' with respect to figure 7.4 suggests that some modification in the profile may be expected.

If two traders requiring cargo storage for their businesses see a

146

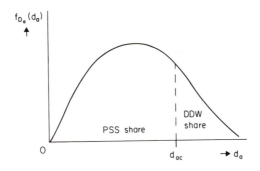

Figure 7.4   PSS/DDW traffic split as a function of d_a

certain trade-off between cargo storage time and accompanying cost,
then they may construct a family of indifference curves as shown in
figure 7.5, with curves A_1 to A_4 belonging to Trader A and curves B_1
to B_4 to Trader B.   The trader is indifferent towards any two or more
points so long as they lie in the same curve.   Trader B is indifferent, for
example, to the difference on curve B_2 between point J (lower cost,
but fewer number of days) and point H.   The shapes, and thus the
family, of indifference curves will vary from trader to trader.   There is

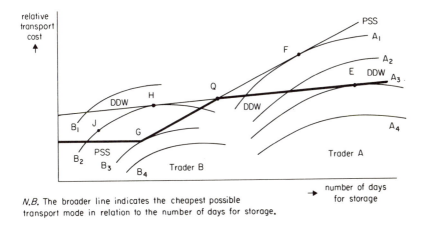

N.B. The broader line indicates the cheapest possible
transport mode in relation to the number of days for storage.

Figure 7.5   Indifference curves in relation to the transport
cost function with respect to the PSS/DDW routes

147

no reason why we should suppose they are as simple to construct as in figure 7.5, since greater storage time does not necessarily imply higher utility. But just for argument's sake the case is presented as simply as possible here.

One thing is common to all families of curves: the higher the curve, the less desirable it becomes to the trader, because this means a higher cost for the same length of cargo storage. If each trader expects to maximise his utility as far as possible, then he will try to choose a length of cargo stay by setting his indifference curve so that it touches one of the given cheapest cost curves at one point only. For example, Trader A should choose point E of his curve A_3, which gives the highest utility under the transport cost structure as in figure 7.5, whereas Trader B should choose point G of his curve B_3 for the same reasons. If there were no DDW route alternative, Trader A would choose point F of his curve A_1. If the PSS route could not be used, then Trader B would choose point H of his curve B_2.

It is clear that a discontinuity occurs at point Q, since no indifference curve can touch the cost curves at this point *and only* this point. Since point Q in figure 7.5 corresponds to the point $d_a = d_{ac}$ in figure 7.4, we may therefore assume a discontinuity also occurs at d_{ac}. And since few people would thus be expected to choose this exact point, the profile of figure 7.4 should be modified to show a slight 'dip' as in figure 7.6.

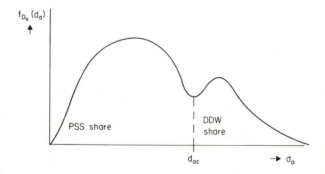

Figure 7.6   PSS/DDW traffic split as a function of d_a: effect of the indifference curves

The choice of the route is, of course, not solely dependent on the length of the storage requirement, but also on the type of storage: refrigeration, protection of various kinds (from erosion, damage, or rotting), and so forth. In order to avoid complication, however, such factors affecting the route choice are not considered here.

Table 7.1
Cargo split among direct, indirect and semidirect routes [4]

Figures are given in tons/month

Port of Karachi (February-March 1971 data for 5 berths)

Throughput	101,300
Indirect route (21.1 per cent)	21,400
Direct route (62.2 per cent)	63,050
Semidirect route (16.7 per cent)	16,850

Port of LaValletta

Throughput	11,600
Indirect route (85.1 per cent)	9,900
Direct route (11.9 per cent)	1,375
Semidirect route (3.0 per cent)	325

Port of Valparaiso

Throughput	46,700
Indirect route (60 per cent)	26,600
Direct route (40 per cent)	20,100

Let us express the ratio of the cargo taking the PSS route by θ with the remainder $(1 - \theta)$ using the DDW route. (For examples of actual cargo split in several ports, see table 7.1). This ratio is further assumed to show little fluctuation over the period concerned. That is, the traffic increase is to be spread out evenly over the whole storage requirement range. Let us start from the steady state situation, where the traffic level is X_L (tons/day), and the working level of the port storage system is at V_s tons $(V_s < C_s)$, with an average length of stay in *port* storage of $\bar{d}$ days. At this stage, the working level of the port storage should roughly satisfy the conditions $\frac{V_s}{\bar{d}} = \theta \cdot X_L$. Thus,

$$V_s = \theta \cdot \bar{d} \cdot X_L \qquad (7.16)$$

In equation 7.16, θ and $\bar{d}$ are not independent of each other; and both are automatically determined from the distribution $f_{D_a} (d_a)$ once the cut-off period d_{ac} is determined from the overall transport cost structure. (See figure 7.3). If the transport cost structure remains unchanged during the short period concerned, and assuming that the

149

inland transport system is not the constraining system of course, the maximum traffic flow which can be coped with by the existing system is bound by

$$\left.\begin{array}{rl} \theta \cdot X_L & \leqslant y_{a_M} \\ \theta \cdot X_L & \leqslant \dfrac{C_s}{\overline{d}} \\ (1-\theta) \cdot X_L & \leqslant y_{b_M} \end{array}\right\}$$

(7.17)

To sum up, expressing maximum possible throughput on average by X_L^* we find

$$X_L^* = \text{Min} \left\{ \frac{y_{a_M}}{\theta}, \frac{C_s}{\theta \overline{d}}, \frac{y_{b_M}}{1-\theta} \right\}$$

(7.18)

If the transfer vehicles are switchable between the direct route and the indirect route, this port could achieve a yet higher maximum throughput (i.e. $X_L^* = y_M$) by setting $\dfrac{y_{a_M}}{\theta} = \dfrac{y_{b_M}}{1-\theta}$. And since $y_{a_M} + y_{b_M} = y_M$, therefore

$$\left.\begin{array}{rl} y_{a_M} & = \theta \cdot y_M \\ y_{b_M} & = (1-\theta) \cdot y_M \end{array}\right\}$$

(7.19)

Equation 7.19 should come as no surprise, since it essentially tells us that the total vehicle force y_M should be allocated between the two routes in proportion to the traffic level of each route. One point, however, should be noted here. This allocation is valid only when there is no problem about storage congestion and, more precisely, is valid only in the situation where

$$\frac{C_s}{\theta \overline{d}} \geqslant y_M$$

(7.20)

This is because what matters among the three values in the bracket of equation 7.18 is the *smallest* of the three; and X_L^* can be improved only by an increase in the value of this smallest one. If equation 7.20 does not hold, and if

$$\frac{C_s}{\theta \overline{d}} < y_M$$

(7.21)

150

then $X_L^* = \dfrac{C_s}{\theta d}$, and is thus dependent on the distribution ratio θ.

The necessary arrangement should then be $y_{a_M} = \dfrac{C_s}{d}$, $y_{b_M} = \dfrac{C_s}{\theta d} - \dfrac{C_s}{d}$

letting $y_M - \dfrac{C_s}{\theta d}$ number of vehicles remain idle.

These considerations do not apply to the case where there is a lot of 'marginal' cargo — by which is meant cargo using the port storage system or the direct route as a matter of convenience, custom, and so forth, without being very cost-conscious. When the storage system or the direct route becomes congested, such 'marginal' users are prone to switch from one route to the other, thus changing the distribution ratio θ. In this case, equation 7.18 should be replaced by

$$X_L^* = \text{Min} \left\{ y_{a_M}, \frac{C_s}{d} \right\} + y_{b_M} \qquad (7.22)$$

And again, in this case if the storage capacity is not the abiding constraint — that is, if

$$y_M \leqslant \frac{C_s}{d} \qquad (7.23)$$

then the maximum throughput X_L^* is y_M, irrespective of the way the vehicle force is split, and not dependent on the distribution ratio θ. If on the other hand

$$y_M > \frac{C_s}{d} \qquad (7.24)$$

then the throughput maximum is achieved by allocating transfer vehicles as follows,

$$y_{a_M} = \frac{C_s}{d}$$

$$y_{b_M} = y_M - \frac{C_s}{d} \qquad (7.25)$$

thus providing the maximum throughput y_M. The distribution ratio θ in this case will become

$$\theta = \frac{C_s}{y_M \cdot d} \qquad (7.26)$$

Let us examine further the condition that the distribution ratio θ is assumed to be fairly unique in relation to the port pricing scheme (e.g. cost comparisons between the port storage charge and the domestic warehouse charge). It was concluded that equation 7.19 gives the optimal vehicle allotment only when equation 7.20 holds (i.e. when the port storage is not the dominant constraint). What occurs when cargo traffic wanting to use the indirect route increases beyond the rate of $C_s/\bar{d}$, thus causing the port storage to become saturated? Some solutions might be to use the open space for temporary stacking, or to take some measure to encourage shorter stay in the port storage system (reduction of $\bar{d}$) or possibly to increase capacity (expansion of C_s).

The first has sometimes been found very effective, especially when the traffic flow has a marked fluctuation so that the high level of traffic flow does not persist for a long time (and therefore the temporary backlog will eventually be absorbed during a later period when the traffic flow is not so robust). This situation occurs when z_{a_M} (the inland terminal maximum off-take capacity) is close to the port storage turnover. Otherwise, the storage working level could well be kept within the storage holding capacity by a higher rate of z_a. This may be termed as a 'higher level equilibrium'. So long as the offtake rate matches the intake rate with respect to the storage system, the distribution of the length of cargo stay (hence the average $\bar{d}$), can be left intact, provided that the rate is less than $C_s/\bar{d}$. That is to say, the port storage system will be oversaturated when the traffic demand flow choosing the PSS route exceeds the offtake rate z_{a_M}.

The traffic flow using the port storage exceeding the rate $C_s/\bar{d}$, but not the rate z_{a_M} ($z_{a_M} > C_s/\bar{d}$), can only be absorbed through this indirect route up to z_{a_M} by the reduction of $\bar{d}$ down to C_s/z_{a_M}. And this can be accomplished through an appropriate increase of the storage charge. (Refer to the section above 'Effects of Storage Tariff Change on Cargo Transit Time', for how this should best be done). If on the other hand $z_{a_M} \leqslant C_s/\bar{d}$, then the maximum allowable traffic level through PSS is bound by z_{a_M}.

As regards the former case, consider an appropriate storage charge increase as shown in figure 7.7. Assuming the invariance of the distribution $f_{D_a}(d_a)$ in relation to the storage charge (tariff) change, the change from k_{s_1} to k_{s_2} will result in the change of d_{ac_1} to d_{ac_2},

152

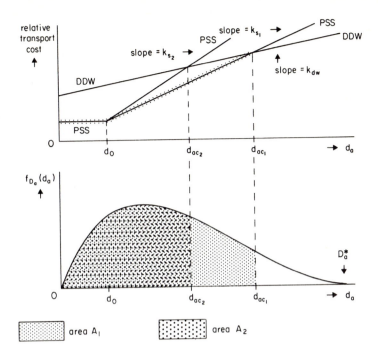

Figure 7.7 Sensitivity of PSS/DDW traffic split as a function of d_a in relation to the relative cost of PSS/DDW

and accordingly a contraction from area A_1 to area A_2. Thus, the average length of stay of cargo in the *port* storage system $\bar{d}$ (as opposed to its *total* storage requirement d_a, where $\bar{d} \leqslant d_a$), is reduced from $\bar{d}_1$ to $\bar{d}_2$, which are uniquely determined from the areas A_1 and A_2, determined in turn by the values d_{ac_1} and d_{ac_2}, respectively.

In sum, the increase of the storage charge necessary to contain the demand in excess of the intrinsic capacity of the storage system, yet less than the offtake maximum z_{a_M}, can be determined by finding a $\bar{d}_{ac_2}$ such that the average length of stay of cargo for the area A_2 gives $\bar{d}_2 = {}^C s/z_{a_M}$, which then determines the corresponding k_{s_2}. If the storage charge is set higher than this rate k_{s_2}, the port storage system will then on average be operated under its full holding capacity, because the inland transport handling rate cannot keep up with a turn-

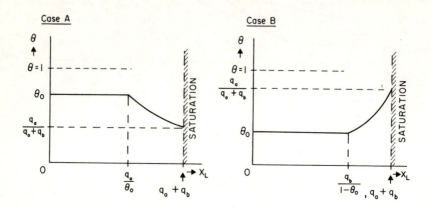

Figure 7.8   Cargo split ratio versus port throughput

over greater than its own maximum z_{a_M}, unless the latter is somehow improved.

   If the storage system is the commanding restraint, and if the improvement of this system through a tariff change is not desired by the port, the question then hinges upon the direct route. The maximum traffic flow through the direct route is bound by Min $\{y_b, z_b\}$. If the distribution rate θ is rather flexible, as shown in figure 7.8, and depending on the state of storage system congestion, the excess cargo traffic might be diverted to this direct route, so long as the total cargo flow through this route does not exceed the Min $\{y_b, z_b\}$. In figure 7.8, q_a represents the maximum throughput through PSS, and q_b the maximum through DDW. The shapes of the θ curves depend on the initial relationships between the values of θ_0 and $\dfrac{q_a}{q_a + q_b}$ as indicated in the two cases illustrated. If the distribution ratio θ happens to be larger than the ratio $\dfrac{q_a}{q_a + q_b}$ (Case A), then this ratio can be maintained until the traffic level

154

reaches q_a/θ_0. And therefore, assuming that the total vehicle force y_M is divided between the two routes according to the ratio θ_0, the transfer vehicle force need not be reallocated until the traffic level reaches q_a/θ_0.

If, on the other hand, θ happens to be less than $\dfrac{q_a}{q_a + q_b}$ (Case B), then again this distribution ratio can be maintained until the traffic level reaches $\dfrac{q_b}{1-\theta_0}$. In Case A of figure 7.8, some cargo will have to switch from the indirect to the direct route, while in Case B the reverse takes place.

The course of the analysis in this section should have made clear one peculiar feature of the storage system. In terms of the handling rates, each of the listed rates has a fixed maximum, with the single exception of the storage system. For example, y_a and y_b are bound by the level of transfer vehicle employment, whereas x is bound by the capacity of cranes and other handling equipment, and z_a and z_b are bound by such factors as the number of rail wagons, trucks, and barges employed. But the storage system can nonetheless vary its turnover through the variation of $\bar{d}$ — namely, the profile of the cargo storage length. The storage tariff change is expected to have a certain effect on this profile, and indeed a higher rate will, as mentioned above, squeeze out the 'marginal' users and encourage its operational improvement. This tariff increase will, in general, provoke a response by the users; and the resulting change in their behaviour will depend on the tariff elasticity of demand.

As in the case considered in this section, if the overall transport cost structure is presented to the shippers, and if they are all cost-conscious, the response they make should be clearly explained by use of the distribution $f_{D_a}(d_a)$ and the overall cost structure. (See for example figure 7.3). However, for the sake of improvement in the port throughput, any storage rate increase which would result in the reduction of the average length of cargo stay down to less than

$$\bar{d} = \frac{C_s}{\text{Min } \{y_a, z_a\}}$$ would lead to little improvement of throughput,

since this theoretical throughput would become greater than actual potential capacity.

Cargo storage time requirement policies

Figure 7.7 gives the aggregate distribution of cargo storage time requirement for cargoes using this particular port with its two alternative routes (PSS and DDW), and shows that the switch-use of these two routes depends on the port charging rate relative to warehouses commercially available elsewhere. The crucial value of d_a, with the port storage charge at k_{s_1} (£/ton/day), is designated as d_{ac_1}, at which point the average cargo transit time will be

$$\bar{d}_1 = \frac{\int_0^{d_{ac_1}} x \cdot f_{D_a}(x)\, dx}{\int_0^{d_{ac_1}} f_{D_a}(x)\, dx}$$

(7.27)

Therefore, the maximum throughput (per annum) achievable by the existing port storage with capacity C_s is expressed as

$$\phi_{as_1} = \frac{L_a C_s}{\bar{d}_1} = \frac{L_a \cdot C_s \cdot \int_0^{d_{ac_1}} f_{D_a}(x)\, dx}{\int_0^{d_{ac_1}} x \cdot f_{D_a}(x)\, dx}$$

(7.28)

If the port storage rate is increased from k_{s_1} to k_{s_2}, which would result in the shift of d_{ac_1} to d_{ac_2}, this potential throughput can, theoretically speaking, be increased to

$$\phi_{as_2} = \frac{L_a \cdot C_s}{\bar{d}_2} = \frac{L_a \cdot C_s \cdot \int_0^{d_{ac_2}} f_{D_a}(x)\, dx}{\int_0^{d_{ac_2}} x \cdot f_{D_a}(x)\, dx}$$

(7.29)

This does not mean, of course, that after this price change the traffic flow through the port storage system increases, but only that the intrinsic capacity (to *accommodate* more traffic) is increased.

The distribution curve of cargo storage time requirement could take almost any form. The curves are usually not so smooth as those shown in figure 7.9. But for practical purposes, we should concern ourselves here with relatively simple, yet sufficiently accurate, ones.

The uniform distribution, though sometimes occurring, seems too simple. The triangular distribution, though analytically simple, can be recommended for practical approximations. Curve Γ_2 is smoothly connected with curve Γ_1 at point $d_a = D_{am}$ since the derivatives of these two curves at this point are both $2 / D_{am}$ and the values of these two are the same (equal to D_{am} /D_a^*). Now, given the holding capacity of the storage system, and the shape of the distribution of cargo storage length, let us consider the effect upon the potential intrinsic capacity of the port storage of an increase in the port storage charge from k_{s_1} to k_{s_2}.

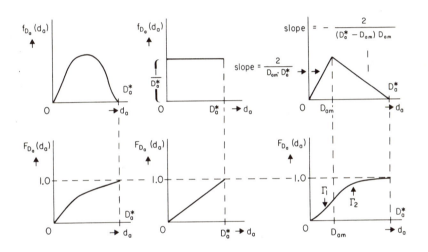

Figure 7.9 Distribution shapes of cargo storage time requirement policies

Example

It is expected that transit containers have to be stored either in the port area or elsewhere in the inland depot. Suppose that all the 'through' containers are to be stored in such a manner that each

157

container needs a ground space of 37m². Assuming 12 tons of cargo on average in each loaded foreign container, we can argue that 12 tons of cargo occupies 37m².

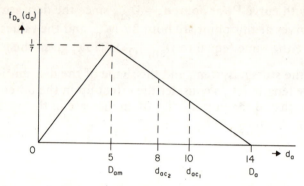

Figure 7.10   Probability distribution of cargo storage length (example)

The probability distribution of cargo storage length is calculated from the nature of the traffic, as in figure 7.10. Suppose that the port storage has 5000 m² for this type of container cargo, and is now fully congested (with cargo requiring fewer than 10 days using PSS). As a result of the storage rate increase, the total transport cost profile changes so that cargoes requiring fewer than, say, 8 days are still expected to use PSS. Then how much does this change lead to an improvement in the port storage intrinsic capacity?

$$\bar{d}_1 = \frac{\left\{ \int_0^5 \frac{x^2}{35} \cdot dx + \int_5^{10} -\frac{x(x-14)}{63} \cdot dx \right\}}{\int_0^5 \frac{x}{35} \cdot dx + \int_5^{10} -\frac{x-14}{63} \cdot dx} = \frac{1.19 + 3.70}{0.357 + 0.516} = 5.6 \text{ days}$$

The saturating level at $k_s = k_{s_1}$ is therefore roughly

$$\phi_{as_1} = \frac{365 \text{ (days)}}{5.6 \text{ (days)}} \cdot \frac{5000 \text{ (m}^2)}{\frac{37}{12} (\frac{\text{m}^2}{\text{ton}})} = 105,695 \text{ (tons/year)}$$

After the increase from $k_s = k_{s_1}$ to $k_s = k_{s_2}$, which is expected to result in a shift from $d_{ac_1} = 10$ (days) to $d_{ac_2} = 8$ days, the intrinsic capacity will increase to

158

$$\phi_{as_2} = \frac{365}{4.87} \cdot \frac{5000}{\frac{37}{12}} = 121{,}538 \ (\text{tons/year})$$

Thus, about 15 per cent more traffic could theoretically be accommodated through the port storage system due to the price increase given, where

$$\bar{d}_2 = \frac{\int_0^5 \frac{x^2}{35} \cdot dx + \int_5^8 -\frac{x(x-14)}{63} \cdot dx}{\int_0^5 \frac{x^2}{35} \cdot dx + \int_5^8 -\frac{(x-14)}{63} \cdot dx} = \frac{1.19 + 2.29}{0.357 + 0.357} = 4.87 \ \text{days}$$

Notes

[1]   *The Financial Times*, 3 August 1976.
[2]   *The Financial Times*, 4 August 1976.
[3]   Hans A. Adler, *Sector and Project Planning in Transportation*, World Bank Staff Occasional Paper Number Four, 1967, p.22
[4]   UNCTAD, *Berth Throughput*, pp 51, 71, 81.

One of the major problems which impinge upon port management is pricing policy. A tariff generally consists of two basic parts: dues for services provided to vessels, and dues for services provided to goods. Since a port is an infrastructure — by which is meant that it functions as the interface between the marine transport sector and the inland transport sector — pricing policy ideally should be developed on the basis of the whole integrated system, which includes everything from the port of embarkation to the final inland destination. The lack of an appropriate tariff could lead to distortions between different transport modes, over- or under-investment in the connecting transport systems, wrongly induced industries, and so forth. Such a comprehensive scheme has, however, never been put into practice in reality, presumably because of the difficulty in co-ordinating all the relevant corporate bodies. In some cases there would seem to be an absence of transport pricing policy altogether.

> . . . in most developing countries, governments do not charge the users of roads, ports, airports, etc. adequately for the cost of these services through fuel taxes, license fees, tolls or other charges.

And as a matter of fact, it would be almost impossible to generalise the set of port pricing policies which have at some time or other been adopted, modified, and sometimes totally revised by individual ports throughout the world. [1]

An optimal tariff structure must nevertheless give due consideration to the behaviour of the port users. If a shipping agent faces an increase in port tariff or other increases in costs incurred by the operation of vessels, he may take any one (or a combination) of the following steps. Firstly, pass the increase on to the consumers (freight rate increase). Second, pass the increase on to the suppliers (traders). Third, absorb the increased cost in his freight structure at the expense of his profit (profit squeeze). Fourth, switch the shipping route to a cheaper one, if there is any alternative (traffic diversion). And finally, reduce the operating frequency of vessels to attain a higher load factor, in pursuit of cheaper cost per unit of cargo. Port management should be aware of all such options open to shippers, not only qualitatively but also as close as possible to reality in quantitative terms, bearing in mind that the shippers' behaviour will be dependent also on the price elasticity of demand in the market.

If there were no congestion and no delays in port, the shippers could derive their freight rate per ton of cargo for the shipment of goods solely from the incurred costs — fuel consumed by the ship, wages for crews, ship depreciation costs, interest, and so on. (See the ship journey cost model in chapter 2). But because of the steady growth of the world economy, at least up until the energy crisis in 1973, and the spectacular increase in (import) demands on the limited port facilities in some oil-exporting countries after 1973, it has become a commonplace for ports to face serious congestion problems. This in turn has driven some powerful shippers to press the port authorities for appropriate compensation for the delays. Obviously, the longer a ship has to wait for services while a port is congested, the more the cost incurred, and thus the higher the cost per ton of cargo. It should be noted, however, that the daily increase in costs for a single ship awaiting servicing is entirely independent of the value of the cargo; and that such delays will have an especially detrimental effect on the shipment of cargoes of low value per unit weight since the proportion of the increase of the price is relatively large. Port management can turn to any of three alternatives. First, simply increase the port tariff without changing the productivity of the port, which would have the effect of rationing the facilities. Second, build new facilities in order to accommodate more traffic, and thus eventually reduce congestion. Finally, though undesirable and temporary a measure it may be, pay compensation for the congestion to shippers.

A remarkable example of the third alternative is found in Nigeria, where the government was forced in 1975 to create a compensation fund, and consequently advertised widely an appeal for co-operation from the shippers not to despatch additional vessels to Nigeria without first getting confirmation that they could be serviced. As one might expect, such a measure seems to be effective only temporarily; and as regards the port development scheme in the long run, new investment should be introduced for expansion.

It goes without saying that some decision must be reached with respect to the first and second alternatives above, in order to provide a sound basis for the long-term development of the port. One example of an attempt to increase port revenues by modifying tariff policy is found in Japan, where an official act of 1953 authorised port authorities throughout the country to collect harbour charges. From the outset, however, there was formidable opposition to the enforce-

161

ment of this provision from port users, who always argued that the effect of such charges would be a kind of double taxation on them, adding significantly to the existing dues on goods as well as the dues for berthing and other services rendered to them. Largely as a result of this opposition, the provision lay dormant for more than twenty years. But the eight biggest port authorities in Japan recently disclosed their intention to impose harbour charges from the beginning of 1976 on every ship over five hundred tons. Faced with imminent financial difficulties, and seriously pressed by ever rising costs, the port authorities have tried to justify their economically logical action by pointing out that the new tariff is to cover the costs of dredging, of scavenging the surface of the waters in the immediate vicinity of the ports, and of improving port environment by surrounding the docks with newly planted greenery. It should be noted that, because of recent outcries against industrial pollution of many sorts in Japan, any proposals for environmental protection and beautification are guaranteed instant popular support, which industry naturally finds it awkward to oppose in a direct fashion. The port authorities' proposals are thus probably calculated to help reduce the overt opposition which might otherwise be expected from port users.

The Yokohama Port Authority estimates that if a charge of two or three yen per ton were introduced under this scheme, the additional annual revenue would amount to two or three hundred million yen (roughly £350,000 to £550,000 at early 1976 exchange rates), since about 27,500 of the 100,000 vessels annually calling at the port are reported to exceed 400 tons. [2] A new tariff scheme was finally negotiated among the various parties concerned, and is expected to be implemented by the end of 1976. [3]

A similar move has been under way recently in Britain as well. At the beginning of 1976 it was publicly announced that

> The British Transport Docks Board, rare among nationalized industries in that it has consistently made a profit, intends to put up its charges in order to make a higher return on assets. [4]

It was reported that the Board now intends to push up its target for return on capital from the current 9 per cent to one of 10 per cent, partly by imposing more robust charges, but primarily through greater efficiency.

Marginal cost pricing

It would be most logical for the port pricing policy to be based on the costs of the particular goods and services rendered. A major consideration in pricing policy is the question of marginal cost.

> The suggestion of marginal-cost pricing in public utilities in a mixed economy appears to have been first made by Professor Hotelling in his article, 'The General Welfare in Relation to Problems of Taxation and of Railway and Utility Rates' (in *Econometrica*, July 1938). [5]

And it has long been argued that

> . . . no approach to utility pricing can be considered truly rational which does not give an important and even a major weight to marginal cost considerations. [6]

But, from the outset, there has been considerable reluctance to deal with marginal cost pricing without some reservations, as the same author admits.

> . . . the principle of marginal cost pricing is not in practice to be followed absolutely and at all events, but is a principle that is to be followed insofar as this is compatible with other desirable objectives, and from which deviations of greater or lesser magnitude are to be desired when conflicting objectives are considered. [7]

One author, writing a few years earlier, had even gone so far as to declare that

> Administrative impossibility, fluctuating prices, and the leaving of an enormous number of small but indivisible changes to the whim of the manager, combine to make marginal-cost pricing impossible in the case of transport. [8]

Enlarging upon this viewpoint, another author pointed out that

> Public policy must be presumed to seek in some sense the general welfare, and hence in the economic sphere it implies a welfare economics. [9]

> Monopoly elements are built into the economic system and the ideal necessarily involves them. Thus wherever there is a demand for diversity of product, pure competition turns out to be not the ideal but a departure from it. Marginal cost pricing no longer holds as a principle of welfare economics (not even for toll bridges); nor is the minimum point on the cost curve for the firm to be associated with the ideal. [10]

It is easy to see the disadvantage of the strict application of marginal cost pricing from the viewpoint of both suppliers and consumers, since

> In so far as there are short-term fluctuations in demand for transport services over time, strict application of marginal cost pricing would be likely to imply substantial changes in prices. [11]

Such frequent changes in prices obviously not only place a burden on the port authority in terms of administrative complications, but also are highly undesirable for port users in assessing their business policies, especially when transport costs play a significant role in the profitability of their businesses and future investment.

Moreover, the adoption of marginal cost pricing must ensure that service-suppliers with decreasing costs be paid subsidies, to enable them to cover their total costs. This raises the difficult question of devising a suitable method for financing such subsidies without violating the marginal conditions.

Since a port provides various types of services and thus the estimation of the marginal cost of the port operations is manifold, it could be the cost of providing extra labour, extra handling equipment, extra storage capacity etc. in order to serve the marginal increase of the traffic. Moreover, users are likely to make use of mixed services (pilotage, quay handling, cargo transfer, storage, etc.), it would seem hardly advisable to apply strict marginal cost pricing across the board, apart from the administrative complications and inconveniences to the users. If a port operating with decreasing cost is expected to be autonomous and commercially viable, without state subsidies or other forms of aid, it may be necessary to adopt a price discriminatory scheme. Although this would result in some degree of cross-subsidisation, it might still be advisable, providing the distortion can be held to a minimum. This would involve setting the tariff higher than the marginal cost for some of the subsystems (for example the direct route, if its elasticity of demand were relatively low), while at the same time setting a tariff lower than the marginal cost for other subsystems (where the elasticity is relatively high). Insofar as the extent of the departure from the strict overall marginal cost pricing does not greatly upset the marginal conditions relative to other industries, this tariff policy could be the second best alternative, since by adopting such a scheme the port could collect enough revenue to cover costs and thus survive as a viable enterprise.

The port operating under decreasing cost function can choose among three basic alternatives in order at least to break even without subsidies. The first is a close modification based in principle on the strict application of marginal cost pricing, but designed to avoid the otherwise inevitable operating cost losses. Such a modification would involve across-the-broad increases for all subsystems, each in proportion to its own marginal cost. In the second, the elasticity of demand would vary among the different subsystems. And since an across-the-board increase as suggested above would most likely not result in the desirable break-even point, then the type of discriminatory pricing scheme discussed above would become necessary. In order to circumvent the cross-subsidisation necessitated by the second alternative, however, a third alternative might be to increase the fixed cost (e.g. port dues) applicable equally to everyone, to a level sufficient to cover foreseeable losses, while maintaining a marginal cost pricing policy for all other costs. This third alternative might draw complaints from shippers because of the high level of port dues in comparison to other ports. But everyone would nonetheless be paying equal amounts. And such a scheme might be advisable, providing the traffic demand for the port facilities is rather inelastic.

Average cost pricing

The variants of marginal cost pricing cannot get away from rejection by the proponents of marginal cost pricing on the grounds of being too complex and actual operational impossibility. Thus even the proponents themselves show their doubts. The proponents of marginal cost pricing, however, while arguing that their own pricing is theoretically optimal, doubtless realise that they themselves are caught up in arguments against marginal cost pricing on precisely the same grounds.

> ... because of this difficulty in raising the revenue required to finance the subsidies, pricing system which would in themselves meet total costs has been proposed as alternatives to marginal cost pricing. [12]

One of the alternatives to marginal cost pricing is the so-called full cost pricing, more often called 'average cost pricing'. Those who support this system stress the point that suppliers (producers) ought to cover the production cost [13], while the proponents of marginal cost pricing seek to achieve an optimal allocation of resources for the sake of the society. Although average cost pricing is usually easier to implement in practice than marginal cost pricing, some firms may not be able to survive under average cost pricing. And the selection of the 'fair return' — which often makes reference to the prevailing market interest rate, the prevailing rate of return of firms, and so on —

is by no means easy. There is also the argument that

> ... doubtless average cost pricing is sometimes misused to
> serve the businessman's interests badly. High prices are
> charged because costs are high at current low output levels —
> without consideration of the possibility that lower prices
> can increase volume and so may reduce unit costs. [14]

Average cost pricing does, nonetheless offer certain advantages in some cases. It tends to maximise throughput, subject to the constraint that revenue must equal costs. [15] Such a pricing policy therefore would seem adequate especially for ports of underdeveloped countries where the overriding objective should be the economic growth of the country, as contrasted to other financial objectives such as profitability and/or the transport co-ordination of the integrated system commonly set by Western countries.

Hybrid pricing policy

While marginal cost pricing schemes are meant to optimise social benefits, and average cost pricing aims to allow the enterprise at least to break even, one should remember that ports as a public service industry are in a peculiar position. They are not necessarily entirely under the thumb of government, nor can they be regarded as purely profit-seeking private firms. One can therefore not recommend a pricing policy which would regard the port as a profit maximiser. As regards marginal cost pricing, it is usually difficult, if not impossible, to appraise the multiplier effect of the port on the economy in general. Although marginal cost pricing is an enticing theory, in practice it is very difficult to appraise socially marginal cost in its true sense. As regards average cost pricing, the port can only be regarded as a quasi-public or quasi-private industry, which suggests that a hybrid pricing policy would be more realistic in order to derive the best advantages of both worlds.

Port authorities nonetheless generally fall within the public sector, partly because of the nature of port functions as public facilities, and also partly due to the fact that port investment and operations involve enormous sums of money. Port authorities, while naturally concerned with the question of profits, are not necessarily profit-orientated. Although it is rare for the financial objectives of ports to be clearly defined (or at least to be made publicly known), they often do exist.

It can be shown that the price should be set lower than marginal cost, if the utility function of the firm is a weighted average of the two (i.e. output and profits), while the pure profit-maximiser seeks to set his price equal to the marginal cost.

> This consideration suggests that the more output-oriented the firm, the greater will be its marginal cost at equilibrium. [16]

The hidden assumption here is, of course, that the firm is in a purely competitive market, so that its output does not affect the aggregate demand, and thus also not the price of its product.

It may be interesting to extend this analysis to such an enterprise as a port which in most cases enjoys some sort of monopolistic power. Moreover, it is natural to think that a port, because of its nature in providing service facilities to the public and in playing a significant role in the national economy, concerns itself with output as well as profits under ordinary circumstances. Though one should by no means jump to the conclusion that the objective of a port is the weighted average of these two, the following analysis yields some informative suggestions.

Suppose that the objective (utility) of the port is

$$U = a\Phi + (1 - a) \cdot \Psi \tag{8.1}$$

where Φ is throughput, Ψ profits, U the utility and where $0 \leqslant a \leqslant 1$. Denoting the total cost of producing Φ units per annum by $C(\Phi)$, and given the demand curve $\Pi = D(\Phi)$, the port profit Ψ is

$$\Psi = \Phi \cdot D(\Phi) - C(\Phi) \tag{8.2}$$

From equations 8.1 and 8.2 we get

$$U = a\Phi + [1 - a] [\Phi \cdot D(\Phi) - C(\Phi)] \tag{8.3}$$

By differentiating equation 8.3 with respect to the level of throughput, and setting this equal to zero, then

$$\frac{\partial U}{\partial \Phi} = a + (1 - a) \left\{ \frac{\partial}{\partial \Phi} [\Phi \cdot D(\Phi)] - \frac{\partial C(\Phi)}{\partial \Phi} \right\} = 0 \tag{8.4}$$

And this is equivalent to

$$\frac{\partial C(\Phi)}{\partial \Phi} = \frac{\partial [\Phi \cdot D(\Phi)]}{\partial \Phi} + \frac{a}{1 - a} \tag{8.5}$$

Equation 8.5 does not give the optimum value of Φ straight away unless the two functions are known; yet what the equation means is quite clearly explained. Since $\frac{\partial C(\Phi)}{\partial \Phi}$ is the marginal cost (MC) to the port at throughput Φ, and $\frac{\partial [\Phi \cdot D(\Phi)]}{\partial \Phi}$ is nothing more than the

167

marginal revenue (MR) to the port at the same throughput Φ, then equation 8.5 means that the optimum is reached where the following condition holds:

$$MC = MR + \frac{a}{1-a} \tag{8.6}$$

If $a = 0$, which means the port is concerned only with profit maximising, equation 8.6 becomes

$$MC = MR \tag{8.7}$$

This, of course, is a well known argument for a monopolistic profit maximiser. If $a = 1$, which means the port is concerned only with its throughput, then equation 8.6 suggests that marginal cost will be infinite; and the port will try to increase throughput as much as possible with no regard to constraints on costs.

The general form of the marginal cost (MC) and the average cost (AC) curves, along with the Demand (DD) and the Marginal Revenue (MR) curves, is shown in figure 8.1, in reference to which the following observations might usefully be made.

1   The four points on the demand curve (T, S, F, E) are equilibrium points for the four pricing policies which might be adopted, showing the volume of traffic which can be expected for each with respect to tariffs. For example, Scheme 1, with port dues fixed at level π_1 (£/ton) should realise a throughput of Φ_1 (tons/year).

2   Since port demand is often relatively inelastic, tariff Scheme 1 tends to be viewed with considerable opposition, on the ground that it will lead to an undesirable level of monopoly profit.

3   If the AC curve were to remain above the demand curve (DD) over the whole range of throughput (perhaps because of an enormous capital outlay and also the co-existence of competing transport industries), then the port would be subject to an operating loss, no matter what tariff policy it were to adopt. And this situation would necessitate a subsidy.

4   The curves in figure 8.1 are such that the intersection points produce rectangles, the areas of which represent profits $AVT\pi_1 > BWS\pi_2 > CGF\pi_3$. π_4 does not form part of a rectangle, because this is a non-profit case.

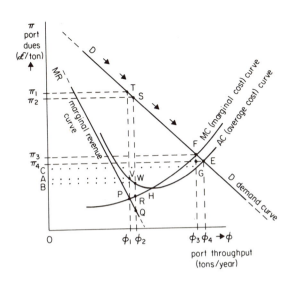

N.B. $\overline{QR} = \frac{a}{1-a}$ and since there is only one segment where MC
exceeds MR by exactly this value, the position of this segment
determines Φ_2.

Figure 8.1 Shift of tariff-throughput equilibrium with respect to
four pricing policies

Equation 8.6 suggests that the port should be operated at through-
put Φ_2 if the weight is a $(0 < a < 1)$, where $\overline{QR} = \frac{a}{1-a}$. In other
words, the port should adopt tariff Π_2, which is lower than the
tariff Π_1 determined by the pure profit maximising condition
MR = MC. The more the port places stress upon throughput, the more
the optimum equilibrium moves downwards to the right along curve
$\overline{DD}$, as shown by the arrows in figure 8.1.

If the relative positions of these curves are such as given in figure
8.1, the Profit Maximising Policy suggests throughput Φ_1 with profit
$AVT\pi_1$. The Output Maximising Policy, with the constraint that
revenue equals cost, gives throughput Φ_4 with zero profit. While

169

Marginal Cost Pricing gives throughput Φ_3 with profit $CGF\pi_3$. (If the port is operated under a decreasing cost structure at this throughput level Φ_3, there occurs an operating loss). And the Mixed Strategy Pricing with weight a gives Φ_2 with profit $BWS\pi_2$.

The throughput Φ_2 lies, of course, between the profit maximising Φ_1 and the output maximising Φ_4. One should not place too much emphasis on these results in practice, because the assumed utility function is the weighted average of two fundamentally different things; and the port is unlikely to set its operation target so clearly as this. Nonetheless, the argument is pregnant with implications and practical suggestions.

At any rate, for the design of a pricing scheme to be optimal in welfare terms, one cannot evade the key issue of interpersonal comparisons of utility, since the revenue, in whatever way it is gained, is not necessarily collected from the people who consume the products (services) of decreasing cost industries, but may, rather, be imposed upon those who, while contributing to the necessary subsidies, do not benefit from these industries.

> The various sectors of the economy differ from one another in the restrictions which they impose on the pricing system, and what is appropriate for one sector may be completely inappropriate for another. No one formula can be established which will be valid as a general principle. [17]

In devising an optimal port tariff scheme, one should first determine whether the port is in keen competition with other transport modes, or commands monopolistic power, and also whether the port is expected to be autonomous (and thus expected at least to break even) or is considered to be just a part of a whole integrated system with subsidies available. Apart from these basic propositions, there are numerous factors to be considered, among which the following are the most important.

1   A clear breakdown of costs incurred, with reference to the type of services rendered, is necessary if the tariff is to be imposed in such a way that users pay for services, in proportion no more no less to what they consume, so that no cross-subsidisation distorts the optimal usage of port facilities.

2   One must have an appraisal of demand characteristics for the port facilities, so that no heavy capacity constraints occur in one subsystem while an abundant slack capacity leads to idleness in another.

3   The port cost structure should be considered with other systems (maritime and inland transport) present in the blue-print as well, since the port transport is only the intermediary phase of the whole integrated transport system of the economy.

Pricing policy with a shifting demand curve

It is a common phenomenon for ports to be faced with continuous traffic growth and therefore a constantly increasing demand for port facilities. In many ports around the world today which are faced with this problem, the expansion may be due merely to the expansion of national or regional economic activity; and in some cases, particularly in the Arab and the central African world, enormous upsurges in imports have been encouraged and even promoted by the governments themselves. A serious problem will occur — as has often been the case in the regions mentioned — when the traffic eventually exceeds the maximum of the handling capacity. Unless remedial measures are taken immediately, the excess traffic will either have to suffer a delay through waiting for services or else it will have to be diverted, to other ports or to alternative transport modes.

There is, of course, a desperate need for transport and communications in developing economies experiencing the phase-transition of the economy — e.g. from agriculture to industry or from industry to trade. As the economy develops, it sees a shift of employment from the primary industry (agriculture) to the secondary (industry) and to the tertiary (services), with trade becoming important. An inadequacy in the transport and communications systems will stand in the way of rapid growth. The importance of this is comparatively greater than in the more mature economies, where transport requirements increase at a lower rate than in developing economies, and in general have a more proportionate relationship with the growth of GNP.

In theory port management could expand existing facilities as much as they like, or even reconstruct and reshape the whole system completely in order to meet the future traffic profile. In practice, of course, port management is never free of the multifarious (and frequently inharmonious) restraints placed upon it, and is always under obligation to give consideration to financial, geographical, technological and even political factors in making any major decisions. It is desirable for management to keep expansion well in hand at all times, to avoid unrestrained increases in demand on port facilities.

And so, management may find itself favouring a somewhat 'negative' option for expansion, by adopting a strategy which allows existing facilities to be increased by only certain units, doing so with a view towards restricting the growth of traffic which, without active restraints, may be statistically forecast to lead to disastrous congestion.

The question which arises is, what kind of pricing policy should be introduced? It must recoup the capital outlay involved, and also be designed to achieve the financial objectives of the port. In order to fix a new tariff system, it will be vital to know the shape of the demand curve for the user of the port. And this is no easy task, because even if one were so optimistic as to expect to find the right kind of data for constructing the curve, there would still remain the formidable task of estimating the set of curves both with and without investment for expansion. Unfortunately, little published research in this connection has yet appeared.

One work on the subject by B. Metaxas examines the supply and demand for tramp shipping services. [18] He concludes that the consumer demand elasticities for the final goods, which are produced from the bulk materials transported by the steamers (possibly excepting timber), tend in fact to be inelastic. He points out furthermore that the smaller the cost of sea transport as a proportion of the total cost of the final goods, the more inelastic the demand for the transport of the raw materials. A World Bank report notes in the more general context that

> ... the elasticity of demand for transport is determined mainly by the elasticity of demand for the things being transported, and by the proportion of transport costs in the value of the delivered product. ... Investigations in developed economies suggest that transportation costs are not a significant proportion of the final price of most manufactured and some mining products (the average is less than 10 per cent) .... The situation is radically different in less developed economies where a larger proportion of the economically important movements are likely to be high-bulk, low-value agricultural and mineral products. The thresholds of viable production or export of these primary products are often determined by externally defined prices. Transport costs on the feeder roads, on the trunk road or railway to the coast, through the port, and on the ship to foreign markets often account for as much as 50 per cent of the receipts from these commodities. [19]

The conclusions derived from the tramp shipping report noted above seem to hold true for the traffic to the port. And one might summarise the generally applicable aspects as follows.

1   It is reasonably expected that the smaller the port dues (cargo dues, vessel dues, etc.) as a proportion of the price of the final goods, the more inelastic will be the demand for the port facilities.

For a country such as Japan, considerably distant from her trading partners (for instance 12,000 kilometres from the Persian Gulf), the ratio of the marine transport cost to the price of the import goods (for instance raw materials) is *relatively* high. The following table expresses the transport cost of two such raw materials as a percentage of the price of the imports to Japan for a period of a decade.

Table 8.1

Transport cost as a percentage of cost of oil and iron ore imports to Japan, 1963 and 1972 (cif prices) [20]

	1963		1972
oil	31%	→ down to →	21%
iron ores	41%	→ down to →	32%

The substantial decrease in terms of this ratio between 1963 and 1972 is, as is explained in the article dealing with the question in the report from which the table is taken, attributed to the technological rationalisation which had taken place during this period — i.e. economies of scale due to increases in ship size, specialisation of ships, and so forth.

If the proportion of the transport cost (which consists, roughly speaking, of freight charges plus port expenses) relative to the price of imported commodities is, say, 20 per cent, even a 10 per cent increase in the port dues is shown to have little effect upon the transport cost and therefore upon the price of the import commodities.

Suppose that the port expenses (of which port dues might amount to 30 per cent, fuel 40 per cent, and others including crew wages 30 per cent) assume about 25 per cent of the total transport cost, of which about 30 per cent is for port dues, then a 10 per cent increase in port dues results in a $0.25 \times 0.1 \times 0.3 = 0.0075$ increase in the transport cost and a $0.0075 \times 0.2 = 0.0015$ increase in the price of the import goods. Roughly speaking, then: tariff up 10 per cent → → price up 0.1 or 0.2 per cent.

2   The more monopolistic the port is because of geographical advantages or for political reasons (such as governmental encourage-

ment), the more inelastic will be the demand.

3   The elasticity of demand depends in part upon the availability of substitutes, which in this case requires alternative means of transport such as other ports close by, road transport, air transport, and so forth.

4   Elasticity of demand further depends upon the quantitative importance of the port dues relative to costs met by the shippers, such as storage costs.

State subsidies and the productivity of ports

In order to identify practices and policies in need of improvement, it would seem most practical and meaningful to make some valid comparisons among ports which can be shown to have a reasonable number of physical characteristics in common, while still exhibiting differing kinds of output. The output (or productivity) of a port can be expressed in terms of either throughput or money. The first can be measured by the physical quantities actually handled per year — general and bulk cargo (measured in tonnage), container boxes (measured by pieces), and so forth. The second can be measured by the annual turnover or by 'value added' (port output produced, minus input used). Money is, in some ways, the less useful of the two measures, for the simple reason that heavily subsidised ports may in fact show a 'negative output' in simple money terms, if we subtract operating costs from revenues received (the negative value being made up by state subsidies). It seems nonetheless useful to give at least brief attention to both aspects, for the potential improvements in some ports which they may bring to light.

In view of the enormous variety of port types, it would be almost impossible to determine a general formula which would indicate productivity in respect to every port with only negligible bias. A few studies of a comparative nature have nonetheless been attempted. A Ministry of Transport (UK) paper of some years ago briefly took up the question of the changing nature of relative costs at British and continental ports. It pointed out that in 1930 the Royal Commission on Transport had felt that

> The figures and evidence given to us all tended to show that the charges in Continental ports are considerably lower than those in British ports, and it was suggested to us that this is accounted for to a large extent by the advantageous physical conditions prevailing abroad. [21]

174

Whatever were the criteria on which this observation was based, the report concludes that more than thirty years afterwards the same trend with regard to charging held true. Despite the differences in port size, types of ship, types of cargo, the labour situations, and geographical positions which had to be taken into account, the Ministry of Transport in 1962

> found that over a variety of ships and cargoes the cheapest
> British port in each case was on average just under twice as
> expensive, and the dearest British port more than three and
> a half times as expensive as the cheapest Continental one. [22]

The report goes on to elaborate on the earlier opinion, indicating that, in addition to the natural physical advantages enjoyed by many European ports, the continental ports served an extensive hinterland which had come to be characterised in the post-war years by 'steady growth and high productivity' and moreover, unlike any British port (in 1962 when the report was completed, at least), the continental ports enjoyed liberal government subsidies.

Similar conclusions are found in the National Ports Council's *Comparison of the Costs of Continental and British Ports* [23]. The NPC concludes in brief by showing that continental ports, in marked contrast to their British counterparts, enjoy extensive financial assistance provided to them in a variety of ways. The report concentrates upon the ports of Rotterdam, Dunkirk, Hamburg and Antwerp, all receiving considerable financial assistance from the state. It is noted, moreover, that the only subsidies received 1967-71 by any United Kingdom port were the Port Modernisation Grant and the Investment Grant, affecting the ports of London, Southampton and Bristol under comparison in the report. These grants did not in fact make a great deal of difference to the finances of the three ports mentioned, owing to the paucity of the grants in comparison to actual investment required. It is then demonstrated that, as a result of their subsidies, continental ports are able to set their charges at levels considerably lower than those which would be necessary were they to operate under the same financial conditions and disciplines as those in the United Kingdom.

There are, however, a variety of criticisms against such subsidies. Among them, probably the most prominent one is that, since subsidies are to be paid out of the public purse, there seems to occur a cross-subsidisation to the consumers by the non-consumers of the industry, in the form of various types of taxes.

> All too often . . . subsidies come from general tax revenue and
> there is no way of knowing which particular source of

taxation to assign to a particular subsidy. It is then tacitly assumed that there is no distortion (or loss of consumers' benefit) to set against the advantages produced by the subsidy. [24]

And moreover,

As Samuelson has pointed out, it is not easy to devise a tax or subsidy which will not affect the marginal conditions, so that it is extremely difficult to change the distribution of income from that which a pricing system automatically yields without violating the marginal condition. [25]

One common observation is that

... it may be argued possibly with some justification, that subsidisation, even when the subsidy is fixed, tends to make managers think that costs do not matter very much, and tends to make them careless about efficiency. [26]

According to this reasoning, state subsidies are bound to be linked on the part of management with expectations of security and further aid, which is thought to lead to inefficiency in the industry through lack of managerial incentive.

The forms which the subsidy may take are numerous. We might break down the cost structure of a typical port in so far as it relates to productivity into the three basic categories and subcategories of capital investment, labour and land as given below. A port often does not have to pay interest or any depreciation charges on the assets with which it is provided, while it may also enjoy capital subsidies by the state, as in the case of Antwerp.

Major port investment factors relating to productivity

Capital

1   Initial construction costs (breakwaters, locks, berths, quays, transit sheds, warehouses)

2   Continuing construction costs (maintenance of real properties, dredging, widening channels)

3   Purchase of capital equipment (tug boats, lighters, cranes, straddle carriers, tractors, forklift trucks, computers)

4   Continuing capital equipment costs (maintenance and replacement of equipment)

Labour

1. Production per head (manning levels used to achieve the existing level of productivity)
2. Unit labour cost (total wage bill, divided by throughput)

Land

1. Purchase cost of land, including land reclamation
2. Rental of land
3. Maintenance cost of land (tends to be relatively negligible, but may assume important proportions where environmental standards have to be upgraded)

State taxation policies

1. Relative to capital equipment
2. Relative to wages
3. Relative to real estate

In some cases the state may also bear some portion of the cost of quays, quay walls and dry docks, as in Dunkirk, or the cost of dredging (as in Hamburg), or the cost of sea dykes and breakwaters (as in Rotterdam). In addition, some ports' operating losses may be borne every year by the state itself, as in the case of Antwerp. Generous grants of land, and light taxation on real estate, may provide another incalculable boost to the port's ability to expand and develop.

The wage bill, probably the most crucial factor in the year-to-year operating costs, once the port is fully operative, may differ greatly from country to country. Pressure for pay claims in countries with highly developed social services are probably kept lower than might otherwise be expected, depending on factors totally independent of the port's control — national policies towards wage controls, income taxes, social security payments and benefits, the level of unemployment, and so on. In a very indirect sense, general social benefits which help to reduce wage pressure among port labour do, in fact, act as a form of state 'subsidy' (though not particularly for the port's benefit *per se*) in reducing potential operating costs. One should observe here, also, that the total wage bill is the labour cost required to achieve a certain throughput. The unit labour cost, while being a useful measure of the relative cheapness of the port, is by no means a measure of port efficiency, simply because one port can offer efficiency together with cheap labour, whereas another may be both expensive as well as inefficient.

The NPC report mentioned above also suggests that much further study is required in respect to comparisons among ports, especially along the following lines.

1   Ultimate effects of subsidies, whether given to all or concentrated on relatively few ports, and the risks of excessive provision of port facilities.

2   The extent to which other forms of central assistance are relevant, e.g. light dues, regional policies, labour policies.

3   The relative effectiveness of financial assistance direct to industry, as compared to such assistance given to ports.

The third question goes far beyond the scope of the present work; and the second is taken up in parts elsewhere. But we might usefully examine here the first of these in further detail.

The four continental ports mentioned above are relatively close together along the same seacoast, and all serve essentially the same vast hinterland of north-western Europe, by way of highly developed systems of railways, roads, and inland waterways.

> . . . Continental ports benefit from an extensive international hinterland which is served by a modern inland transport network and where steady growth and high productivity have been marked features of the post-war years. [27]

They are thus in direct competition with one another for through traffic, as well as each for its own place in the industrial development of the region. It is natural for a country to view a particular port, under these conditions, as an integral part of the economy of its region and not necessarily as an enterprise which is a commercially viable entity of itself. British ports, by contrast, are generally expected to be self-supporting. The total amount of goods through the British ports is suspected to be rather inelastic to tariff change, because the proportion of the port cost is relatively small, and there are few alternatives anyway. In the absence of any non-British competitor ports, the external benefits accruing from the state subsidies are expected to be minor, whereas among the continental ports they are expected to be comparatively great because of the 'floating' traffic, the volume of which in any one port is very much affected by the tariffs of the competitor ports. Of course, cheap production sites, more efficient shipping services, and better labour relations could be significant for the United Kingdom to induce foreign industries to re-site around British ports. But such considerations are, of course, far beyond the scope of this work.

178

If port revenues were increased in the continental ports to the point where they approximated more nearly the actual operating costs — which would probably entail raising charges to shippers — then the volume of shipping might become somewhat depressed. This is doubtless an eventuality which all the nations involved wish to avoid. These continental port authorities and their governments are obviously agreed that any loss incurred by the port operations them-selves, as a result of encouraging greater throughput by keeping costs to shippers as attractively low as possible, are greatly offset by the advantages to be gained in other sectors of the economy.

It is not within the scope of this work to show quantitatively the effects of higher throughput on the prosperity of the inland transport sector, the retail industry, and all industries dependent on an abundant supply of imported raw materials — just to name a few examples. But the general concept of this policy is nonetheless clear. State subsidies to ports can be regarded in one sense as a form of capital investment of the multiplier-effect variety, from which these other sectors reap proportionally great benefits. Any government desiring the best possible return on investment of this sort will have to base the types and quantities of subsidies as a matter of policy on the expected gains to be enjoyed by the other sectors, and not particularly with regard to the port alone.

Methods of comparing ports in terms of charges and productivity

The NPC report has adopted two particular methods for comparing the ports listed above. The first is to calculate the theoretical costs of a continental port, assuming that there were no capital subsidies and that all services associated with the port had to be paid for fully by the port itself. The general results of this method are illustrated concisely in table 8.2, suggesting the changes in port charges which would theoretically be necessary for the port to break even. The second method is to consider the effects on the costs of each United Kingdom port, assuming it were operated under the same subsidised financial conditions as the continental ports. Both methods cited here are the obverse and reverse of a single coin. The conclusion is that, just to break even without subsidies, the continental ports would have to earn revenues considerably higher (something on the order of 30 to 80 per cent higher), as indicated in table 8.2, than they do at present.

Table 8.2
Revenue required to break even (7 major European ports) after bearing full cost of port authority's operations [28] (percentages of actual revenue)

178% Hamburg
176% Antwerp
136% Dunkirk
129% Rotterdam
 97% Southampton
 96% Bristol
 95% London

N.B. 'Full cost' covers overhead as well as operating cost.

The figures given in the table must be taken with some reserve, however, firstly because without subsidies they would doubtless have to increase their charges, either to cover operating costs and capital costs, or else to enable them to invest in future expansion. One cannot expect *a priori* that the demand curve will be inelastic; hence an increase of 76 per cent in charges for Antwerp (theoretically to break even) might cause such a drastic diminution in the traffic volume that the port would still be operating at a loss because of a resultant general depression of the revenue. In any event, potential revenue cannot be sensibly estimated without a knowledge of price elasticity of the traffic demand, which itself is no easy task.

Secondly, the effects of subsidies in relation to the financial conditions of the ports are hard to quantify and even more difficult to use as criteria for comparing different ports, unless two ports selected for comparison are similar enough in terms of geographical position, handling capacity, types of ships and cargoes served, and so on. If, for example, one port is subsidised in such a way that some portion (say half) of the cost of quays is borne by the state, what would be the equivalent of this subsidy in terms of a second port which may be handling different types of cargo, using a dissimilar tariff structure, serving another hinterland (or at least other markets), and thus having different needs of its own? Should the second port be given a subsidy of half the cost of its quays? Or would a monetary subsidy of the same magnitude be more appropriate? Since quays are different in both type and cost, and since the handling rates of quay-side relative to the rest of the whole of the two systems would probably differ, and furthermore since equal amounts of money invested in different ways would not necessarily produce effects of equal magnitude on productivity anyway, neither possibility seems to satisfy the equivalence requirement.

Thirdly, a quantitative comparison would not be very significant, unless two ports were in direct competition in attracting the same types of traffic. Unless the major share of the traffic handled in a port originates from, or is destined for, some particular regions which overlap with those served by the other port, the traffic is unlikely to switch from one port to the other merely upon consideration of differences in charges.

It should be noted, in reference to the Ministry of Transport and NPC reports, that these conditions do not much apply to the ports of Britain, except in so far as supplying the British hinterland is concerned, since British ports can rarely be considered in direct competition with ports on the continent. But there are isolated cases where the question of costs in a British port in comparison to those of a continental port can emerge. Some British North Sea oil is already flowing to Norwegian ports because it is easier to build pipelines there than to the Scottish coast. Leaving aside the jobs and other benefits created by handling and refining the oil, one might suggest that British 'export' of this oil by way of a Norwegian or other port might bring greater profits to the oil industry than would export from a Scottish port, because of differences in charges.

Needless to say, subsidies in any form will certainly help a port relieve at least some portion of its financial burden. And if two ports of more or less the same size and type are in competition, the one which gets subsidies will of course be in a more advantageous position than the other. And it will also help contribute to an increase in the total traffic serving the hinterland. However, the order of magnitude of this increased traffic (hence increased revenue to the port) remains to be seen, until some reliable estimations of the potential traffic actually subject to changes in charges are to hand.

There is a pronounced danger in the argument that if only a port were to get a subsidy equal to that of another port, then it could achieve a level of performance close to the other. The cost structures of the two (share of capital costs, wage bills, land rents, etc.) may be totally different, as may the tariff elasticity of traffic demand, geographical factors, regional economic factors, and so on. If all these factors are taken into consideration with reasonable accuracy — for ports within similar categories — then some comparative analysis seems possible. In sum, finally, in appraising the financial structure of a port, it is of vital importance to place special emphasis on its tariff structure and the related responsiveness of the traffic using the port.

181

Notes

[1]   See for a full discussion, Ian Heggie's 'Charging for Port Facilities', *Journal of Transport Economics and Policy,* VIII/1, January 1974, pp 3-25.

[2]   *Nihon Keizai Shimbun*, 9 January 1976.

[3]   Ibid., 4 August 1976.

[4]   *The Guardian,* 28 January 1976.

[5]   I.M.D. Little, *A Critique of Welfare Economics*, 2nd edition, Oxford, 1973, p.185.

[6]   W. Vickrey, 'Marginal Cost Pricing' in D. Munby (ed.), *Transport*, Penguin, 1968, p.116. The essay was published originally in 1955.

[7]   Ibid., p.98

[8]   Little, *A Critique of Welfare Economics*, pp 195-6. This work was first published in 1950.

[9]   E.H. Chamberlin, 'Product Heterogeneity and Public Policy' in G.C. Archibald (ed.), *The Theory of the Firm, Selected Readings,* Penguin, 1971, p.191. The essay is reprinted from Chamberlin, *Towards a More General Theory of Value*, Oxford 1957.

[10]   Ibid., p.199.

[11]   A.R. Prest, *Transport Economics in Developing Countries, Pricing and Financing Aspects*, London 1969, p.24.

[12]   Nancy Ruggles, 'Recent Developments in the Theory of Marginal Cost Pricing' in R. Turvey (ed.), *Public Enterprise, Selected Readings*, Penguin, 1968, p.32.

[13]   Included in 'production cost' for private firms is the so-called 'fair return' to enable the firm to achieve an appropriate growth.

[14]   W.J. Baumol, 'On the Theory of Oligopoly' in Archibald (ed.), *The Theory of the Firm*, p.266

[15]   E. Ames, 'The Economic Theory of Output-Maximizing Enterprises' in ibid., pp 280-1.

[16]   Ames, op.cit., pp 272-3.

[17]   Nancy Ruggles, 'Recent Developments', p.43.

[18]   B.N. Metaxas, 'The Future of the Tramp Shipping Industry', *Journal of Transport Economics and Policy*, VI/3, September 1972, pp 271-80.

[19]   *World Bank Operations : Sectoral Programs and Policies*, p.144.

[20]   Source of table: *Nihon Kai un no Genkyo*, p.1, Japan Ministry of Transport, Tokyo, 1974.

[21]   Ministry of Transport, *Report of the Committee of Inquiry into the Major Ports of Great Britain*, p.72.

[22]   Ibid., p.73.

[23]   See also the NPC, *Summary of a Report to the National Ports Council by Touche Ross and Company*, London 1974, which is a shorter version of the above.

[24]   Thomson, *Modern Transport Economics*, p.136.

[25]   Ruggles, 'Recent Developments', p.23.

[26]   Little, *Critique of Welfare Economics*, pp 193-4.

[27]   Ministry of Transport, *Report of the Committee of Inquiry into the Major Ports of Great Britain*, p.73.

[28]   Table adapted from NPC, *Comparison of the Costs of Continental and British Ports — 1974*.

9 Strategies for port investment

Introduction

Materials do not last for ever. Equipment suffers from deterioration. New machines are destined to be replaced as they become obsolescent. There is hardly anything which remains unchanged for long. Economic activities experience cyclical ups and downs, as well as shifts in their patterns. The transition of an economy will be reflected upon the pattern of trade; and the importance of the infra-structure increases in weight as the economy develops, which in turn triggers off innovations in related technologies.

Investment doubtless plays a key role in the course of economic development and can take many forms. Whatever the form, the most important questions are whether the project is worthwhile carrying out, which one should be selected out of a number of alternatives, when to undertake and how large the size should be, and so on. Though none of these points seems easy to answer, investment with no regard to these questions is bound to result in the misallocation of scarce resources and the distortion of sound economic development.

The enumeration of costs and benefits is only one among the numerous things to be considered. There are all sorts of complications here especially in terms of measuring benefits accruing from invest-ment. In theory, the stream of future costs and benefits due to investment should be discounted at appropriate rates back to the present; and if the benefits exceed the costs, the project should be undertaken. In practice, however, it is not that simple. Apart from the difficulties in measuring benefits, there is the question of distribution of such benefits, which necessitates for example the task of appraising who are to be the beneficiaries. Furthermore, public investment projects doubtless give rise to questions of externalities assessment. In order to value the costs and benefits of a project, market prices are mostly used. But this approach is by no means immune from hot debate, particularly where market imperfections in consumer goods and production goods exist.

The choice of an appropriate discount rate is yet another big issue. There are abundant arguments about whether the market rate of interest serves as the closest representative to the marginal productivity of investment, or what should be the right social time preference rate? Or should there be any difference at all between the rates of interest adopted in the private and the public sectors? And so on and so forth.

It is beyond the scope of this study to discuss these problems in detail. The main part of this chapter is devoted to the investigation of investment co-ordination among the constituent subsystems, and to a simple example of the various policies possible in choosing projects, given the alternative technologies in the course of port expansion.

Investment co-ordination among subsystems in series

The bottleneck of the whole port system lies in the subsystem whose intrinsic capacity is the smallest of all. Faced with expansionary investment planning, therefore, it would be sensible to try to allocate the budget in such a way as to achieve a balanced improvement among all the constituent subsystems — or at least to close the imbalance gap as much as possible.

Let us consider a simple model first. Supposing there are two fundamental subsystems with existing intrinsic capacities ϕ_{A_0} and ϕ_{B_0}. The intrinsic capacity of the whole system is dictated by the smaller of the two, since the two are in series. Now, given the budget constraint I_s, what should be the most efficient allocation scheme? It will depend, of course, on the cost of expanding the facilities for each subsystem. There are two cases to be considered here. One is the case where the cost is proportionate to the scale (i.e. linear cost function); and the other is where there is economy of scale which, simply put, means 'the bigger the cheaper' per unit. Increasing the number of vehicles for a higher level of handling may fall in the former category, whereas the latter may be viewed more favourably for the expansion of warehousing.

Let us denote the two cost functions for Systems A and B by $\Psi_A(\phi_A)$ and $\Psi_B(\phi_B)$, respectively, and also suppose that the present capacities of these two subsystems are given by ϕ_{A_0} and ϕ_{B_0}. Without diminishing our generality, let us assume $\phi_{A_0} > \phi_{B_0}$ so that Subsystem B is the dictating bottleneck system at present. Thus $\Delta\phi_0 = \phi_{A_0} - \phi_{B_0}$ is the initial gap. Simply put, the problem is to ration the budget between these two subsystems in such a way that the new level of capacities of these two will be in balance. Formulating first the

185

Budget Constraint and then the Co-ordinating (Balance) Constraint, we get

$$\Psi_A(\phi_A) + \Psi_B(\phi_B) = I_s \qquad (9.1)$$

$$\phi_{A_0} + \phi_A = \phi_{B_0} + \phi_B \qquad (9.2)$$

where ϕ_A, $\phi_B \geqslant 0$. Equations 9.1 and 9.2 can be solved once the function forms of Ψ_A and Ψ_B are given. And if either ϕ_A or ϕ_B is found to be negative, from equations 9.1 and 9.2 the solution should be to allocate the total budget to whichever gives the non-negative value.

If both cost functions $\Psi_A(\phi_A)$ and $\Psi_B(\phi_B)$ are differentiable to the first order, equations 9.1 and 9.2 can generally be computed with a simple method such as Newton-Raphson. Denoting the computational sequence of each variable at stage k by ϕ_{Ak} and ϕ_{Bk}, the following relation is immediate.

$$\phi_{A(k+1)} = \phi_{Ak} - \frac{\Psi_A(\phi_{Ak}) + \Psi_B(\phi_{Bk}) - I_s}{\Psi'_A(\phi_{Ak}) + \Psi'_B(\phi_{Bk})} \qquad (9.3)$$

$$\phi_{B(k+1)} = \phi_{A(k+1)} + \phi_{A_0} - \phi_{B_0} \qquad (9.4)$$

where Ψ'_A and Ψ'_B designate the first order derivative of Ψ_A and Ψ_B. The convergence of the series ϕ_{Ak}, ϕ_{Bk} is guaranteed under such smooth monotone cost functions as shown in figure 9.1.

Linear cost function

If both are linear functions, then the solution requires no extensive computation. Suppose $\Psi_A(\phi_A)$ and $\Psi_B(\phi_B)$ are expressed for convenience as

$$\Psi_A(\phi_A) = k_A \phi_A \qquad (9.5)$$

$$\Psi_B(\phi_B) = k_B \phi_B \qquad (9.6)$$

where k_A and k_B are the unit costs of expansion for each subsystem. (Equations 9.5 and 9.6 assume strict linearity without a constant term; but this is not required for the basis of the following analysis.) From equations 9.1, 9.2, 9.5 and 9.6, we get

186

$$\phi_A = \frac{I_s + k_B(\phi_{B0} - \phi_{A0})}{k_A + k_B} \tag{9.7}$$

$$\phi_B = \frac{I_s + k_A(\phi_{A0} - \phi_{B0})}{k_A + k_B} \tag{9.8}$$

The initial 'capacity gap' between the existing facilities is $\Delta\phi_0 = \phi_{A_0} - \phi_{B_0}$ (if $\phi_{A_0} > \phi_{B_0}$). Therefore, the optimal budget allotment in this case is to allocate $\dfrac{k_A I_s + k_A k_B(\phi_{B0} - \phi_{A0})}{k_A + k_B}$ of the

total budget I_s to Subsystem A and $\dfrac{k_B I_s + k_A k_B(\phi_{A0} - \phi_{B0})}{k_A + k_B}$ to

Subsystem B. If, at the time of expansion, there were no imbalance between Subsystems A and B (i.e. if $\phi_{A_0} = \phi_{B_0}$), then this allocation rule means simply that one should allocate the budget to each subsystem in proportion to the unit cost of the two subsystems. One more point to note is that, if $I_s \leqslant k_B(\phi_{A_0} - \phi_{B_0})$, then the solution will be to allocate the entire budget to Subsystem B, since this means I_s is not big enough even to level up the capacity of Subsystem B in order to match that of Subsystem A.

Cost function with continuous economy of scale

Coming back to equations 9.1 and 9.2, a representation is given in figure 9.1 for the case where there is economy of scale. Curves K_A and K_B represent the cost functions of subsystems A and B. (The way they are shown here assumes continuous economy of scale; but the whole argument holds for a linear case as well). Curve K'_A is obtained by shifting the curve K_A by a distance of $\overline{OT}$ to the right along the ϕ_A, ϕ_B axis and K''_A is symmetric with curve K_A with respect to the same axis.

If $I_s \leqslant \overline{TU}$, the whole budget should be allocated to Subsystem B, where

$$\overline{TU} = \Psi_B(\phi_{A_0} - \phi_{B_0}) \tag{9.9}$$

This case means that the budget is too small even to level up the capacity of System B with that of System A at the time of expansion. More interesting, however, is the case where $I_s > \overline{TU}$ in general.

187

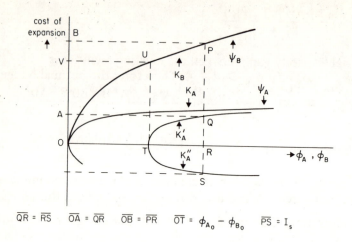

Figure 9.1 Graphical solution for finding optimal budget allotments

Supposing such monotone curves as in figure 9.1, the optimal capital allotment is given by finding a $\overline{PS}$ with the exact value of the budget I_s. $\overline{PS} = I_s$ means $\overline{PR} + \overline{RS} = I_s$, since $\overline{PR} = \Psi_B(\phi_B)$ and $\overline{RS} = \overline{QR} = \Psi_A(\phi_A)$. This gives the relation $\Psi_A(\phi_A) + \Psi_B(\phi_B) = I_s$, which satisfies equation 9.1. And since K'_A is drawn by shifting K_A by the distance $\overline{OT} = \phi_{A_0} - \phi_{B_0}$, therefore $\overline{OR} = \phi_B = \overline{OT} + \overline{TR} = \phi_{A_0} - \phi_{B_0} + \phi_A$, which satisfies equation 9.2. Thus, the optimal capital allotment is to give $\overline{OA}$ to System A and $\overline{OB}$ to System B.

Extension to pseudo-parallel channels

The case of only two systems in series has been treated in the previous section. But the budget allotment analysis can be extended in a similar way to many systems in series. However, a port is peculiar in the sense that it has subsystems not only in series but also in parallel —

188

for example, the two parallel alternatives, the direct route and the indirect route. Both routes have, nonetheless, one subsystem in common: the quay handling system. The chief reason for not separating the two routes entirely by providing separate quay handling systems is, simply, that it would be more expensive to do so. At any rate, since the two distinct routes have one subsystem in common, and each route has two subsystems in series, this peculiarity may be termed 'pseudo-parallel' channels, in contradistinction to the genuinely parallel channels.

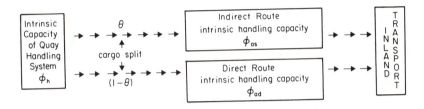

Figure 9.2   Handling systems intrinsic capacities

Leaving aside the inland transport system, which is mostly out of the port's control, let us denote the intrinsic capacity of the quay handling system by ϕ_h, that of the indirect route by ϕ_{as}, and that of the direct route by ϕ_{ad}, as shown in figure 9.2, and the cargo distribution ratio by θ. Given the existing capacities ϕ_{h_0}, ϕ_{as_0}, ϕ_{ad_0} (tons/annum), and the budget I_s, what should be the optimal capital allotment to achieve the maximum possible port throughput? Supposing the split ratio θ remains unchanged over the expansion period, [1] the intrinsic capacity of the indirect and direct routes should, in general, be matched to the expected flow of cargo through each subsystem. And, of course, no cargo can avoid the quay handling system. The following analysis reveals the most efficient means of investment, given an arbitrary budget.

With the cost functions of each subsystem denoted as $\Psi_1(\phi_h)$, $\Psi_2(\phi_{as})$, $\Psi_3(\phi_{ad})$, the problem can be formulated as

$$\Psi_1(\phi_h) + \Psi_2(\phi_{as}) + \Psi_3(\phi_{ad}) = I_s \tag{9.10}$$

189

$$\theta \, (\phi_{h_0} + \phi_h) = \phi_{as_0} + \phi_{as} \qquad (9.11)$$

$$(1 - \theta) \, (\phi_{h_0} + \phi_h) = \phi_{ad_0} + \phi_{ad} \qquad (9.12)$$

where ϕ_h , ϕ_{as} , $\phi_{ad} \geqslant 0$

If all three cost functions Ψ_1 , Ψ_2 , Ψ_3 are differentiable, the solution will be at hand again by such computational methods as Newton-Raphson.

Linear case

As before, for the sake of reasoning, let us consider a simple case where all the cost functions are linear (no economy of scale). Suppose we have simply

$$\left.\begin{aligned}
\Psi_1(\phi_h) &= k_1 \cdot \phi_h \\
\Psi_2(\phi_{as}) &= k_2 \cdot \phi_{as} \\
\Psi_3(\phi_{ad}) &= k_3 \cdot \phi_{ad}
\end{aligned}\right\} \qquad (9.13)$$

where k_1 , k_2 , k_3 are the unit costs for expansion of each subsystem. The equation 9.10 becomes

$$k_1 \cdot \phi_h + k_2 \cdot \phi_{as} + k_3 \cdot \phi_{ad} = I_s \qquad (9.14)$$

For simplicity, let us introduce new variables q_1 , q_2 , q_3 :

$$\left.\begin{aligned}
q_1 &= \frac{k_1}{I_s} \cdot \phi_h \\
q_2 &= \frac{k_2}{I_s} \cdot \phi_{as} \\
q_3 &= \frac{k_3}{I_s} \cdot \phi_{ad}
\end{aligned}\right\} \qquad (9.15)$$

Rewriting equations 9.10, 9.11 and 9.12, we then get

$$q_1 + q_2 + q_3 = 1 \qquad (9.16)$$

$$q_2 = a_1 + a_2 \cdot q_1 \qquad (9.17)$$

$$q_3 = \beta_1 + \beta_2 \cdot q_1 \qquad (9.18)$$

$$0 \leqslant q_1, q_2, q_3 \leqslant 1 \qquad\qquad (9.19)$$

where $a_1 = \dfrac{k_2}{I_s}(\theta \cdot \phi_{h_0} - \phi_{as_0})$, $a_2 = \theta \cdot \dfrac{k_2}{k_1}$,

$\beta_1 = \dfrac{k_3}{I_s}\left\{(1 - \theta) \cdot \phi_{h_0} - \phi_{ad_0}\right\}$, $\beta_2 = (1 - \theta) \cdot \dfrac{k_3}{k_1}$

Equation 9.19 means that the allotment to any one of the subsystems cannot exceed the budget and should, of course, be non-negative. All the points (q_1, q_2, q_3) which satisfy equations 9.16 and 9.19 can be nicely represented by an equilateral triangle such as the one following. Any point within or on the boundaries of $\triangle ABC$ (point P, for example) will satisfy equations 9.16 and 9.19, since $q_1 = \overline{CE}$, $q_2 = \overline{AF}$, $q_3 = \overline{BD}$ and since $\overline{CE} = \overline{PS} = \overline{DS}$ and $\overline{AF} = \overline{PT} = \overline{PE} = \overline{SC}$. Therefore, $q_1 + q_2 + q_3 = \overline{CE} + \overline{AF} + \overline{BD} = \overline{DS} + \overline{SC} + \overline{BD} = 1$.

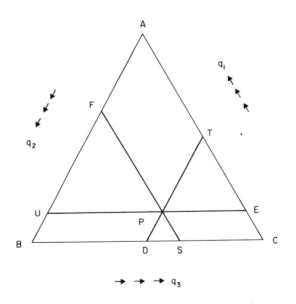

N.B. $\overline{AB} = \overline{BC} = \overline{CA} = 1$

191

Figure 9.3 provides an example where $\frac{k_2}{k_1} = 0.5$ and $\frac{k_3}{k_1} = 0.2$. That is, the unit cost in this case for expanding the quay handling system is double that for the indirect route, and five times as great as the cost for the direct route. For simplicity it is assumed that no capacity gap exists initially among the two link-ups (i.e. $\theta\phi_{h_0} = \phi_{as_0}$, and $(1 - \theta) \cdot \phi_{h_0} = \phi_{ad_0}$).

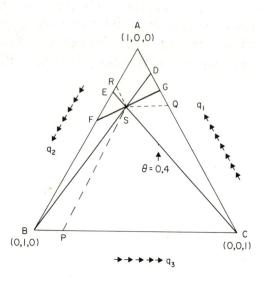

Figure 9.3   Figurative solution for finding optimal budget allotment

Point S gives the optimal allotment for the case of $\theta = 0.4$ (40 per cent of cargo flow using the indirect route and 60 per cent using the

192

direct route). Equation 9.17 becomes $q_2 = \theta \cdot \dfrac{k_2}{k_1} \cdot q_1 = 0.2\, q_1$.

Equation 9.18 becomes $q_3 = (1 - \theta) \cdot \dfrac{k_3}{k_1} \cdot q_1 = 0.12\, q_1$. The straight line $\overline{CE}$ is $q_2 = 0.2\, q_1$ (point C (0, 0, 1) is on this line). The straight line $\overline{BD}$ is $q_3 = 0.12\, q_1$ (point B (0, 1, 0) is on this line). The point S is the intersecting point of these two straight lines, i.e. $q_1 = \dfrac{25}{33}$, $q_2 = \dfrac{5}{33}$, $q_3 = \dfrac{3}{33}$. With the cargo distribution ratio $\theta = 0.4$, the optimal allocation is to allot the budget I_s by $\overline{CQ}$ $(= \dfrac{25}{33})$ to the quay handling system, $\overline{AR}$ $(= \dfrac{5}{33})$ to the indirect route system, and $\overline{BP}$ $(= \dfrac{3}{33})$ to the direct route system.

Now, another question is how should the optimal allocation be altered with a variance of the cargo distribution ratio θ? The optimal solution point corresponding to each value of θ can be found by the same procedure as in the case of finding point S for $\theta = 0.4$. However, the loci of these solutions can be readily found by a simple manipulation. Coming back to equations 9.17 and 9.18 again, leaving θ variable, we get

$$q_2 = 0.5\,\theta \cdot q_1 \tag{9.20}$$

$$q_3 = 0.2\,(1 - \theta) \cdot q_1 \tag{9.21}$$

The solution is given, therefore, in general together with equation 9.16.

$$q_1 = \frac{1}{1.2 + 0.3 \cdot \theta}, \quad q_2 = \frac{0.5\,\theta}{1.2 + 0.3 \cdot \theta}, \quad q_3 = \frac{0.2\,(1 - \theta)}{1.2 + 0.3 \cdot \theta} \tag{9.22}$$

Eliminating θ from equations 9.20 and 9.21, the loci is given by the equation

$$0.2\, q_1 - 0.4\, q_2 - q_3 = 0 \tag{9.23}$$

Equation 9.23 is shown by the straight line $\overline{FG}$ in figure 9.3. Point F is determined by setting $q_3 = 0$ (since the equation for $\overline{AB}$ is $q_3 = 0$), which is equivalent to $\theta = 1$. Therefore, from equation 9.23, $0.2\, q_1 - 0.4\, q_2 = 0$. Remembering $q_1 + q_2 + q_3 = 1$, point F is found as F $(\dfrac{2}{3}, \dfrac{1}{3}, 0)$. Point G is determined by setting $q_2 = 0$ (since the equation for $\overline{AC}$ is $q_2 = 0$), which is equivalent to $\theta = 0$. Therefore, from equation 9.23, $0.2\, q_1 - q_3 = 0$. Remembering $q_1 + q_2 + q_3 = 1$, point G is found as $G(\frac{5}{6}, 0, \frac{1}{6})$. Thus $\overline{FG}$ represents the loci of optimal allotment, with θ varying from $\theta = 0$ (point G) to $\theta = 1$ (point F), through $\theta = 0.4$ (point S).

Where initial capacity gaps exist, the loci of optimal allotment is not necessarily represented by a straight line. The case discussed by use of figure 9.3 is, as a matter of fact, a rather special case. The basic reasoning, nonetheless, holds for a general case.

For this case, the conclusion becomes easy to grasp by introducing $\Delta\phi_1$, $\Delta\phi_2$ to denote the initial gaps between the quay handling system, on the one hand, and the indirect route and the direct route, respectively, on the other, where

$$\left.\begin{aligned}
\Delta\phi_1 &= \theta \cdot \phi_{h_0} - \phi_{as_0} \\
\Delta\phi_2 &= (1 - \theta) \cdot \phi_{h_0} - \phi_{ad_0}
\end{aligned}\right\}$$

(9.24)

supposing both $\Delta\phi_1$, $\Delta\phi_2$ are non-negative. Combining equations 9.16, 9.17, 9.18 and 9.19, and using the denotations from equation 9.24, we get

$$q_1 = \frac{k_1}{k_1 + \theta \cdot k_2 + (1 - \theta) k_3}\left[1 - \frac{k_2 \cdot \Delta\phi_1 + k_3 \cdot \Delta\phi_2}{I_s}\right]$$

$$q_2 = \frac{\theta \cdot k_2}{k_1 + \theta \cdot k_2 + (1 - \theta) k_3}\left[1 - \frac{k_2 \cdot \Delta\phi_1 + k_3 \cdot \Delta\phi_2}{I_s}\right]$$
$$+ \frac{k_2 \cdot \Delta\phi_1}{I_s}$$

$$q_3 = \frac{(1 - \theta) k_3}{k_1 + \theta \cdot k_2 + (1 - \theta) k_3}\left[1 - \frac{k_2 \cdot \Delta\phi_1 + k_3 \cdot \Delta\phi_2}{I_s}\right]$$
$$+ \frac{k_3 \cdot \Delta\phi_2}{I_s}$$

(9.25)

Equation 9.25 may be interpreted as follows. Since the budget is to fill the initial gaps first, if there are any, then $\Delta\phi_1$ and $\Delta\phi_2$ should be filled at a cost of $k_2 \cdot \Delta\phi_1 + k_3 \cdot \Delta\phi_2$. If I_s is less than this sum, the budget will not be big enough to level up all the subsystems, but can only be allocated so as to squeeze the capacity gaps. Then capital should be allotted to the cheapest subsystem first, to level it up as

194

much as possible, and then the leftover capital can be allotted to the other remaining subsystem. If I_s is greater than the sum, after allotting $k_2 \cdot \Delta\phi_1 + k_3 \cdot \Delta\phi_2$ to each subsystem, there should be no capacity gap; and the problem then will be to allocate the residual capital to the three subsystems. Equation 9.25 explains the process — allocate the residual capital to each subsystem in proportion to k_1, $\theta \cdot k_2$, $(1 - \theta) k_3$, respectively, instead of using the proportions k_1, k_2, k_3, which are the unit costs for expanding each subsystem. This is because of the peculiar nature of the port as a system of pseudo-parallel channels. The solution to the problem with a certain extent of initial capacity gap could be presented in figure 9.3 by use of curvatures.

Although the analysis has proceeded thus far leaving θ as a given value, the cargo distribution ratio θ is not a policy constant imposed by the port, but rather a resultant ratio showing the users' choice depending on the port tariff for each route. A port, however, could try to change this ratio by introducing a new tariff scheme to make either route less attractive than the other. For example, if the indirect route were the more expensive to expand, given a limited amount of money available, the port might well increase the tariff for the indirect route. Such a policy would be expected to divert a certain proportion of the traffic towards the direct route, and then expand the direct route accordingly to absorb the traffic increase, since the latter is cheaper to expand in this case. The cargo distribution ratio will, in such a case, be made smaller by the new policy. If, however, the indirect route were relatively cheap to expand, and the direct route is expected to be congested, the port may increase the handling charge for the direct route, thus shifting some demand to the indirect route while expanding the latter.

We have dealt with the problem of how to allocate an arbitrarily fixed budget among the constituent subsystems, all of which are closely interrelated. But, there is another fundamental question as to the port investment : whether the investment should actually be made or not. If it should, then when? And how much? Once the size of the investment and the timing are decided, then the problem is to allocate it in a most efficient way. An appraisal of port investment should be based on various factors. If the port fails to expand to cope with the traffic, then the obvious outcome will be an inability to meet demand. The question then is the trade-off between the saving of the cost and the penalty (or potential loss) of doing nothing. Therefore, the traffic diversion should be properly estimated, effects of the policy upon the state of congestion should be reliably forecast, and so on. Furthermore, other internal policy changes should be investigated. For example, the upshot of the tariff change expecting a modal shift of cargo flow within the port hinges upon the users' responsiveness; and it is open to their criticism since an unreasonable tariff policy would disrupt the whole picture of sound port operations.

In sum, it is possible to increase the throughput by achieving better co-ordination of subsystems, among which for example is the change of cargo distribution ratio – i.e. higher utilisation of the whole system. However, the actual policy change should take account of such important issues as its effect upon the users' behaviour, upon the state of congestion, potential loss of traffic and so on. And a sound investment scheme should only be made on the basis of sound port pricing policy, the economic implications of which are discussed in chapter 8. In the following section, the problem of project choice with available technologies is taken up, although only two technologies will be considered. The port, facing a steady traffic growth over a long period, is to choose one of the two. And the port must try to contain the traffic by installing new technology whenever the overall capacity becomes saturated.

Project choice with demand increase

If a port expects steady growth of cargo traffic over a fairly long period of time ahead, and tries to contain the growth without any loss, the problem of a serial expansion programme would arise, with various technical possibilities available to meet it. Here we consider only two possibilities: Technology A with instalment cost a_A and capacity C_A, and Technology B with instalment cost a_B and capacity C_B. Furthermore, to help elucidate the implications of the analysis, it is assumed that A has the same unit operating cost as that of B, and is constant over the whole range of output.

In order to take the economy of scale into account, let us assume for the capacity that $C_A > C_B$ and assume that

$$\frac{a_A}{C_A} < \frac{a_B}{C_B}$$

(9.26)

for the average fixed costs. If there is no lag time for the instalment of facilities, the port will install either A or B at the point of reaching capacity saturation.

Bearing in mind that it is of considerable importance, yet no easy task, to procure the demand curve for an investment decision, let us suppose two types of demand curve, shifting with time, as shown in figure 9.4. Type A, corresponding to any tariff change, implies that the demand curve resumes its initial gradient as time passes, whereas Type B implies that the gradient becomes less steep as time passes. In the following analysis, only Type A is considered, since it is the easier to illustrate; but the basic argument holds true for the other as well.

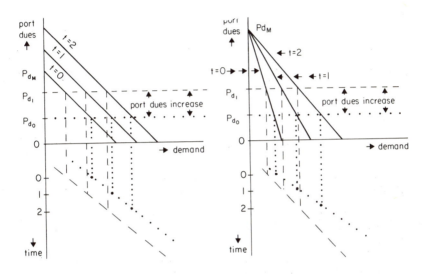

Figure 9.4   Two simple types of shifting demand curve

Let us now make a comparison between the two technologies in terms of *net present value* of capital cost, with the real discount rate r_d, assuming the traffic trend lasts over a long period which inevitably necessitates a serial expansion programme. (Inflation is taken into account with respect to the instalment cost by using the *real* discount rate).

$$\text{NPV(A)} = a_A + \frac{a_A}{(1 + r_d)^{t_A}} + \frac{a_A}{(1 + r_d)^{2t_A}} + \ldots \quad (9.27)$$

$$NPV(B) = a_B + \frac{a_B}{(1 + r_d)^{t_B}} + \frac{a_B}{(1 + r_d)^{2t_B}} + \ldots$$

$$(9.28)$$

where $t_A = \dfrac{C_A}{R_g}$ and $t_B = \dfrac{C_B}{R_g}$, denoting R_g as annual growth of

traffic. Since $\dfrac{1}{1 + r_d} < 1$, the values of these infinite series are

given as

$$NPV(A) = \frac{a_A}{1 - \left[\dfrac{1}{1 + r_d}\right]^{t_A}}$$

$$(9.29)$$

$$NPV(B) = \frac{a_B}{1 - \left[\dfrac{1}{1 + r_d}\right]^{t_B}}$$

$$(9.30)$$

If the port confines itself to the period of LCM (least common multiple) of t_A and t_B, equations 9.27 and 9.28 will give the finite series, and equations 9.29 and 9.30 should be modified accordingly. But this yields no more fruitful a result, and is thus not considered here.

The relative cheapness of the two technologies, therefore, depends on equations 9.29 and 9.30. If

$$\frac{a_A}{1 - \left[\dfrac{1}{1 + r_d}\right]^{t_A}} < \frac{a_B}{1 - \left[\dfrac{1}{1 + r_d}\right]^{t_B}}$$

then Technology A is the more economic to choose; otherwise, the reverse is true. If both sides are equal, then of course there is no difference between A and B in terms of installation cost. In order to clarify the implication of this result, consider the following Taylor expansion.

$$(1 + r_d)^{t_A} = 1 + t_A r_d + \frac{t_A(t_A - 1)}{2} r_d^2 + \ldots$$

$$(9.31)$$

$$(1 + r_d)^{t_B} = 1 + t_B r_d + \frac{t_B(t_B - 1)}{2} r_d^2 + \ldots$$

$$(9.32)$$

If t_A and t_B are both

$$t_A, t_B \ll \frac{2}{r_d} \qquad (9.33)$$

then the values beyond the third term of equations 9.31 and 9.32 can be neglected. This will not be an unreasonable condition for many cases, since the real discount rate r_d is usually on the order of one tenth. Equation 9.33 would then mean $t_A, t_B \ll 20$ (years); and we are, of course, concerned here with a continuous expansion of relatively small scale and not with a once-and-for-all type investment. Therefore, we see t_A, t_B at most as a few years.

Now, approximating $(1 + r_d)^{t_A} \simeq 1 + t_A \cdot r_d$ and $(1 + r_d)^{t_B} \simeq 1 + t_B \cdot r_d$, then

$$NPV(A) = \frac{(1 + t_A \cdot r_d) \, a_A}{t_A \cdot r_d} \qquad (9.34)$$

$$NPV(B) = \frac{(1 + t_B \cdot r_d) \, a_B}{t_B \cdot r_d} \qquad (9.35)$$

From equations 9.34 and 9.35, the following observations can be concluded.

Policy 1   Choose A :   if $\dfrac{a_A}{C_A} < \eta_{AB} \dfrac{a_B}{C_B}$

Policy 2   Choose B :   if $\dfrac{a_A}{C_A} > \eta_{AB} \dfrac{a_B}{C_B}$

Policy 3   Indifferent :   if $\dfrac{a_A}{C_A} = \eta_{AB} \dfrac{a_B}{C_B}$

$$\text{where } \eta_{AB} = \frac{1 + \dfrac{C_B}{R_g} \cdot r_d}{1 + \dfrac{C_A}{R_g} \cdot r_d} \, .$$

R_g is the constant addition to the demand level (tons/annum) and is represented in figure 9.4 (Type A) by the slope of the straight line (Demand vs Time). These are stricter conditions for judging the

199

relative cheapness of the two technologies than would be the case of comparing the average fixed costs of the two. If $C_A > C_B$ is assumed, η_{AB} then is less than unity; and taking Policy 1 for example, this means that the fact of the average fixed cost of A being less than that of B is not a sufficient condition to recommend Technology A. Rather, the above given condition for Policy 1 requires that the average fixed cost of A should be *less than* the average fixed cost of B *times* a factor which is less than unity, before A can be recommended. Obviously this is a much stricter condition than mere economy of scale in an ordinary sense would imply. The latter might be expressed simply:

Technology A, which is larger than Technology B, is said to enjoy economy of scale, if $\dfrac{a_A}{C_A} < \dfrac{a_B}{C_B}$.

Although intuitively clear, Policies 1, 2 and 3 show that it is sensible to choose the technology with the smaller capacity if there is no economy of scale, i.e. if $\dfrac{a_A}{C_A} = \dfrac{a_B}{C_B}$.

A port investment planning in general should comprise, of course, a lot of complex factors closely interrelated with each other and thus necessarily requires a far more sophisticated economic appraisal, e.g. a feasibility study as well as a thorough impact study. However, the design of this book is to present a gateway to the methodology for the techno-economic analysis of the port transport system by taking up only very much simplified models throughout.

Notes

[1]   See *Infra*, p.193, for the effects of variation in the cargo split ratio.

Bibliography

Adler, Hans A. *Sector and Project Planning in Transportation*, World Bank Staff Occasional Paper Number Four, 1967.

Archibald, G.C., (ed.), *The Theory of the Firm. Selected Readings*, Penguin, 1971.

Ashby, Sir Eric, Chairman, *Royal Commission on Environmental Pollution, Third Report, Pollution in Some British Estuaries and Coastal Waters*, HMSO, 1972.

Aziz, U.A., S.J. Gilani, Jock Hoe and Lim Chong Yah, *Traffic Flow through Port Swettenham Projected to 1975*, Department of Economics, University of Malaya, 1964.

Bertlin and Partners, Consulting Engineers, *Research Project on Tidal Berths and Locked Basins*, National Ports Council, London 1969.

Buckley, D.J. and S.G. Gooneratne, 'Optimal Scheduling of Transport Improvements to Cater for Growing Traffic Congestion', *Journal of Transport Economics and Policy*, VIII/2, May 1974, pp 122-35.

Central Office of Information, London, *British Industry Today. Freight Transport*, HMSO, 1971.
British Industry Today. Ports, HMSO, 1974.

Chang, W.H., L.S. Lee, S.J. Yang, and C.G. Vandervoort, 'Harbour Expansion and Harbour Congestion Charges', *Journal of Transport Economics and Policy*, IX/3, September 1975, pp 209-29.

Churchman, C.W., R.L. Ackoff and E.L. Arnoff, *Introduction to Operations Research*, Wiley and Sons, 1957.

Comer, Eugenia C. and Pedro N. Taborga, 'Port Simulation Model (GSM) Release (I) User's Guide', World Bank, unpublished paper, 1974.

Crowley, James A., 'Towards an Integrated Freight Transport System', National University of Ireland PhD thesis 1973.

Dasgupta, Ajit K. and D.W. Pearce, *Cost-Benefit Analysis*, Macmillan, 1972.

DeSalvo, J.S. and L.B. Lave, 'An Analysis of Tugboat Delays', *Journal of Transport Economics and Policy*, II/2, May 1968, pp 232-41.

Devanney, J.W. and L.H. Tan, *The Relationship between Short-Run Pricing and Investment Timing : The Port Pricing and Expansion Example*, Transportation Research, IX/6, December 1975, pp 329-37.

Devlin, Lord. *Final Report of the Committee of Inquiry under the Rt Hon. Lord Devlin into Certain Matters Concerning the Port Transport Industry*, HMSO, 1965.

Drummond, Spencer H., 'The Maritime Trade of North West Europe : A Study of Its Pattern, Importance and the General Problem of Its Protection', University of Southampton M.Phil. thesis 1972.

Edmond, E.D., 'Uses and Abuses of Queue Theory in Port Investment Appraisal', unpublished paper, University of Liverpool Marine Transport Centre, 1975.

Edmond, E.D. and R.P. Maggs, 'The Utilisation of UK Ports by Scheduled Container Services and Its Effect on Port Investment Appraisal', unpublished paper, University of Liverpool Marine Transport Centre, ca 1974-5.

Edwards, S.L., 'Transport Cost in British Industry', *Journal of Transport Economics and Policy*, IV/3, September 1970, pp 265-83.

Eidem, Frode, *Port Development Planning*, Oslo, Transportøkonomisk Institutt, 1973.
A Simulation Model for a Multi-Port System, mimeographed paper, Transportøkonomisk Institutt, 1974.
A Simulation Model for a Multi-Port System. Annex. Listing of the Computer Program 'Multi-Port', Example of Input and Output, mimeographed paper, Transportøkonomisk Institutt, 1974.

Financial Times, The. London.

Gaisford, R.W., *A Simulation Model of a Large Multi-Purpose Sea Port and Its Application in Two Large International Sea Ports*, Rendel, Palmer and Tritton, Consulting Engineers, London, ca 1970.

Gilman, S. 'The Feasibility of Containerising Routes to Developing Countries', unpublished paper, University of Liverpool Marine Transport Centre, 1975.

Gilman, S., and G.F. Williams, 'Cost Influences on the Geography of Multi-Port Systems — An Investigation into the Economics of General Cargo Routes', unpublished paper, University of Liverpool Marine Transport Centre, 1974.
'The Economics of Multi-Port Itineraries for Large Container Ships', *Journal of Transport Economics and Policy*, X/2, May 1976, 137-49.

Goss, R.O., *The Cost of Ships' Time*, HMSO, 1974.
Costs and Benefits of Navigational Aids in Port Approaches, HMSO, 1971.
'Port Investment' in D. Munby (ed.), *Transport. Selected Readings*, Penguin, 1968, pp 276-312.
Studies in Maritime Economics, Cambridge, 1970.

Grusky, Maurice, 'Harbor Engineering' in R.W. Abbett (ed.), *American Civil Engineering Practice*, New York 1956, II, pp 78-81.

Guardian, The. London.

Gulbrandsen, Odd, and Frode Eidem, *Port Development Planning*, Oslo, Transportøkonomisk Institutt, 1973.

Heggie, I.G. 'Charging for Port Facilities', *Journal of Transport Economics and Policy*, VIII/1, January 1974, pp 3-25.

Heggie, I.G. and C.B. Edwards, 'Port Investment Problems : How to Decide Investment Priorities' in Institution of Civil Engineers, *Conference on Civil Engineering Problems Overseas*, 18/19 July 1968, London 1968, pp 31-49.

Hay, William W. *An Introduction to Transportation Engineering*, New York 1961.

Holt, J.A. and R.R. Morton, 'The Economics of Congestion in Port Approaches', unpublished paper, Liverpool Polytechnic, n.d.

Institution of Civil Engineers, *Conference on Civil Engineering Problems Overseas*, 18/19 July 1968, London 1968.

Israel Ports Authority, Reports and Statistics Center, *Yearbook of Israel Ports Statistics, 1963/64*, Haifa, 1965.

Jansson, Jan Owen, 'Intra-Tariff Cross-Subsidisation in Liner Shipping' *Journal of Transport Economics and Policy*, VIII/3, September 1974, pp 294-311.

Japan Ministry of Transport, Bureau of Marine Transport, *Kai jo yu so no gen kyō ('Present State of Marine Transport')*, Tokyo 1973. *Nai kō kai un no gen kyō shi ryō ('Statistics Relating to the Present State of Domestic Marine Transport')*, Tokyo 1974. *Nihon kai un no gen kyō ('Present State of Japanese Marine Transport')*, Tokyo 1974.

Johnson, K.M. and H.C. Garnett, *The Economics of Containerisation*, London 1971.

Kendall, P.M.H., 'A Theory of Optimum Ship Size', *Journal of Transport Economics and Policy*, VI/2, May 1972, pp 128-46.

Knudsen, Olav, 'The Politics of International Shipping : Interaction and Conflict in an International Issue-Area', University of Denver PhD thesis 1972.

Laing, E.T., 'Economic Appraisal Criteria for Port Investments', mimeographed lecture, University of Liverpool Marine Transport Centre, 1974.

Layard, Richard, (ed.) *Cost-Benefit Analysis*, Penguin, 1972.

Little, I.M.D., *A Critique of Welfare Economics*, Oxford 1973, 2nd edition.

Little, I.M.D. and J.A. Mirrlees, *Project Appraisal and Planning for Developing Countries*, London 1974.

Lyon Associates, Inc., Consulting Engineers, *Korea Port Development Study. Draft Final Report, Volume III of IX, Determination of*

Port Development Priorities. Prepared for the Government of the Republic of Korea and the International Bank for Reconstruction and Development, *ca* 1971.

Maggs, R.P., 'Computer Simulation Applied to a Container Park', unpublished paper, University of Liverpool Marine Transport Centre, 1975.

Marine Transport Centre, University of Liverpool, 'An Investigation into the Effects of New Handling Technologies on the Structure of Marine Transport Systems', unpublished paper, n.d. (1974 or 1975).

Mauritius, Government of, *Mauritius Port Study. Volume I. Main Report*, prepared by Sir Alexander Gibb and Partners, and Freeman Fox and Associates, London 1973.

Metaxas, B.N., 'The Future of the Tramp Shipping Industry', *Journal of Transport Economics and Policy*, VI/3, September 1972, pp 271-80.

Mettam, J.D., 'Forecasting Delays to Ships in Port', *The Dock Harbour Authority, No.558* April 1967.

Mills, G., 'Investment Planning for British Ports', *Journal of Transport Economics and Policy*, V/2, May 1971, pp 119-52.

Mishan, E.J., *Cost-Benefit Analysis*, London 1971.

Munby, Denys (ed.), *Transport. Selected Readings*, Penguin, 1968.

National Ports Council, *Comparison of the Costs of Continental and British Ports, 1974. A Report to the National Ports Council by Touche Ross and Company*, London 1974.
Equipment Evaluation. An Examination of the Use of Fork Lift Trucks in the Ports, London 1973.
'Methods of Evaluating Cargo Handling Equipment', mimeographed paper, n.d.
National Ports Council Bulletin, London, trimestrial, from Spring 1972.
National Ports Council Research and Technical Bulletin, nos 1-8, 1964-71. Superseded in 1972 by the National Ports Council Bulletin.
Summary of a Report to the National Ports Council by Touche Ross and Company, London 1974.

Nihon Keizai Shimbun ('*The Japan Economic Times*'), Tokyo. (The translations of all quotations from this newspaper are my own).

Nishimura, Hajime, '*Ji dō sha yu sō no Technology Assessment*' ('*Technology Assessment of Motor Transport*'), *Kō gai kenkyū* ('*Research on Pullution*'), IV/1, July 1974, pp 48-59.

Observer, The. London.

Omtvedt, Petter C., *On the Profitability of Port Investment*, Oslo 1963.

Parzen, Emanuel, *Stochastic Processes,* San Francisco 1962. 'Planning for the Increased Throughput of a Common User Container Berth', *National Ports Council Research and Technical Bulletin*, VI, 1970, pp 285-93.

Prest, A.R., *Transport Economics in Developing Countries, Pricing and Financing Aspects*, London 1969.

Road Research Laboratory Leaflet, May 1970.

Rochdale, Viscount, Chairman, *Committee of Inquiry into Shipping. Report.* HMSO, 1970.

Saaty, Thomas L., *Elements of Queuing Theory, with Applications*, McGraw-Hill, 1961.

Saggar, R.K., 'Turnround and Costs of Conventional Cargo Liners. UK– India Route', *Journal of Transport Economics and Policy* IV/1, January 1970, 53-65.

Shneorson, D., 'Price Discrimination in Liner Sea Transport', University of London PhD thesis 1972.

Slettenmark, Rolv., 'Optimising of Port Facilities', *Norwegian Maritime Research*, III/2, 1975, pp 41-3.

Summerskill, Michael, *Laytime. 2nd edition.* London 1973.

Taborga, Pedro N., 'Determination of an Optimal Policy for Seaport Growth and Development', mimeographed paper, Massachusetts Institute of Technology, Department of Civil Engineering, 1969. 'Port Simulation Model (GSM) Release (I) User's Guide', mimeographed paper, International Banking for Reconstruction and Development 1974.

Thomas, Simon, 'India–Nepal Transit System', unpublished paper, University of Oxford Transport Studies Unit, 1976.

Thomson, J.M., *Modern Transport Economics*, Penguin, 1974.

Thorburn, T., *Supply and Demand for Water Transport*, Stockholm Business Research Institute, 1960.

Transport, Ministry of UK. *Report of the Committee of Inquiry into the Major Ports of Great Britain*, HMSO, 1962, reprinted 1967.

Turvey, R., (ed.), *Public Enterprise. Selected Readings*, Penguin, 1968.

UNCTAD (United Nations Conference on Trade and Development), *Berth Throughput, Systematic Methods for Improving General Cargo Operations*, New York 1973. *Development of Ports*, Geneva 1967. *Development of Ports. Improvement of Port Operations and Connected Facilities*, New York 1969. *Port Pricing*, New York 1975.

United Nations Department of Economic and Social Affairs. *Physical Requirements of Transport Systems for Large Freight Containers*, New York 1973.

Vickrey, W., 'Marginal Cost Pricing' in D. Munby (ed.) *Transport. Selected Readings*, Penguin, 1968, pp 98-116.

Watson, P.R. and A. Stewart, 'Shiphandling Simulation and Marine Training', in *Universities Transport Studies Group, Seventh Conference* : University of Surrey, 6-9 January 1975, (no page numbers).

Weille, Jan de, and Anandarup Ray, 'The Optimum Port Capacity', *Journal of Transport Economics and Policy*, VIII/3, September 1974, pp 244-59.

Whittington, M., 'A Study of the Importation of Grain into the United Kingdom', unpublished paper, University of Liverpool Marine Transport Centre, *ca* 1974-5.

Williamson, Oliver E., 'Peak-Load Pricing' in R. Turvey (ed.), *Public Enterprise, Selected Readings*, Penguin, 1968, pp 64-85.

World Bank, *World Bank Operations : Sectoral Programs and Policies*, Baltimore, 1972.